Carnival and Theater

Carnival and Theater

Plebeian Culture and the Structure of Authority in Renaissance England

Michael D. Bristol

ROUTLEDGE

NEW YORK AND LONDON

First published in 1985 by
Methuen, Inc.
Paperback published in 1989 by
Routledge, an imprint of
Routledge, Chapman and Hall Inc.
29 West 35 Street
New York, NY 10001
Published in Great Britain by
Routledge
11 New Fetter Lane
London, EC4P 4EE

*Library of Congress
Cataloging in Publication Data*

Bristol, Michael D., 1940–
    Carnival and theater.

    Bibliography: p.
    Includes index.
    1. English drama – Early modern
and Elizabethan, 1500–1600 – History
and criticism. 2. English drama –
17th century – History and criticism.
3. Authority in literature – England.
4. Theater and society – England.
5. England – Popular culture.
6. Theater—Political aspects.
7. Politics and literature. I. Title.
PR658.A89B75 1985   822′.3′09
85-11426

ISBN 0 416 35070 4
ISBN 0-415-90138-3 (pb)

*British Library
Cataloguing in Publication Data*

Bristol, Michael D.
    Carnival and theater: plebeian culture
and the structure of authority in
    Renaissance England.
    1. Theater – England – History
    2. England – Popular culture
    I. Title
    792′.0942   PN2585

ISBN 0 416 35070 4
ISBN 0 415-90138-3 (pb)

For Doris

CONTENTS

ACKNOWLEDGEMENTS

S OME of the ideas discussed in Parts II and III were originally presented under the title 'Carnival and the Institutions of Theatre in Elizabethan England', *ELH*, 50 (1983), 637–55. The earliest source for the argument I have tried to work out here was the experience I had during the late 1960s with an experimental theater in Urbana, Illinois, called The Depot, Inc. That experience showed me what a theater might be as the expression of collective life and collective struggle, and I'm happy now to reaffirm solidarity with my many friends and associates in that endeavor. In particular I would like to thank Professor James Hurt, whose performance as the first gravedigger in *Hamlet* provided me with a powerful image of the themes developed here.

I wish to thank my unfailingly contentious colleagues at McGill for the opportunity to discuss the issues addressed here, especially Professors Darko Suvin, Leonore Lieblein, John Ripley, Michael Maxwell, Irwin Gopnik, Kate Shaw, and George Szanto. For advice, encouragement, and practical aid and comfort I would like to thank Charles Frey, Donald Hedrick, Barbara Mowat, Nancy Hodge, Terence Hawkes, and Naomi Liebler. Don Bouchard, Paisley Livingston, and Benjamin Weems read early versions of the manuscript, and, although I dislike criticism, especially when it is constructive, I am obliged to admit that their 'refusal to understand' has made this a better book. At a later stage the text was read by Maurice Charney, Stephen Orgel, and Walter Cohen. The editorial comments and suggestions of this heterogeneous readership have helped me to incorporate important second thoughts and have also kept me mindful of why I wanted to do this in the first place. The sense of community I have experienced in working with and against the members of this diverse group has been the most personally rewarding part of the project for me, and I hope that this at least is reflected in the final result.

The Social Science and Humanities Research Council of Canada provided me with a generous research grant to carry out this project. I would like to express my appreciation for that support, and for the support provided by McGill University in the form of a sabbatical leave. Hectorine Leger typed the manuscript and corrected my French. Final editing and proofreading have been done with the highly professional assistance of Marta Meanna.

Doris Bristol has faithfully kept me company through all the struggles; she has sustained me with a truly serio-comic attitude to my efforts and, always, with love.

PART I
THEORETICAL PERSPECTIVE

THEATER is an art form; it is also a social institution. By favoring a certain style of representation and a particular etiquette of reception, the institutional setting of a performance informs and focuses the meaning of a dramatic text and facilitates the dissemination of that meaning through the collective activity of the audience.[1] The social and political life of the theater as a public gathering place has an importance of its own over and above the more exclusively literary interest of texts and the contemplation of their meaning. Because of its capacity to create and sustain a briefly intensified social life, the theater is festive and political as well as literary – a privileged site for the celebration and critique of the needs and concerns of the *polis*. The critical intensification of collective life represented and experienced in the theater, and the possibility it creates for action and initiative, is the subject of this book.

The richest material for the elaboration of the argument pursued here is the dramatic literature of Renaissance England and its complex relationship to the traditions of Carnival. For most of its more recent history, theater has functioned with a diminished capacity to achieve its social and political purpose. In Renaissance England, however, the theater objectified and recreated broadly dispersed traditions of collective life that were also represented and disseminated through anonymous festive manifestations such as Carnival. The dramatic literature produced by this theater retains much of the power and the durable vitality of these strong political forms. Unlike the theater of later periods, that of Elizabethan and Jacobean England is not exclusively or even mainly a specialized institution of literary production and consumption. In this theater, literature as *objet-d'art* or as ideological finished product is subordinated to more active, though more ephemeral forms of institution-making carried over into theater from the traditions of popular festive form.

These collective traditions give rise to dramatic forms that are intensely critical and even experimental in their representation of social and political structure. There is, first, a negative critique that demystifies or 'uncrowns' power, its justificatory ideology, and the tendency of elites to undertake disruptive radicalizations of traditional patterns of social order, and to introduce novel forms of domination and expropriation. In addition, there is a positive critique, a celebration and reaffirmation of collective traditions lived out by ordinary people in their ordinary existence. That positive critique, which articulates the capacity of popular culture to resist penetration and control by the power structure, is a central theme of this text.

For the first few decades of its existence, the public playhouse of Elizabethan England was not yet fully differentiated from more dispersed and anonymous forms of festive life, play and mimesis. Theatrical spectacle and the theatricalization of social and intellectual life were common to virtually all social groups, corporations, and communities in Renaissance England, primarily in informal, amateur organizations. The performance traditions of these homogeneous groups usually emphasized the immediate social purposes of theater, in particular the enjoyment of corporate or communal solidarity, over the specialized appreciation of durable literary values. Theater and popular festivity were closely related forms of social life, neighboring institutions with similar patterns of representation and similar orientations to political and economic practice.

> In the months of June and July, on the vigils of the festival days, and on the same festival days in the evenings after the sun setting, there were usually made bonfires in the streets, every man bestowing wood or labour towards them; the wealthier sort also, before

their doors near to the said bonfires, would set out tables on the vigils, furnished with sweet bread and good drink, and on festival days with meats and drinks plentifully, whereunto they would invite their neighbours and passengers also to sit and be merry with them in great familiarity, praising God for his benefits bestowed on them. These were called bonfires as well of good amity amongst neighbours that being before at controversy, were there, by the labour of others, reconciled, and made of bitter enemies loving friends.[2]

The midsummer watch was a collective celebration, combining spectacle and festive abundance with the social and political functions of the town meeting and the family court. The practice was repeated 'time out of mind'; it took place outside any formal administrative apparatus.

The same functions, according to Stow, have been accomplished through other traditional sports and collective pastimes, and, in his own day, these functions have been extended into the new institution of the public playhouse.

These, or the like exercises, have been continued till our time, namely, in stage plays . . . [and] of late time, in place of those stage plays, hath been used comedies, tragedies, interludes, and histories, both true and feigned; for the acting whereof certain public places, as the Theatre, the Curtain, etc. have been erected.[3]

Stow's brief account describes theater as a continuation of popular festive activity in which the social purpose as well as the playful atmosphere of other popular sports and pastimes are sustained. The public playhouse, then, must be considered a politically significant *mise-en-scène*, where the energy and initiative of collective life are forcefully manifested in texts, in performance convention, and in the reception and appreciation of theatrical spectacle.

Renaissance drama is important in that it invites consideration of forms of collective life and of subjectivity other than those proposed and legitimated by a hegemonic culture. The problem of specifying the relationship among subjectivity, collective life and the structure of formally constituted or 'official' authority is obviously very complicated, and the difficulties are compounded by the accumulated prestige and literary authority of canonical texts by Shakespeare and his contemporaries. The present analysis proceeds against the grain of traditional literary scholarship and also of its more recent, radically critical variants. The problem addressed here is not whether Shakespeare's plays, for example, represent a traditional world picture of some kind, whether Christian humanist or its secular counterpart in the Tudor Myth, or, on the contrary, represent a critical and subversive demystifying of a dominant ideology. The second position is certainly an advance over the first, both in its emphasis on discontinuity and rupture within the Tudor consensus, and in its insistence that the problem of meaning cannot be considered independently of the problem of authority. But the larger issue of authority and its allocation between the centers of political power and exceptional individual subjects, such as Shakespeare, has been, even in the most strongly revisionist critical texts, analyzed primarily in light of the image power has of itself as an infinitely resourceful center of initiative, surveillance and control. The existence of a popular element in the cultural landscape of the period has either been ignored or been treated as yet another instrument of political and cultural domination. But the problem of authority cannot be fully elucidated by focusing exclusively on the relationship between what purports to be a virtual monopoly of significant political power and a few individual centers of avant-garde consciousness uneasily balanced between alternatives of affiliation or critical rejection of the imperatives of a ruling elite.

The problem of 'authors' and of their 'authority' is discussed here not only in the light of their relationship to de jure authority, but also and more centrally in the light of their relationship to a coherent, diverse and energetic popular culture that struggles to retain its own particular and local authority over the ordering of social and economic life. Before proceeding to any detailed analysis of that popular culture, however, it is useful to place the problem in a more fully developed theoretical context. That context has three significant elements. First, there is the problem of the literary text and how it is most effectively situated in relation to the non-literary. Though interpretation of literature is an important element in the discussions that follow, it does not take precedence over other issues, nor is the 'reading of texts' invested with decisive teleological importance. For this reason the perspective developed in the work of Mikhail Bakhtin has been adopted as a primary 'literary' or interpretive strategy. Second, there is the general problem of festivity and ritual form, and its evidently conservative function in sustaining the continuity of social life. That problem has been most powerfully addressed in the sociology of Emile Durkheim, and in recent revisions of his theory in the work of René Girard and Victor Turner. Third, there is the problem of specifying exactly what is meant by popular or plebeian culture, the degree to which that culture retained any degree of independent initiative, and the ability of that culture to articulate and carry out its own partisan agenda in the face of a powerfully organized hegemony. This is recognizably the problem of class struggle, but it is also an aspect of the social 'architecture' proposed by Fernand Braudel, in which the history of the *longue durée* and its embodiment in the diverse patterning of everyday life proceeds in accordance with its own interior rhythms independently of any mobility in the political superstructure.

The project undertaken here is informed by a range of materialist critical traditions. It is also animated by the attitude of materialist 'sadness' described so eloquently by Walter Benjamin in his *Theses on the Philosophy of History*:

> this sadness stands out more clearly if one asks with whom the adherents of historicism actually empathize. The answer is inevitable: with the victor. And all rulers are the heirs of those who conquered before them. Hence, empathy with the victor invariably benefits the rulers. Historical materialists know what that means. Whoever has emerged victorious participates to this day in the triumphal procession in which the present rulers step over those who are lying prostrate. According to traditional practise, the spoils are carried along in the procession. They are called cultural treasures, and a historical materialist views them with cautious detachment. For without exception the cultural treasures he surveys have an origin which he cannot contemplate without horror. They owe their existence not only to the efforts of the great minds and talents who have created them, but also to the anonymous toil of their contemporaries. There is no document of civilization which is not at the same time a document of barbarism. And just as such a document is not free of barbarism, barbarism taints also the manner in which it was transmitted from one owner to another.[4]

CHAPTER 1
PLAYING THE OLD WORKS HISTORICALLY

DRAMATIC texts imply theatrical performances and thus a concrete social and institutional *mise-en-scène*. Although in some cultural settings theater has a relatively clear and well-defined relationship to the social structure as a whole, the theater of Elizabethan England was situated quite ambiguously in relation to the established categories and fully legitimated functions of the formally constituted social order. Despite this initially marginal status, a significant body of texts has not merely *survived* from this institution but been sustained within the canon of literature as a central and privileged tradition. The fate of an old play in a contemporary performance or reading presents many complex difficulties, but the most elusive of all these problems is the recognition and recuperation of their initially uncanonical literary and social status.

The dramatic texts remain, but the social and institutional setting in which they were performed has changed greatly. The problem of reading and performance is thus necessarily historical.

> We too are at the same time fathers of a new period and sons of an old one; we understand a great deal of the remote past and can still share once overwhelming feelings which were stimulated on a

grand scale. And the society in which we live is a very complex one, too. . . . What really matters is to play these old works historically, which means setting them in powerful contrast to our own time. For it is only against the background of our own time that their shape emerges as an old shape, and without this background I doubt if they could have any shape at all.[1]

Diverse ideological orientations to both past and present are possible, and every historical analysis is grounded, at least implicitly, in a purposeful and usually self-conscious political stance. For Brecht, history is an indispensable part of his central critical purpose and of the requirement that the 'spectator must master the incidents on the stage'.[2] Neither the actions represented, nor the techniques of any such representation, are to be considered as 'natural' or 'universal', since 'man is the sum of all the social conditions of all times'. The spectator masters the incidents by dispelling the illusion of a trans-historical 'human nature', and by discovering the dynamic and contingent movement both of 'man' and of 'social conditions' through history.[3]

Brecht's project for 'playing the old works historically' begins from the observation that Elizabethan dramatists were engaged in 'global experiments' testing social possibilities and mimetically working through abrasive social conflicts. In retrospect these experiments have a powerfully tragic feel, in that they represent forms of collective life that have almost entirely disappeared. The contrast between the old works and the cultural forms of our own time dramatizes the impermanence of that older way of life, and, equally, the impermanence of presently existing social and political arrangements.

To describe these plays as 'global experiments' suggests that literary artists and their audiences were immediately and objectively aware of struggle and change. This is certainly the view put forward by E.M.W. Tillyard, although his position contrasts very sharply with Brecht's. Tillyard is currently regarded as outmoded both in his methodology and his interpretation of particular works. Nevertheless, he remains a powerfully influential figure, even among scholars who explicitly reject his views. *The Elizabethan World Picture*, for example, establishes the position that the literature of the past is part of a larger cultural and ideological totality, and that its interpretation consequently requires a disciplined act of historical imagination in which the willingness to discover and acknowledge difference is paramount.

Tillyard argues that, in the Elizabethan period, there is only one significant culture and that unanimity exists among those who share that culture in the form of a comprehensive 'world picture' or intellectual frame of reference. Literature, drama and theatrical activity are the reflection and the instrument of that world picture, which has an autonomous and virtually objective existence, independent of its actualization in concrete literary, theological or political writing. Even when a text depicts social disintegration, the idea of hierarchical order is the implicit prior standard that rationalizes the image of disorder. Although images of social conflict are common in Elizabethan literature, Tillyard argues that 'pictures of civil war and disorder . . . [have] no meaning apart from a background to judge them by'.[4] This 'background' is both a teleology and a durable social consensus that rejects any inference that disorder could ever be regarded as 'natural'.

> Such a way of thinking was abhorrent to the Elizabethans (as indeed it always has been and is now to the majority), who preferred to think of order as the norm to which disorder, though lamentably common, was yet the exception.[5]

Loyalty to the idea of order is the preference of the majority, even when the contingent circumstances of history seem to deny the very possibility of order, or when the exceptions occur more frequently than the instances of the norm. There are, however, important qualifications in the claims of unanimity and consensus.

The social and political boundaries of unanimity are acknowledged in a discussion of Richard Hooker, who represents for Tillyard the central and most accessible spokesman for the shared ideals of Elizabethans.

> Hooker's elaborated account must have stated pretty fairly the preponderating conception among the *educated*. . . . He writes not for the technical theologian but mediates theology to *the general educated public* of his day. . . . He has the acutest sense of what the *ordinary educated man* can grasp and having grasped ratify. It is this tact that assures us that he speaks for the *educated nucleus* that dictated the current beliefs of the Elizabethan Age.[6] [Emphasis added]

Cultural unanimity exists among a narrowly circumscribed group, as the constantly reiterated term 'educated' suggests. The 'world picture' shared by Elizabethans is a selective tradition disseminated by an 'educated nucleus' and ratified by a somewhat wider community of 'ordinary educated men'. The educated nucleus who share this outlook and responsibility for its dissemination are treated as unproblematic. Furthermore, though Tillyard's argument emphasizes differences between past and present in ideological content, terms such as 'art' and 'literature' are not regarded as historical categories, much less 'educated' or 'public'. The production of literary meaning, the use to which it is put by the 'educated nucleus' and the authority of that educated elite are not treated as questionable elements in a specific historical dialectic. On the contrary, there is a strong implication that the selective tradition and its interpretive community are continuous, and that their authority is above serious criticism.

Tillyard's position represents one side of a debate about Renaissance culture – that which maintains that it is primarily a continuation of the unified, theocentric cosmology of the Middle Ages. The alternative view is that Renaissance culture is authentically 'heterocosmic', and that its art represents a tension between opposing but equally valid social and ontological systems. Norman Rabkin identifies this opposition as 'complementarity', a pattern created by the coexistence in a literary structure of symmetrically opposed meanings, each of which has a double valuation.

> Shakespeare tends to structure his imitations in terms of polar opposites – reason and passion in *Hamlet*, for instance, or reason and faith, reason and love, reason and imagination; Realpolitik and the traditional political order, Realpolitik and political idealism. . . . Always the dramatic structure set up the opposed elements as equally valid, equally desirable, and equally destructive, so that the choice the play forces the reader to make becomes impossible.[7]

Rabkin opposes the reductionist tendency of critics who derive their interpretations from strategies such as Tillyard's; his aim is to put Shakespeare 'out of the reach . . . of the special pleader for a particular ideology [or] Renaissance orthodoxy'.[8] In order to accomplish this, Rabkin argues that polyvalence and polysemy are implicit governing principles in many of the greatest works of world literature. The contrasted meanings in literary texts do not cancel each other, but instead conform to a higher level of organization in symmetrically contrasted dualisms.

One of the strengths of this position is that it acknowledges a distinctive existence for literature as a socially significant practice possessed of its own authority. The literary text is an independent structure rather than the expression or reflection of an ideological tendency external to itself. The quality of 'literariness' is the polysemic character of literary language and of larger narrative patterns. Rabkin acknowledges that this does seem to disengage literature and its interpretation from political struggle and tendency. However, he argues that 'complementarity' represents a commitment both to the fundamental contradictoriness of real, social experience and to the 'common understanding' seeking to interpret that social experience.

> . . . the aesthetic presentation of the world as complementarity
> . . . provides a writer with the basis of a mimesis which appeals to
> the common understanding because it recalls the *unresolvable*
> *tensions that are the fundamental conditions of human life*. It is a
> mode of awareness, an option for a certain and essential kind of
> openness to human experience.[9]

Even though Shakespeare's plays dramatize irreconcilable contradictions, there is no dialectical clash and dissonance, no sense of compelling pressure in the historical process. In fact, as Rabkin suggests in an important essay on Shakespeare's *Henry V*, mimetic action transforms historical conflict and the contest of ideologies into a kind of optical illusion in which the opposing forces appear as either 'rabbits' or 'ducks', eliding violent historical struggle into a trick of perception and purely formal duplicity.[10]

Both Tillyard and Rabkin view the social activity of theater as fundamentally reassuring and harmonious, rather than as the disruptive and alarming spectacle it appeared to be to some sixteenth-century observers. This view corresponds to the wish to identify ideas and images about which all reasonable men and women might agree, and to derive secular authority from the views of that anonymous collective. Tillyard interprets the past as a social unity made possible by the uncontested cultural and political hegemony of an intellectually unified elite. Rabkin is committed to a more egalitarian outlook in which social harmony flows from the authority of a 'common understanding' very widely shared by people of imagination and goodwill, regardless of their specific social position or level of education.

Tillyard and Rabkin are both committed to a reconciliatory view of the problem of 'playing the old works historically'. The critical debate as defined by their respective positions, therefore, tends to minimize interpretive conflict in the articulation of meaning. This is clear in a tendency to speak of 'Elizabethans' or a 'common understanding', rather than to differentiate and distinguish gender, social rank and economic position. Because conflict is viewed as having only marginal or subordinate interest for interpretation, reconciliatory strategies overlook the application of creative practice to limited partisan ends. Both Tillyard and Rabkin ignore the purposeful and limited character of traditions of everyday life and social observance that give rise to and are the precondition of any individual act of creativity. They also disregard one social group's expropriation of the forms created by another. Elizabethan drama was not created by and for 'Elizabethans' in general: both institutions and specific texts were created by well-defined communities with economic and political interests to advance, and with a great many internal conflicts about the form and purpose of their own art. Plays were performed in a variety of settings, sometimes with a homogeneous audience, sometimes in a more diversified and heterogeneous setting. And in any period a radically unbalanced view may take precedence over broader conceptions sanctioned by orthodoxy and consensus. All this suggests that historical reconstruction of 'the old works' must place struggle, social difference and cultural antagonism at the center of critical analysis, rather than consensus, harmony and accommodation.

Whether it is based on tactics of exclusion, as in Tillyard, or on tactics of harmonious integration, as in Rabkin, the reconciliatory strategy of conventional literary scholarship has been committed to a view of literature as a benign, and thus a culturally and politically innocuous, institution. This commitment is radically challenged in a number of recent critical texts that focus on discontinuity, struggle and the realities of power. In all the variants of this revisionist stance, including the present text, literature is viewed as a troubling and indeed troublesome institution, imprecisely defined and yet decisively correlated with structural ambiguity in the social and cultural context. To present an exhaustive survey of all the important variations of this position is beyond the scope of this discussion. There are, however, two recent critical tendencies in the study of Renaissance culture that have particular pertinence for the present inquiry. The first of these is the 'anthropological' perspective exemplified by the influential work of Stephen Greenblatt and grounded in the theories of discontinuity and rupture proposed by Michel Foucault. The second is the avowedly Marxist approach exemplified by the work of Jonathan Dollimore and informed by the cultural poetics of Raymond Williams, as well as by a comprehensive knowledge of the 'history of ideology' practiced, though in a much more limited and selective way, by Tillyard.

Stephen Greenblatt, and several other scholars who share a similar perspective, notably Jonathan Goldberg and Louis A. Montrose, is centrally concerned with the theme of power and with the objective of its decipherment. In *Renaissance Self-Fashioning*, Greenblatt pursues these interests by proposing a reading of Renaissance culture in the form of a theory of the avant-garde. The ingenuity of this strategy is greatly enhanced by the decision to focus on a few exceptional subjects who are widely acknowledged to be central to the received canon of literary and intellectual history, but whose exact position in relation to their own artistic and intellectual milieu has been energetically and indeed acrimoniously debated. The 'talented middle class men' studied here – More, Tyndale, Wyatt, Spenser, Marlowe and Shakespeare – exemplify a complex social mobility that gives rise to various strategies of 'self-fashioning'. This process requires the elaboration of a richly textured social integument or 'self', and at the same time demands that something be held in reserve, so that distance is maintained between the self and the center of power or its objectification in ideological material. The subjectivity achieved in this way permits a reading of power and the shifting of its center of gravity so as to demystify its claims to divine sanction. Thus More and Tyndale, between them 'undermined the two great pillars of the European social order from feudal times, exposing their pretensions to divine sanction as mere ideology, ridiculing their attempts at mystification, insisting on their human origin and their material interests'.[11] As with any statement about demystification, this one depends to some extent on an alleged prior condition – here, feudal times – that is both mystified and monolothic, and thus in need of critical decipherment. It is, of course, doubtful that any such situation ever existed, but this kind of academic objection does not seriously weaken the force of Greenblatt's argument. The text of *Renaissance Self-Fashioning* carefully delineates the role of a critical avant-garde in the hazardous enterprise of tracking the shifts of power and making it a possible object of knowledge. The main objection to this thesis is not with Greenblatt's estimate of the importance of an avant-garde subjectivity within the cultural landscape of early modern Europe. But the thesis has only a limited domain of application; in adopting certain conceptions of the individual or self in relation to power, Greenblatt relies on a greatly reduced conception of social and collective experience.

In a brief but important passage on the poetry of Thomas Wyatt, Greenblatt takes pains to distinguish his concept of individuality and the self from modern, romantic notions of selfhood. 'I would suggest that there is no privileged sphere of individuality in Wyatt, set off from linguistic convention, from social pressure, from the shaping force of religious and political power.'[12] This observation reveals a general and pervasive refusal to adopt any aesthetic based on invidious comparisons between some inviolable core of subjectivity and personal integrity on the one hand, and 'mere' social convention and conformity to outward pressure on the other. Despite this careful separation of the concept of self-fashioning from the contemporary ideology of individualism, Greenblatt's work rests on a disembodied and abstract conception of the social, in which collective experience is apprehended only through secondary refractions, codes, conventions, ideological formations and images of power. These have a tenuous, alien and sometimes baleful relation to the self, which is consistently presented in the condition of isolation.

In Greenblatt, as indeed in Foucault, whose work underlies so much of *Renaissance Self-Fashioning*, the critique of power often seems to be a glorification of the powerful, despite the conscientiously sustained determination to disclose the impostures of power and to repudiate its claims. Power is always singular, a unity and also a plenitude. Authority is indistinguishable from power: it is the name power gives to itself, its guise of civility, its exterior sanction, its claim to ulterior purpose. Opposition to such a center of authority/power is a cat-and-mouse game played out within an abstract field known as language or discourse. Since opposition can be initiated only by the isolated subject, it is at best a delaying tactic, at worst a 'suicidal folly'. *Renaissance Self-Fashioning* thus vividly depicts the pathos of individual opposition by meditating on the shifts in power itself and on such choices as conformity, impotent rebellion or 'subversive submission'. The main limit to this view – and it is a serious limit – is the tendency to confuse the wishful thinking of powerful people with an objective description of social reality. Fantasies of unlimited freedom of action, and of freedom of the consequences of one's actions, do express the will to violence, just as Greenblatt maintains. But these fantasies do not actually produce social wealth, or bring about social order, or cause all suffering and anxiety. The powerful inertia of social production is itself a primary form of opposition to the impositions of power, but the thesis of self-fashioning necessarily excludes any consideration of this aspect of the problem.

The theme of production is, of course, a central preoccupation of Marxism and of Marxist literary criticism. In its earlier manifestations, this preoccupation focused on literature as a reflection of material production and on the instrumental possibilities of certain genres, most notably 'realism'. This position has proved unsatisfactory in a number of ways, most notably for contemporary Marxists, who now propose that literature is a form of production in its own right, not merely an epiphenomenon of the 'base'. Unfortunately, the abandonment of 'reflection' in favor of the 'production of ideology' leads to the virtual disappearance of material production in all its mundane particularity. The strengths and the weaknesses of this position for the interpretation of the cultural history of the Renaissance are exemplified by Jonathan Dollimore's *Radical Tragedy*.

Dollimore's text pursues two arguments at once. Jacobean tragedy is described as a radical and subversive genre, eroding a dominant ideology of Christian providentialism from within. At the same time the text undertakes a critique of contemporary literary scholarship as the expression of a partially occulted ideology that Dollimore refers to as 'essentialist humanism'. This strategy is, of course, a version of the one recommended by Brecht, namely that the past be read 'in powerful contrast to our own time'. Dollimore shows in detail that the literature of the past is not only read but in fact administered by contemporary institutional scholarship, and that such cultural administration is itself a significant element in the production of ideology.

The theme of radical subversion is presented as a broad intellectual program that questions established or officially authorized beliefs in every area of cultural activity.

> . . . this was a drama which undermined religious orthodoxy . . . its challenge in this respect generates other, equally important subversive preoccupations – namely a critique of ideology, the demystification of political and power relations and the decentering

of 'man'. Emerging from the interaction between these concerns was a radical social and political realism.[13]

Since Jacobean England was not an open society, such an agenda could not be pursued openly and explicitly. Dollimore argues that the formal peculiarities of Jacobean drama, its disjunctive combination of 'realistic' and 'conventional' techniques of representation, constitute a strategy for the evasion of official persecution. Furthermore, this strategy of evasion would be intelligible in the light of a widespread and pervasive Renaissance skepticism occasioned by a 'breakdown' of a unified, Christian world-view.

This revisionist project is parallel to a sustained critique of the 'essentialist humanism' that governs so much of traditional literary scholarship. Dollimore argues that universalizing conceptions such as 'human nature', the 'great tradition' and the 'common understanding' all advance the implicit claim that the forms of consciousness and of social character experienced within capitalist society constitute 'man'. This universalization of 'bourgeois' subjectivity is, moreover, a commitment to a political fatalism and to the repression of 'difference and otherness, a fear of disintegration through democracy and change'.[14] The scholarly ideals of civility and detachment are themselves a tactical element in a comprehensive strategy to forestall and to discourage any serious consideration of alternative forms of collective life. This analysis of the dominant tendencies of 'humanist' criticism is not, of course, unique to Marxism. A similar critique of universalizing interpretation is advanced, though from the opposite end of the ideological spectrum, by D. W. Robertson.[15] In his brief and polemical reading of *Hamlet*, Robertson suggests that the prince is a sorry example of every possible kind of 'cupidity' – morally and socially degenerate, pathetic and ludicrous.[16] A reading like this is bound to irritate most Renaissance scholars, especially as Robertson is at pains to reveal that sympathetic interpretation of Hamlet's character is an expression of 'modern' – that is, bourgeois – sentimentality.

What this work shows is that there is no such thing as an ideologically unconditioned discussion of the literature of an earlier period. Both Dollimore and Robertson reveal the implicit ideological bias of 'essentialist humanism' by virtue of their own strong, indeed corrosive, ideological commitments. Such commitments are perhaps less a matter of formal doctrine than of historical empathy for excluded or forgotten experiences of social and cultural reality. In the light of such specific convictions, it is possible to investigate the question of relationship between a tradition and its latter-day heirs, and to consider various strategic deployments, ranging from celebratory identification to critical resistance.

Dollimore's revisionary interpretation of Jacobean tragedy is effective as an aspect of his decipherment of contemporary literary scholarship. As a reading of Renaissance drama and theater, however, it has limitations that seriously weaken the overall force of the argument. *Radical Tragedy* describes the diversity of thought and opinion so characteristic of the Renaissance as a consequence of the 'breakdown' of an earlier, comprehensive, intellectual and social unity. In effect, Tillyard's 'Elizabethan World Picture' is pushed back, or chronologically transplanted, to an earlier though indefinitely specified period. The question raised by all such theories of 'breakdown' is not as much when the process of decay and disintegration began, as whether the prior condition of unity ever existed. In fact, D.W. Robertson has argued at length for a unity of outlook during the fourteenth century, but this argument is persuasive only if all of Robertson's strategic exclusions are accepted uncritically. Robertson finds unity in the specifically Pauline and Augustinian doctrines of charity and cupidity, but in order to do this he must dismiss all speculative thinking on purely abstruse philosophical topics such as language, all social protest of the sort conducted by the Franciscans, and, of course, all popular culture, where – according to Robertson – nothing interesting ever happens. It is not clear why Dollimore finds it necessary to retain such a reactionary conception, even as a target for his radical, subversive dramatists, since Marxism offers the far more powerful and persuasive doctrine that struggle and difference are a constant feature in all periods of history. On the other hand, given the diachronic and teleological bias of Marxism, and the emphatic re-articulation of that bias in Raymond Williams's scheme of dominant/residual/emergent cultures, the appeal of an idea such as 'breakdown' is not hard to understand.

A second objection to *Radical Tragedy* is its reliance on a reductionist model of the theater as a social and communicative space. In this model, plays are entities that occupy center stage and convey messages, subversive or otherwise, to an audience. All these terms are treated as largely unproblematic: the peripheral interferences in the institutional *mise-en-scène* are ignored. A play is discussed as if it were an academic demonstration of some kind that could, for example, 'show how individuals become alienated from their society'.[17] The decision to make the case for a 'radical tragedy' by treating it primarily as a question of intellectual history is, moreover, a vindication of the supposedly super-seded Tillyard. This decision perpetuates the exclusion of popular culture and the consequential exclusion of all forms of knowledge that do not achieve recognition within some kind of circle of 'educated' men and women.

The revisionist strategies of Greenblatt and Dollimore advance our understanding of Renaissance culture by turning the traditional debate, as exemplified by Tillyard and Rabkin, inside out. A divided subjectivity and its polysemic text are placed at the center of a detailed history of ideology. That divided subjectivity is invested with an historically specific psychology in the form of anxious self-fashioning and with an historically specific social character in the form of radical subversion. As in traditional literary scholarship, authority is divided or allocated between established power and the exceptional subject. The possibility of a further complication in the form of authority invested in productive life or material culture is not considered. The literary subjects in question, however, produced their work not only by 'looking up' towards a sinister but powerfully seductive image of 'power', but also by 'looking down' towards the vitality, the continuity, the relative stability and abundance of popular culture. The full articulation of the possible impact of such a popular culture on literature, as well as on 'power', requires a more comprehensive theory of literature and its relationship to the articulation of collective struggle in other public language than any of those discussed so far.

The most comprehensive recent theory of struggle and difference as the central presupposition of interpretive and historical concern is constituted by the sociological poetics of Mikhail Bakhtin. This 'theory' is characterized by a very high degree of openness and is not merely unsystematic but at times willfully *anti*-systematic.[18] Bakhtin is a theorist of heterogeneity, not only in literature, but also more generally in language defined as a concrete and material form of social activity. But his interest in heterogeneity is very much more than a novel and picturesque version of critical pluralism. The poetics of culture worked out by Bakhtin require careful attention to the history of ideology as practiced by Tillyard; they also require appreciation of polysemy as a central feature of texts, as in the work of Rabkin. In Bakhtin's theory, however, neither of these approaches is fully adequate either by itself or in combination. All reductionist historicism, whether Marxist or non-Marxist, diminishes literature to 'the status of a simple servant and transmitter of ideologies, [and] dogmatized ideological points reflected by the artist in his work, thus turning active and generating problems into ready theses, statements, and . . . conclusions'.[19] Bakhtin is equally opposed, however, to the idealizing of abstract polyvalence as a purely aesthetic manifestation cut off from concrete social entities engaged in active, sometimes violent, struggle, maintaining that 'in the ideological horizon of any epoch and any social group there is not one, but several mutually contradictory truths, not one but several diverging ideological paths'.[20]

The 'divergent paths' do not coexist peacefully, not even in their represented form within literary texts. Literature in this view does not simply provide the occasion for an interesting diversity of critical opinions of a purely contemplative kind, but is instead the site of active and partisan ideological contestation.

Literary language and indeed language in general is a mediation between 'things' and 'consciousness'.[21] Its particularizations in individual utterances have, moreover, a concrete, material existence.

> All the products of ideological creation – works of art, scientific works, religious symbols and rites, etc. – are material things, part of the practical reality that surrounds man. . . . Nor do philosophical views, beliefs, or even shifting ideological moods exist within man, in his head or in his 'soul'. They become ideological reality only by being realized in words, actions, clothing, manners, and organizations of people and things – in a word: in some definite semiotic material.[22]

The insistence on concrete utterance and on 'definite semiotic material' corresponds to the view that language is always saturated with specific social and communicative purpose. Language in Bakhtin's sense is, therefore, deeply identified with collective life and with human agency.

A central feature of this theory is the sustained consideration given to the social diversity of speech types, a phenomenon of all actual language activity to which Bakhtin assigns a term translatable as 'heteroglossia'.[23] This concept, as well as the related concept of 'dialogism', does not belong to a theory of language at all, if the term 'language' is understood to refer to an abstract system of lexical items, rules and grammatical functions that exists in some way prior to utterance or speech. In fact, 'heteroglossia' or the plenitude of actual prior utterance takes the place of any concept of formal system as the context and ground for every concrete instance of speech. This is actually a theory of human action, social initiative and collective authority rather than a theory of 'discourse', but, since social action has no reality unless and until it is realized in some definite semiotic material, language becomes a most useful central conception. But this is a greatly expanded, comprehensive view of language that includes not only verbal expressions of every kind, but also gestures, physical actions such as 'thrashing', and even the organization of space and time, to which Bakhtin gives the designation 'chronotope'. This set of terms provides for a general account of verbal, that is to say social, creativity and for the dissemination of authority. To deploy these concepts in a reduced sense as the expression of a purely formal and ideal polyvalence, or as the detached appreciation of different 'points of view', is to forestall serious consideration of the history of collective life most forcefully suggested by Bakhtin's work.

The idea of distinguishing literary works into univocal texts where only the author's voice is heard, multivocal texts where the author's voice is not heard at all, and a third category combining the first two is articulated in Plato's *Republic* and reformulated in Aristotle's *Poetics*. Although Plato views all poetry as philosophically dubious, tolerable only under the strictest surveillance, it is the multivocal or mimetic forms of comedy and tragedy that are most corrosive and threatening to the well-being of the *polis*. Mimicry or 'seeming-to-be-other' is inadmissible because it is socially debased, and because it confuses the categories of identity and difference. Bakhtin's theory reverses this view, favoring the promiscuous creativity of mimetic forms, with their dispersion of authority among multiple voices, as against philosophically unified forms that reveal a singular, sovereign voice. In this view of the hierarchy of genres, the novel with its dispersed, plural, collective speech is given priority over lyric, as the site of individual subjectivity, and over epic, which expresses a fixed and conclusive ideology.

Authority, in the context of this theory, is identified with the power to influence and to disseminate thought and opinion as well as feeling. When this power approaches from without, in the form of an official mandate or sacred writ, it is likely to be coercive and deadening in its effects. Authority in this sense is actualized by means of discourse enjoining obedience to a person, an institution or an ideological formation in final and definitive form. By mobilizing allegiance to prescriptive writ, authority is an expropriation of creative energy and social initiative. However, the word 'authority' is derived from Latin *augēre*, 'to grow, increase, augment'. In this sense it refers directly to any power of creative utterance or action, and the gradual augmentation of persons through social experience. Authority is thus the quality or state of being an author, that is, an originator, creator, one who conceives and brings to completion even the humblest social initiative or artistic project. In this sense, authority is not a special talent or the exclusive privilege of a small minority of great statesmen and artists, but is, on the contrary, initially dispersed among all men and women with basic linguistic competence.[24] Authoritative discourse, or the coercive expropriation of this widely dispersed verbal creativity, is always limited, constrained – in fact *preempted* – by the diffuse authority of collective life as it is actually lived in everyday experience. This diffuse or heteroglot authority is actualized in the collective and anonymous forms of Carnival.

Bakhtin describes Carnival as a 'second life' or 'second culture' sustained by the common people or plebeian community throughout the Middle Ages and well into the early modern period. During the Renaissance, this culture engages with and directly opposes the 'official' culture, both in literature and in the public life of the marketplace and city square. The 'ennobled language' of official ideology, official religion and high literature becomes saturated with the language of everyday productive life. The genres of literature become 'Carnivalized', their structures 'permeated with laughter, irony, humor, elements of self-parody, and finally – this is the most important thing – Carnival inserts into these structures an indeterminacy, a certain semantic open-endedness, a living contact with unfinished, still-evolving contemporary reality'.[25]

By bringing privileged symbols and officially authorized concepts into a crudely familiar relationship with common everyday experience, Carnival achieves a transformation downward or 'uncrowning' of de jure relations of dependency, expropriation and social discipline. The basic principle of grotesque or Carnival realism is to represent everything socially and spiritually exalted on the material, bodily level. This includes cursing, abusive and irreverent speech, symbolic and actual thrashing, and images of inversion and downward movement, both cosmological (the underworld, hell, devils) and anatomical (the buttocks, genitalia, visceral functions). The transformation downward and re-interpretation of the social world is, moreover, cyclical: uncrowning, devouring and death are always linked to rebirth and social renewal. Carnival images reflect 'the material needs of the organized human collectivity. The bowels study the world in order to conquer and subjugate it.'[26]

As a critical and interpretive concept, Carnival draws attention to the radical 'otherness' of literary works, even those by the most canonical of authors. Bakhtin is not concerned with abstract and universalized 'otherness': he focuses on one specific form of the social 'other', that is 'the people', and in particular the culture and patterns of collective life of the common people in early modern Europe. The insistently cheerful and hopeful populism of this idea has been characterized as naively idyllic, vague and even silly, but both the substance and the tone of its elaboration contribute to the overall coherence and strategic versatility of the theory. The presentation of the people as unfailingly generous, hopeful and continually oriented to a better life in the future is not, of course, an objective description of any actual state of affairs that ever existed in history. It functions in Bakhtin's various analyses as a teleology, inserting into every analysis of the past the idea of a purpose-ful drive toward an authentic socialization of both practical and spiritual life. In addition, 'the people' is a concept that embodies the relationship between productive energy and expropriation, continuously affirming the thesis articulated by Walter Benjamin to the effect that the monu-ments of civilization derive in part from conquest and violent repression. Unlike the 'sadness' expressed by Benjamin, the primary theme of Bakhtin's analysis of the 'anonymous toil' that creates great cultural monuments is the cheerful conviction that these monuments are marked and contaminated by that toil. The social life of common people in early modern Europe is described in terms of cooperation, engagement with material life, and a resourcefulness that enables them to conserve valuable institutions and to create new ones. By virtue of this capacity, 'the people' are able to retain authority and initiative, and thus to act purposefully and reciprocally on the dominant culture.

Bakhtin's concepts of heteroglossia and Carnival, his interest in mimicry and indirect discourse, and his appreciation of the informally organized social life of the public square, all seem to imply that theater is the most vital institutional setting for literary and verbal creativity.

When Pushkin said that the art of the theater was 'born in the public square,' the square he had in mind was that of 'the common people,' the square of bazaars, puppet theaters, taverns, that is the square of European cities in the thirteenth, fourteenth, and subsequent centuries. He also had in mind the fact that the state and 'official society' . . . were located by and large beyond the square. But the square in earlier times itself constituted a state (and more – it constituted the entire state apparatus, with all its official organs), it was the highest court, the whole of science, the whole of art, the entire people participated in it.[27]

This image of the interpenetration of theatrical mimesis and of immediate, practical political life is extremely suggestive with respect to the dramatic literature produced by Marlowe, Shakespeare and their contemporaries. Apart from a few scattered comments on Shakespeare, however, Bakhtin does not pursue the implications of this observation, and, perhaps anomalously, identifies the novel rather than drama as the exemplary genre in which heteroglossia and carnivalization are most powerfully manifested. There are no doubt circumstantial reasons for Bakhtin's decision to focus on the novel. A more important reason for this orientation, however, is that, since the late seventeenth century, the theater has been an essentially moribund social form. Dramatic literature in this context consists mainly of reduced and diminished genres – comedy of manners, satire, sentimental naturalism – giving way to a protracted endgame in the twentieth-century avant-garde. The lack of any sustained consideration of Elizabethan and Jacobean drama in Bakhtin's work is, however, a consequential omission, since this material was created *before* the collapse of the theater as a strong social institution.

Bakhtin's account of Carnival suggests the possibility of a more detailed and circumstantial account of the relationship between popular culture, theater and dramatic literature in Elizabethan England. 'The essential Carnival element in the organization of [Elizabethan] drama . . . does not merely concern the secondary, clownish motives. . . . The logic of crownings and uncrownings, in direct or in indirect form, organizes the serious elements also.'[28] But, although Bakhtin draws attention to what is perhaps a central and decisive application of his own thesis, the full implications of these observations are never pursued in any detail. Any attempt to develop more fully the implications of this brief observation would have to consider Carnival as something much more than a system of images and transgressive rhetorical devices. To interpret the relationship between theater and Carnival, it is necessary to take Bakhtin somewhat more literally and to view Carnival as a concrete social reality in the context of early modern Europe. Such a project must take into account the unselfconscious, ritual character of Carnival, and its utility as a durable strategy for maintaining social cohesion, as well as its selfconsciously pragmatic character as an instrument for altering the status quo. Carnival, in the present text, is assumed to have *both* a social and an antisocial tendency. The existence in even the simplest community of material differences among households suggests that stable collective life is only maintained against the grain of chronic stress and incipient violence. The analysis of festivity that develops out of the sociology of Emile Durkheim proposes that social harmony must be periodically renewed by the ritual intensification of collective experience. Even the apparently secular and informal manifestations of Carnival can be interpreted in the light of such reconciliatory functions. As the next two chapters will show, however, such a view in no way excludes the possibility of coherent social protest and the displacement of the sacred by partisan economic and political concerns.

CHAPTER 2
THE SOCIAL FUNCTION OF FESTIVITY

IN PREINDUSTRIAL society, men and women live and work according to a double time, alternating between the annual cycles of everyday productive life and the parallel cycles of festivity.[1] The familiar distinction between the sacred and the profane, however, can obscure the complex relationship between these two manifestations of social time. Social labor is itself invested with a sacred character in traditional society. And, as Emile Durkheim has shown, the time of sacred observance is neither a collective delusion nor a transcendental experience of supernatural entity, but rather a full and coherent experience of real social life. In this view, festivity interprets the structure of collective traditions, and promotes the continuity of social existence, even when the forms of festive observance seem to manifest an overtly antisocial character.

Festivals typically combine solemn and stately formalities with a suspension of some of the ordinary rules of social life. Both formalities and informalities are playful in that they contrast sharply with the routines of ordinary practical life, and yet it is clear that the play element has a serious, perhaps a sacred purpose, even in the most secularized societies.[2] Misrule and festive misconduct may take the form of a traditionally permitted, stylized transgression or it may be an over-extension of sanctioned liberties where celebrations 'go too far'. But celebrations *usually* 'go too far', the profane intrudes upon the sacred, religious observance becomes compromised by secular interests. Role reversal, the transgression of social boundaries, and even the erosion of the 'true meaning' of the festival are as intrinsic to its structure as is the painstaking observance of correct ceremonial form.

Despite the often lamented ambiguity or deterioration of festive form, it persists as a vital element of social life. That persistence is generally accounted for by an analysis of the function of all festivals in reinforcing social order and in promoting feelings of communal or corporate solidarity. The functional theory acknowledges the complexity of festive form and seeks to incorporate apparently dysfunctional elements into a unified explanation. In its reduced form, the theory that festivity promotes social cohesion explains festive form and its customary violation as a catharsis or 'safety valve'. In this view, people who are oppressed, expropriated or in some way constrained by an unwelcome social discipline are permitted to release their accumulated resentment at regular intervals so that they may then be reincorporated within the repressive regime. There is certainly some element of truth in this analysis for any society characterized by inequality in the allocation of wealth, and by division into masters and servants. Nevertheless, the view that festivity, especially festivity of the Carnival type, is fully accounted for by describing it as an instrument of oppressive manipulation is far too limited.

The 'safety valve' theory assumes that 'rulers' always possess the capacity to permit or to withhold permission. Furthermore, though this theory acknowledges that things usually get out of hand and is in fact an attempt to account precisely for that element of festivity, it nevertheless asserts that nothing is ever changed by the excesses of festive liberty. People may 'go too far' in their celebratory activity, but they can always be brought back into conformity with established social discipline. For catharsis to actually work in such a reliable way, however, it would be necessary for festivals to be completely unselfconscious occasions in which nothing was ever learned, and for the participants to cooperate, year after year, in an oppressive routine contrary to their interests.

The participants in a festival are, in fact, often unreflective and unanalytical about what they are doing, and much festive usage does retain an apparently archaic character. The persistence of certain festive forms down the ages, and the relative inability of participants to account for them, have given rise to the notion that, in historically recent times, festivals persist as a residual survival of a forgotten sacrifical cult from an earlier, purely agrarian, primitive society. E.K. Chambers, who relies heavily on the voluminous descriptions of folk festival and folk religion collected by Sir James Frazer in *The Golden Bough*, describes folk drama as a reenactment of the annual sacrifice of a priest-king whose death and resurrection were vital to the renewal both of agricultural and of sexual fertility.

> . . . festival usage is both conservative and reconstructive. The death remains, but its old significance has been forgotten, and it is given a new one. The mimetic instinct appears again, in a new aspect, as an element of play, which accompanies the serious business of the festival with the free and self-sufficing activities of minds and limbs released from labour, and stimulated by unusual meat and drink. Thus arises a simple drama, in which a revival is added to the death, and a consciousness of the waning and waxing of the seasons is reflected.[3]

The meaning of the festival is ancient, but it is unavailable for immediate critical scrutiny. The annual reenactment of the same narrative and gestural forms, the deployment of old masks and symbols, is a powerful mechanism for perpetuating a narrow and parochial interest in agricultural routine. As in the theory of the 'safety valve', the festival is an instrument of control, though in the theory of 'archaic survival' people are controlled not by rulers but by their ancestors.

Both catharsis and the survival of traditional form are incorporated into a more comprehensive analysis of ritual and festivity in Durkheim's *The Elementary Forms of the Religious Life*. This analysis begins with the distinction between the sacred and the profane, and identification of the domain of the sacred with social life. 'The sacred principle is nothing more or less than society transfigured and personified.'[4] The sacred is experienced through ritual, ceremonial form and festivity, all of which have an heuristic function.

> Society exists and lives only in and through individuals. If the idea of society were extinguished in individual minds and the beliefs, traditions, and aspirations of the group were no longer felt and shared by the individuals, society would die.[5]

Since it is the manifestation of shared social experience, the sacred has a material and objective existence: it is a 'moral being' to which individuals return through the observance of ritual and ritual-like practices. This powerful integrating and reconciliatory force pervades economic, cultural and interpersonal aspects of communal experience.

> Even the material interests which these great religious ceremonies are designed to satisfy concern the public order and are therefore social. Society as a whole is interested that the harvest be abundant, that the rain fall at the right time and not excessively, that the animals reproduce.[6]

Durkheim is most immediately concerned with preindustrial and preliterate societies, but his analysis is equally pertinent for complex social organizations of more recent time. Even in advanced societies where many techniques for sustaining and administering collective life are available, ritual and ceremony persist as a favored resource for enhancing the cohesiveness of social order. The external form of the ceremony is relatively unimportant; no matter how arbitrary or even grotesque the festive manifestation may be, the important thing is that people continue to celebrate in conformity with traditional practice. Every festival reunites the individual with the collective. It reawakens and strengthens feelings of solidarity among persons who will actually benefit from it. In that sense Durkheim's view of society is conservative, since the needs of each individual are presumably best satisfied when he or she is identified with and supported by the collective. Festive life, however, has relatively little to do with covert manipulation or with social control by an extrinsic authority or political monopoly.

Durkheim stresses the function of festival, but is less concerned with its form. The general pattern of ritual and ceremonial form most pertinent to the analysis of the festival was initially worked out by the Belgian folklorist Arnold van Gennep to account for 'rites of passage' in a variety of cultural settings. In order to change status or social position, individuals are required by their society to undergo liminal rites, or rites of transition, in which they leave one category and cross the threshold into another. The structure of these liminal rites is tripartite:

> rites of passage . . . may be subdivided into rites of separation, transition rites, and rites of incorporation. . . . Rites of separation

are prominent in funeral ceremonies, rites of incorporation at marriages. Transition rites may play an important part, for instance, in pregnancy, betrothal, and initiation.[7]

The most obvious application of this concept would be to the stages of individual life, and the various transitions indicated by periods of growth and maturity. The three-part structure of liminal rites is not limited to passages in the life of the individual. The seasonal festivals observed by communities are also liminal events that dramatize significant social transitions, commemorate origins and mark out the annual cycles of productive life.[8]

Van Gennep's analysis of the liminal process is, like Durkheim's analysis of the function of ritual, strongly reconciliatory. The full working out of any ritual leads to the reintegration of the social group. However, in the concept of liminality proper, the middle stage of every transition, van Gennep introduces a novel and important dialectical element. After separation and before incorporation, the liminary participants enter a peculiar and ambiguous social space. 'Betwixt and between' the categories of social life, liminality is the experience of the social 'other'. Neither here nor there, the participant in the liminal experience is, socially speaking, 'elsewhere'. This confers immunity for otherwise unlawful acts; it provides an alibi and an excuse. It is also, perhaps, the fulfillment of wishes that ordinarily cannot be satisfied, or, in other words, utopia. Nevertheless, the experience of otherness is governed by the impulse to return to the already constituted, traditional patterns of social organization. Society means the same thing for all its members. Dissidence, hostility, even rebelliousness are anticipated and respected in and through the festival, which provides for an accommodation of difference. The social group is all-inclusive and supportive. Festivity, ceremonial form and the transgression of social boundaries are animated with the strongest possible feeling of solidarity and community affiliation.

Shakespeare's Festive Comedy, by C.L. Barber, is a minutely detailed application of the theory of festivity discussed in the preceding paragraphs to the social customs of Elizabethan England. Barber's analysis of festivity reveals a 'Saturnalian pattern' that moves 'through release to clarification'.[9] This is in fact a three-part scheme, very much like van Gennep's description of rites of passage and the stages of separation, transition and incorporation. Release necessarily implies a release from something; in the case of Elizabethan England, Barber argues that the participants are released from the routines of productive labor, and from the rules of a hierarchically organized society with its demands for the decorous observance of precedence and social position. Release – separation from the everyday – leads to merrymaking proper, a varied ensemble of activities that may include wooing games, folk pageants and processions, and various forms of symbolic and not-so-symbolic misrule. The 'saturnalian attitude' is overwhelmingly positive in Barber's account.

> The holidays in actual observance were built around the enjoyment of the vital pleasure of moments when nature and society are hospitable to life. In the summer, there was love in out-of-door idleness; in the winter, within-door warmth and food and drink. . . . the celebrants also got something for nothing from festive liberty – the vitality normally locked up in awe and respect.[10]

Finally, the celebrants experience clarification, 'a heightened awareness of the relation between man and "nature"'. This awareness includes 'mockery of what is merely natural, a humor which puts holiday in perspective with life as a whole'.[11] Clarification is thus equivalent to concepts such as those of incorporation and reintegration, but Barber emphasizes obedience to a 'hospitable' society as the existential basis of the individual's relationship to the collective, so that the idea of solidarity becomes compatible with the complex distinctions of a hierarchical social structure. The patterns of reaffirmation and reintegration are archaic survivals of earlier forms of social organization or cultural practice. The saturnalian pattern is depicted as a well-understood social custom that reflects quite consistently the shared ideological horizon of Elizabethan England.

The great strength in Barber's study of festivity and of festive comedy is his picture of a social and cultural milieu in which the themes of harmony, reconciliation and the universe's 'hospitality to life' are the dominant patterns. This stress on the reconciliatory power of festive experience does not mean that he is unaware of real antagonism in Elizabethan society. In his treatment of the lawsuits surrounding the quarrel between the Earl of Lincoln and the Dymoke family, however, he attributes the friction primarily to the aberrant personalities involved, rather than focusing on any substantive clash of interests between opposing social classes. But this is inherent both in his model of the festive process and in his focus on comedy, in which accommodation, unanimity of outlook, the healing of social wounds – in other words 'happy endings' – are regarded as the norm and the purpose of social activity. In this perspective, conflict is always seen as deviant, a misunderstanding or delusion to be corrected by a clarification and reinterpretation of social rules rather than through struggle, negotiation and strategic action leading to social change.

The saturnalian pattern is in fact a complicated version of the 'safety valve', which explains festivity according to a theory of necessary and beneficial repression. Festive comedy ends happily in the return of a repressive order characterized by a wise and tolerant acceptance of individual waywardness. In this reduced but influential application of Durkheim, collective life is portrayed as an opposition between a social 'order' and an isolated individual who desires and may even need 'freedom' from the restrictions of society. Saturnalian release and repression mediate this opposition by redirecting the energy of individual desire back towards the necessary imperatives of social discipline. The suppression of difference is the social expression of an abstract order outside the scope of human action – the universe's 'hospitality to life'. Because it incorporates the basic presuppositions of an individualistic ideology, Barber's reading of festivity and of social life in general necessarily favors a benevolent repression as the source of collective harmony.

Durkheim's sociology is very much more than a theory of repression, because Durkheim does not view social life as an imposition on individuals. In fact, his theory is a sustained critique of the ideology of individualism in all its forms. Collective experience is prior to any experience of individuality; solidarity and identification with communal life are themselves objects of desire as well as preconditions for viable personal existence. Social life is not a strategic compromise between a transcendental order and the divergent energies of individuals pursuing their own interests, but rather the first and most basic resource of human existence. In Durkheim's view, people choose to perpetuate their own collective traditions, not in conformity with nebulous metaphysical conceptions such as the universe's 'hospitality to life', but because those traditions continue to satisfy real needs and real desires. In this context, the analysis of festive accommodation and reintegration must be read, not as resistance to change or suppression of difference, but rather as the active promoting of social continuity.

Durkheim maintains that harmonious collective life is beneficial to its members, who therefore participate willingly in activities that will promote and conserve such harmony. However, to imagine that harmony arises from a natural sociability, or that unanimity is a normal state of affairs prior to any incidental disharmony, is clearly wishful thinking. Feelings of solidarity are probably intermittent at best, and it is just as likely that members of a community may be animated by strong feelings of distrust, animosity and chronic hostility towards one another. The violence of festive misrule is not always symbolic and, whether symbolic or not, it is certainly not an incidental feature. If a theory of catharsis and reintegration is to account even partially for the overall shape of festivals such as Carnival, it must acknowledge that the transgressions connected with festive misrule are real and that, in the violence of festive misconduct, real and sometimes irreparable damage will be done.

For Durkheim, society is the governing category of any science of human culture: individual men and women, as well as their conceptions of the sacred 'other', are most fully accounted for by the complex forms of their social existence. But this is not equivalent to saying that people are naturally disposed towards peaceful cooperation. As René Girard points out, people are just as naturally disposed towards indiscriminate reciprocal violence. In fact, Girard argues, festivals reenact an historically specific act of violence in which a substitute victim is murdered in order to ward off a more terrifying, indiscriminate violence among the members of the same community. This sacrificial murder is the partly hidden meaning of all religion and thus of all social life.

> Durkheim asserts that society is of a piece, and that the primary unifying factor is religion. His statement is not a truism, nor does it dissolve religion in social institutions. . . . Durkheim never fully articulated his insight, for he never realized what a formidable obstacle violence presents and what a positive resource it becomes when it is transfigured and reconverted through the mediation of scapegoat effects.[12]

In this revision of Durkheim, people are drawn towards a collective solidarity as a strategic choice or necessity, but not from a purely altruistic love of neighbor. Ceremonial form and festive transgression are a kind of public rehearsal in which the desirability of social peace and economic cooperation are re-derived from the sacrifice of a carefully selected substitute victim.

The violence of the festival is treated as its central feature by Roger Caillois, in his study *Man and the Sacred*. The process of ritual catharsis is characterized by 'transgression' and 'paroxysm'. Renewal and the reintegration of the individual into the social order are achieved through the release of repressed energy and resentment, through elimination of waste matter and defilement, and finally through sexual excess and debauchery. These violations are not merely tolerated – they are required for the overall purpose of eventual reconciliation.

> . . . in its pure form, the festival must be defined as the paroxysm of society, purifying and renewing it simultaneously. The paroxysm is not only its climax from a religious but also from an economic point of view. It is the occasion for the circulation of wealth, of the most important trading, of prestige gained through the distribution of accumulated reserves. It seems to be a summation, manifesting the glory of the collectivity, which imbues its very being.[13]

Somehow the most intensive periods of antisocial behavior and the pursuit of individual gratification of every kind manifest the 'glory of the collectivity' and help to sustain it. This is perhaps not so much a 'safety valve' as it is a theory of social exhaustion. By depleting reserves and leaving everyone bruised and sore, a collective binge brings on a collective hangover and sets the stage for vows of sobriety and getting back to work. The 'paroxysm' brings about a condition of relative privation, scarcity and discomfort that constrains each individual to turn his attention to economic strategies required to overcome necessity – in short to survive.

To Caillois, the festival in its pure form belongs primarily to small, cohesive social organizations and reflects the collective outlook of ancient cultures. The reversal of social order permitted in the Roman Saturnalia is typical of this kind of festive manifestation in that it is completed by the actual murder of the mock-king. This final and conclusive act achieves the underlying purpose of the social inversion, which is to eliminate all dissonant impulses. Since the victim of the sacrifice is, in all likelihood, a slave, the entire complex of events has a clearly admonitory function as well: it 'permits' mutiny and inversion in mimetic form so as to prevent the real thing. Without a real willingness to carry out the execution, however, the full force of the festival is seriously vitiated. Burning or hanging an effigy, 'burying carnival' or 'expelling winter' are weak after-images of a more sinister but finally more authentic social form.

> . . . the modern carnival [should] be viewed as a sort of moribund echo of ancient festivals of the Saturnalian type. . . . in these latter-day manifestations, no more should be seen than the automatic application in a new environment of a kind of atavism, a heritage of the times in which it was felt vitally necessary to reverse everything or commit excesses at the time of the new year.[14]

This is more than a simple 'survivalist' account, however. The 'latter-day' manifestations no longer have the purposeful direction of festive celebrations in ancient societies because the integrating function of the festival has been taken over by the administrative apparatus of the state, which opposes and seeks to suppress all traditional, collectively sustained techniques of social organization. The functional equivalency between festivity and administrative technique suggests, moreover, that the social order objectified in the festival is a rival and antagonist to state power. In fact it is precisely such a rivalry that gives rise to the historical suppression of many festive forms during the early modern period in Europe, including the cutting down of maypoles and the proscribing of 'lewd, pagan rites'. The state and its accompanying collateral administrative cadres arrogate to themselves the functions of defining and excluding the social 'other', so as to maintain social peace.

In van Gennep's theory of liminal rites, the experience of social 'otherness' is defined in accordance with norms of the prevailing order. Transgression and outsiderhood are recognizable by virtue of their difference from these norms. Caillois's observation that 'festivity' and 'administration' are rivals, rather than just functional equivalents, implies that society might be inherently divided, not in the sense that there are contending social classes, but in the more confusing sense that it might consist of conflicting and even incommensurable experiences for the same group of individuals. Society may be characterized, not by its reconciliatory capacity, but by structural ambiguity that actually gives rise to more or less permanent dissonance. This chronic disharmony persists independently of extrinsic factors of conflict such as the existence of social classes or the unequal allocation of social wealth. If this ambiguity could be resolved into a system of rigorous, mutually exclusive oppositions, then, of course, unity would be recuperated at a higher level of abstraction. However, if society is an unsystematic aggregate of more or less *ad hoc* institutions that has grown by historical accretion, then unity gives way to dispersion of social life into several different modes of collective interrelating. Festivity in this context would continue to function as a force of cohesion by mediating some of the structural ambiguity. However, it would no longer be possible, according to this view, to treat festivity as a clarification of the social rules to which it is in some sense hierarchically subordinated. Festivity would carry with it a genuine capacity for social creativity and would demand to be recognized as a substantive action rather than as a sign with some hidden social meaning.

One way to specify the multiplicity or dispersion of social experience within what is ostensibly the unity of society is by way of the distinction proposed by Victor Turner between 'social structure' and 'communitas'.[15] Social structure is the authorized and legitimated system of categories, roles and consciously recognized social imperatives that ordinarily provide order and coherence in the day-to-day experience of each member of the community. 'Communitas' is a term that refers to the many shifting, informal and spontaneous forms of affiliation and affective loyalty that may be generated by participation in a common task, by shared life experiences among men or women of the same age or marital status, or by transient and ephemeral social activity such as a celebration or a journey. Structure favors differentiation and the organized division of labor; it is often hierarchical, though it need not be. Communitas, on the other hand, favors non-differentiation and is likely to be egalitarian. In Turner's view the social world is composed of accumulated 'debris' or 'fallout' from earlier strata of social organization. Every society, therefore, provides both an elaborated, usually ambiguous or complex structure, together with rich and varied opportunites to experience communitas. Individuals function best when their willingness to conform or become reconciled is accompanied by considerable social versatility.

Communitas has a strong link, in Turner's analysis, with the experience of liminality, the transitional state 'betwixt and between' the roles, functions and predetermined identities provided for in the social structure. The benefits of participation in the social structure are those of an ordered social world with a system of regulations and control that protects each individual from wanton or whimsical interference. The difficulty with structure is in its tendency to promote conformity at the expense of appropriate versatility, to oppose growth, change of status and social mobility, even when such transformations are prompted naturally by maturation or by altered economic conditions. The experience of liminality is a resource that facilitates alteration in one's social situation. The liminary participant leaves the social structure and at the same time enters communitas, a state that enhances sociability and provides support for 'becoming different'.

Caillois, in his analysis of the festival, argues that festivity can have only a diminished function under modern conditions, since, beginning in the late medieval and early modern periods, the administrative state preempts the living function of older ritual forms. Turner acknowledges the pressure exerted on festival by modern political formations, but nevertheless maintains that it still functions as an effective social resource. The anonymous, ludic and symbolic action of liminality in tribal societies tends to lose its relatively unreflective character in more advanced cultural settings. However, liminal experiences do not simply disappear, but are reinvented in the form of a self-conscious, often parodic, mimesis that maintains both the form and the function of older liminal observances. These re-creations of liminal phenomena are described by Turner as 'liminoid'.

> Liminal phenomena tend to be collective, concerned with calendrical, meteorological, biological, or social-structural cycles and rhythms . . . liminoid phenomena develop most characteristically outside the central economic and political processes. . . . Liminoid phenomena, being produced by specific named individuals or particular groups, 'schools', 'coteries', tend to be more idiosyncratic and quirky than liminal phenomena. They compete with one another in the cultural market, and appeal to specific taste – while liminal phenomena tend to have a common intellectual and emotional meaning for all the members of the widest affective community.[16]

Among liminoid phenomena Turner particularly mentions both theater and Carnival. In this view the evidently archaic ritual practices of Carnival are read as a deliberate and purposeful mimicry. There is no question of a 'moribund' survival of earlier forms. And while it is clear that the liminoid form retains its social function, it is no longer appropriate to consider that function as exclusively reconciliatory.

> Liminal phenomena may, on occasion, portray the inversion or reversal of secular, mundane reality and social structure. But liminoid phenomena are not merely reversive, they are often subversive, representing radical critiques of the central structure and proposing alternative models.[17]

In a liminoid event the participants are likely to find their experience of solidarity and communal affiliation in the idea of a radical departure from or resistance to the constraints of the social structure.

The distinction between liminal and liminoid phenomena suggests that the concept of the festival ought to be extended so as to include both organized mimesis of an apparently non-ritual kind, such as theatrical performances and spectacles, and unplanned, contingent outbreaks of misrule and resistance, such as riots. Turner argues that an actual crisis in social life is very likely to manifest itself as a 'social drama'.[18] Despite the unanticipated and purely circumstantial character of many disputes or quarrels, the participants in such an event often act in accordance with a familiar 'script' or 'scenario'. In other words, their cultural experience provides the actors with a socially derived text which provides form, purpose and narrative resolution to the crisis. This conception is, in Turner's view, applicable to domestic crises and neighborhood disputes, as well as to events on a larger scale, such as general uprisings.

Turner's development of the theoretical conception of the festival derived from Durkheim and van Gennep takes account of conflict and dispersion as well as unity in considering the social function of festive form. In addition, his distinction between social structure and communitas, with its elaboration into the concepts of liminoid phenomena and social drama, proposes a much more central role for human agency, both constructive and destructive. This distinction recalls the more general ones that Bakhtin makes between 'official culture' and 'popular culture' or Carnival, and indeed Turner acknowledges an indebtedness to

Bakhtin. In this more complex version of the theory, festivity retains its character as an expression of the sacred in the sense originally intended by Durkheim, and therefore it retains its function as a force for social integration.

However, all these terms must now be read as historical categories. Carnival in the early modern period is not simply festivity in general, though all festivity is very likely to have a 'conservative' social function. In considering a particular historical instance of festivity, however, it is necessary to ask who is conserving what and at whose expense. The forms of festive life are always available for appropriation to particular social and political purposes. In early modern Europe such appropriation is by no means exclusively confined to the dominant culture.

CHAPTER 3
CARNIVAL AND PLEBEIAN CULTURE

CARNIVAL was celebrated throughout Europe in the early modern period, reaching its climax on Shrove Tuesday or Mardi Gras, just before the beginning of Lent. The specific pattern of celebration varied from one locality to another, although the general features of Carnival were quite similar in a variety of cultural settings.[1] Carnival is a time of festive abundance and overindulgence; meat is consumed in large quantities, there is much drinking, and special foods such as pancakes mark the celebration. Along with lavish consumption of food, Carnival encourages drunkenness, disruptive behavior and symbolic disorderly conduct. There is also actual misrule, including increased sexual promiscuity, street violence and civil commotion. Finally, Carnival is the occasion for masquerade, disguise and processions, often featuring role-reversal and gender-switching, together with special performance activities featuring both topical dramas and traditional narratives. Because it is a winter festival, Carnival has always had its largest outdoor manifestations in southern Europe, but, even in cities where the climate is not well suited to street celebrations during the months of February and March, Carnival was nevertheless an annual event.

In the strict sense of the term, 'Carnival' refers to the feast enjoyed every year in the days immediately preceding Ash Wednesday and marks the 'taking away of meat', in preparation for the penitential fast of Lent. Carnival is not an isolated episode, however, but a relatively protracted season extending throughout the somewhat indefinite period of time between the fixed feasts of the Christmas cycle and the movable feast of Easter. One of the functions of Carnival is to facilitate the annual transition from celebrations fixed by the solar calendar, including All Souls' and the Twelve Days of Christmas, and ending with Candlemas on February 2, to celebrations fixed by the juxtaposition of the lunar calendar with the vernal equinox, including Lent and Easter, and ending with Ascension Day.[2] Because it occurs 'betwixt and between' these liturgically recognized cycles but is not strictly speaking part of the liturgical year, Carnival's annual arrival is 'untimely' and is marked with customs like ringing the church bell at the wrong time or changing the hands on the clock. As the liminal event *par excellence*, Carnival is the pivotal link in the annual cycle of festivity, and carnivalesque manifestations pervade every celebration, those of May and midsummer no less than the winter observances.

As with every festival, Carnival was observed among all the various social strata. Despite the customary crossing of social barriers, however, important distinctions were observed. Wealthy and privileged households had their own Carnival celebrations featuring lavish masquerades and private entertainments. Carnival had particular significance for the common people who made up the vast majority of the populace, for whom it was 'our yeere of Iubile: and when the pancake bel rings we are as free as my lord Maior'.[3]

Whether Carnival was a mere holiday in the most limited sense of the term, or in fact a 'second life for the people' characterized by a spirit of social equality and cooperative allocation of material wealth, is not so readily determined. To begin with, it is necessary to define exactly what is meant by such terms as 'the common people', or 'plebeian society', and to account for both the uniting and disuniting tendencies within such a large and diverse 'group'. Further, the nature of popular or plebeian culture needs to be specified, as well as the degree to which any such culture is accessible to historical research. Finally, if Carnival is a distinct and purposeful working out of the ethos of plebeian culture, then it must be a self-conscious, 'liminoid' rather than 'liminal', manifestation that overlaps with a definite political outlook, whether this is an explicit ideology or a more nebulous, implicit sentiment animating direct action that challenges the status quo.

The social structure of Elizabethan England is, or purports to be, a 'chain of being' or 'ladder of degree' that accounts for all differences in birth, *métier* and wealth, and that determines both the correct order of precedence in society and the correct division of labor, responsibility and authority. The social practice of the period, however, was characterized by considerable economic and social disruption, religious and political controversy, and extensive upward and downward social mobility.[4] Despite the complexity of the structure, and despite the various factors of change and uncertainty, the identity of the common people or, as they were sometimes known, 'the inferior sort' was clear to virtually everyone. The most fundamental of all the divisions in society was that between the small elite entitled to some degree of participation in both de facto and de jure power, and everyone else – regardless of actual wealth and power – without such de jure entitlements.[5] That elite was composed mainly of all those of 'gentle birth', from the humblest mere gentleman to the great lords. Obviously this group, though small, was extremely diverse in its interests and political outlook. Nevertheless, the recognition of gentility was of undeniable importance and consisted primarily in the conviction of some kind of objective difference from the socially and politically excluded 'other' – that is from virtually all the populace. Neither the ruling elite nor the common people as a whole are in any way homogeneous groupings; and, furthermore, the barriers to gentle status by no means precluded the permanent promotion of a family to gentility. But the basic distinction between a small elite that rules, or purports to rule, and a large, diverse body of 'little people', between a patrician society and a much larger though much less powerful plebeian culture, is extremely pertinent historically, and has particular cogency for understanding both the form and the objectives of popular culture in the early modern period.

The plebs, and thus plebeian culture, is a broad, socially inclusive category, but it does not correspond either to an abstract conception of a 'unified populace' or to the modern phenomenon known as 'mass society'. The plebs is unified by virtue of its exclusion from privileges of gentle birth. Perhaps even more important, the plebeians are a broad social grouping that includes everyone directly identified with actual production, including farmers, craftsmen and merchants, along with their dependents and allies among such disadvantaged groups as apprentices, journeymen and servants. The plebeians are thus in themselves a class society, rather than a social class. But the plebeians are also a political entity, nominally excluded from rule, but nevertheless exerting constant pressure on the ostensible ruling elite through the weight of sheer numbers and through innumerable local contestations of the extent of surveillance and supervision, and the nature of property rights.[6] The identification with material life and productive effort, and the exclusion from material benefits that accrue to certain households with privileged status, give rise to a heightened sense of local authority and proprietary right. The plebs is not a working class in the modern sense, but it is the complex ensemble of producing classes, *métiers* and corporations, all of which are animated by the conviction that they are entitled to the wealth created by their labor.[7] This culture tends also to promote an ethos in which the pursuit of wealth for the sake of accumulation must be subordinate to the purpose of sustaining and reproducing the men and women who produce that wealth.[8]

The common people thus have a distinct and definite existence, separate from the nobility and gentry who rule them. At the same time, these common people experience complex and multiple forms of social dissonance among themselves, quite apart from the constant friction with the ruling elite. There are more or less permanent structural oppositions between rural and urban interests and, in addition, newer structural conflicts brought about by the introduction of new techniques and new sources of wealth. These structural oppositions are superimposed on traditional patterns of alliance and rivalry between various guilds or between different towns and settlements. There are also important informal associations that figure prominently in the social landscape of plebeian communities, particularly the 'youth groups' or confraternities that included unmarried males from adolescence up to and in some cases beyond the age of 30.[9] Among the diverse functions of these associations were those of surveillance of weddings and sexual conduct, especially through the charivaris, organization and implementation of festive misrule, and local defense and popular justice. The internal organization of these associations was cooperative rather than hierarchical. Their internal sociability was likely to be expressed in socially aggressive conduct, however, and 'youth groups' were often denounced for disturbing the peace. Finally, if the frequency with which sureties of the peace were asked and usually granted is any indication, the ambient level of social and domestic violence must have been relatively high.

The patterns of dissonance and conflict within the society of common people do not resolve neatly into a simple scheme of class struggle or transition from feudalism to capitalism. In order to account fully for the chronic discord of social life in the early modern period, E. Le Roy Ladurie suggests that two explanatory paradigms are necessary.[10] Some conflict certainly appears to take the form of a class struggle in which solidarity is primarily horizontal and in which groups of unequal status oppose each other vertically. However, there is also conflict in which the community is split into rival factions or coalitions. In this situation solidarity is experienced vertically and the contention is between opposing parties or religious affiliations. In light of this pervasive discord, and the ominous and virtually constant potential for violence, plebeian culture developed an ensemble of implicit strategies and cooperative resources for achieving communitas and for modulating but not eliminating social conflict.

The common people lived in a system of interlocking communities, and much of their attention and creative energy was connected with the day-to-day management of their own social life. Since a good deal of their cultural activity was objectified in relatively impermanent and even ephemeral semiotic material, traces of popular culture have not always been easy to discern or to contextualize accurately. One approach to the problem of popular culture has been to posit a radical and substantive inferiority in the collective traditions of the subordinate classes. Only the elite possess a culture in this view; the popular element is characterized as naive and parochial, or simply dismissed as uninteresting. Whatever culture the subordinate classes do possess would be a debased and simplified version of the elite culture, disseminated in a form suitable to untutored minds. This view does, however, concede that something resembling a cultural life does exist among the common people, but in too reduced a form to require any serious attention.

Although such a view is discouraging, an even more troubling objection to any study of popular culture has to do, not with a prejudgement of quality, but with the basic difficulty of access. The most radical problem for the analysis of popular culture is not whether evidence exists, but whether any evidence that does exist could be regarded as genuinely popular.[11] To put the question another way – could any evidence of the socially and culturally excluded 'other' ever exist even in principle? According to this argument, no real trace of a popular culture can exist that in some way speaks for it; what survives to be noticed are images, descriptions and characterizations of popular culture that are primarily useful for its suppression or at least marginalization. These images at best provide a distorted picture of the subordinate classes, as do the similarly false and flattering images of madness, criminality and every other socially excluded form of subjectivity or collective life. This bafflement of scholarly inquiry is predicated on the concept of two exclusive and mutually unintelligible 'discourses' – the madman and his medical attendants, the criminal and his judges, or the popular element and the dominant culture. The project of translating the unintelligible does nothing other than reproduce the discourse of the dominant culture and is therefore futile. The excluded 'other' remains mute, unreadable and powerless.[12]

In the light of this challenge to the very possibility of any analysis of popular culture, it is important to ask to what extent subordinate classes were in fact subordinated. An intent to hold people in subordination is not the same as achieving an effective control over every aspect of their social conduct, to say nothing of their subjective outlook. A wish to discourage or ignore manifestations of popular culture will not of itself cause that culture to disappear. The exploited or unprivileged population is not, perhaps, altogether powerless, even if its strength is primarily in sheer numbers. Similarly, an uneducated, even illiterate, population is not by virtue of that exclusion ignorant or deficient in intellectual capacity, substantive knowledge and practical skills. And many common people took advantage of the available access to formal education. In England, much of the literature that has survived was created by individuals whose origin was among the subordinate classes, and who were therefore fluent in the verbal idiom and the intellectual traditions of popular culture, as well as conversant with the resources of formal education. Many common people have the capacity to mimic the idiom of the elite, and vice versa, just as madness has the capacity effectively to mimic reason. But all mimicry is a feature, not of mutually unintelligible discourses, but of a 'heteroglot' world of socially diverse speech types. These speech types overlap, interpenetrate, exchange terms and expressions, and in general shadow each other so intimately that no monopoly of knowledge is ever achieved without contamination by what it purports to exclude. Instead of an inference that popular culture cannot be observed anywhere, it seems more useful to assert that popular culture existed everywhere, though never in a 'pure' and uncontaminated form. The hypothesis of a dominant culture effectively secured from intrusions of the popular element and capable of administering the culture of the subordinate classes must be discarded in favor of a picture of a numerically small elite absolutely surrounded by a veritable demographic and cultural ocean of the 'inferior sort'. Popular culture is thus not hidden from view; virtually everything that survives is likely to contain some traces of its impact or to reveal a deflection from its enormous mass.

The existence of a popular tradition or 'folk culture' in sixteenth-century England has been acknowledged for some time, undoubtedly because that popular culture had such a substantial impact on the dramatic literature created by the great Elizabethan and Jacobean playwrights. Documentary evidence of this popular culture is scattered and fragmentary, although Robert Weimann has shown that a considerable amount of quite useful evidence does in fact exist and that the real problem is devising a strategy for analyzing that evidence.[13] Weimann has been criticized for relying too heavily on secondary materials without discovering any new evidence of his own. However, this criticism overlooks what is undoubtedly Weimann's most striking accomplishment. Through an exhaustive survey of the voluminous scholarly literature produced over a period of many decades, *Shakespeare and the Popular Tradition in the Theater* demonstrates how much is already known about popular culture in the early modern period and how energetically that culture contributed to the growth of learning, of art, and of political and social institutions. His project, drawing together under a single unifying rubric all the scattered and specialized studies of isolated aspects of the problem, effectively displays the scope and coherence of popular culture so that it can no longer be marginalized as a quaint, folkish curiosity.

Weimann's analytic perspective relies very extensively on the themes of development, emergence and transition. 'Folk' or 'popular' elements are described as simple or early forms that evolve toward the greater complexity of a fully achieved and perfected dramatic art. This pattern of development of folk drama into the complex literature of the great Elizabethans parallels a larger narrative that describes the overall historical transition from feudalism to capitalism. By using development as a central organizing scheme, it is a foregone conclusion that manifestations of popular culture will be read as 'less developed'. Weimann does not wish to denigrate popular culture, but generally he describes it as a source of forms, practices and fragmentary images that achieve fuller and more complex realization in the masterpieces of dramatic literature and in the professional theaters where these works were produced. Such a view imposes a false teleology on popular culture, and obscures the distinctive objectives and sense of collective life characteristic of the community that produces the various popular forms of festive and mimetic activity.

A similar objection can be raised to the use of the transition from feudalism to capitalism as the primary analytical scheme for interpreting popular culture. There is no doubt that feudalism once existed, that capitalism has now almost completely displaced it, and that therefore a transition must have happened.[14] Further, a significant consequence of that transition was the virtual disappearance of the plebeian culture of the early modern period and the splitting apart of the social grouping that sustained it. For many historians, including most Marxists, England is the exemplary case for understanding the specific over-determinations that led to the abolition of the manorial economy, and to the creation of the institutions and practices most favorable to a capitalist economy and a bourgeois culture. There is, however, considerable disagreement as to how, why and when this transition happened and who was most affected by it. The theme of transition is undoubtedly a valid interpretive strategy for elucidating social change in the Elizabethan period, despite the controversy over detail. However, the focus on a long-term pattern of overall development tends to obscure more subtle forms of political struggle within the period.

No matter how much foresight they may have had, contemporary observers could not possibly have anticipated all the ramifications of future capitalist development from the perspective of the late sixteenth century. Analyses of the transition show, moreover, that the distinction between regressive, feudal tendencies and emergent capitalist tendencies does not correspond in any clear way to the social and political hierarchies and distinctions thought to be important at the time. Finally, though proposals for the restructuring of society were not unknown, it was rare to find anyone openly advocating radical social change on the grounds that innovation, progress or evolution were either inevitable or necessarily good in themselves. Millenarian schemes bear little resemblance to emerging capitalism in any case, and their existence did not make the objective conditions of the transition clearer to the men and

women of the sixteenth century. The nature and the eventual outcome
of the transition remained obscure, and in general people devised their
political and cultural strategies in the light of more immediately intelligible considerations. The diachronic themes of emergence and transition have, therefore, relatively limited value for any analysis of popular
culture, especially since that culture operated in the light of values that
were neither feudal nor bourgeois. Plebeian culture is equally excluded
from both the terms of the transition. In Carnival and in other popular
festive customs it must endeavor to represent and possibly to actualize
other choices for the organization of collective life and for the allocation
of temporal goods.

The transition from feudalism to capitalism certainly had some impact
on plebeian culture, since in the long term the imperatives of a large-
scale capitalist economy penetrated very deeply into the patterns of
everyday life. In the early modern period, however, plebeian culture still
retained some degree of immunity from the destructive effects of
capitalism. The history of plebeian culture is best understood in the
context of what Fernand Braudel has called *longue durée* or the 'structure of everyday life'. In Braudel's theory of social change, this *histoire
quasi immobile* includes a vast ensemble of durable social and economic
practices, including land use and patterns of settlement, the selection of
staple crops, the characteristic etiquette of everyday social usage, and the
extensive production for immediate domestic use and local consumption
before it passes into the market, where it becomes exchange value.
The history of everyday life is the most basic of the three levels in
Braudel's 'architecture'. This routine activity of ordinary men and
women, together with the things they use, lies outside the more lively
unfolding of historically notable events, but nevertheless determines
the 'limits of the possible' for the levels of social activity that lie
above.[15]

Braudel distinguishes two additional levels of social activity from the
quotidien routines of the *longue durée*. Economic life constitutes a
highly visible and relatively mobile middle stratum. At this level of
activity, production enters into the market, where the rules and procedures of exchange become the dominant concern. For Braudel, economic
history is the history of trade and commerce, and also the history of
social relations. It is moreover the history of technological innovation,
exploration and conquest. Above this middle level is a more obscure
sphere of activity which Braudel calls 'capitalism'. This is the highly

abstract manipulation, exchange and accumulation of abstract wealth that has been allocated to the peculiar function of acquiring still further abstract wealth. This sphere of activity is much less visible than the sphere of economic activity itself, but it eventually comes to dominate economic life throughout the world.

Braudel's model conserves the traditional Marxian dialectic of a mutually determining relationship between production (economic life) and capital. But in the concept of 'everyday life' a novel complication is introduced. Whatever happens in the relationship between base and superstructure, that relationship must itself be seen vis-à-vis the inertia of material culture.

> On the one hand, peasants lived in their villages in an almost autonomous way, virtually in an autarchy; on the other hand, a market-oriented economy and an expanding capitalism began to spread out, gradually creating the very world in which we live, and, at that early date, prefiguring our world. Thus we have two universes, two ways of life foreign to each other, yet whose respective wholes explain one another.[16]

This theory suggests that material culture holds something in reserve, that the 'limits of the possible' determine the tempo of social change and may even deflect or soften its effects. It also suggests that capitalism does not emerge as a perfected and finished system, but remains incompletely rationalized, with numerous blank spaces in which resistance can take shape. In the early modern period, the blank space of popular festive form remained very large and therefore offered considerable scope for critical reflection on all forms of domination, feudal as well as capitalist.

The relationship between Carnival, social regulation and militant, organized political protest is the subject of an extensive study by Emanuel Le Roy Ladurie. In 1580, in the small town of Romans, the annual Carnival turned into a genuine 'people's uprising'. The rebels, mainly urban craftsmen and laborers, together with a significant number of peasants from local villages outside the town, evidently planned to murder the well-to-do landowners and the wealthy town merchants who lived as nobility. Their plan was anticipated by the local elite, who secured the city gates and proceeded to massacre the leaders of the mutiny and many of the participants. Both sides had used the Carnival of the previous year to symbolically act out and even to rehearse the bloody encounters of the climactic days and nights of February 1580. Le Roy Ladurie's account shows that Carnival was useful as a way to communicate grievance, threat and counter-threat. The mummery and symbolic violence were equally valuable for purposes of concealment, cloaking the extent of the planned assaults, disguising the intended tactics, and hiding the identity of the actual murderers. The specific social and political setting for the massacres included a number of long-standing and particularly abrasive sources of conflict and disagreement between rich and poor, between various commercial and artisan interest groups, and between Protestant and Catholic. Although the feelings of bitterness between the two sides were clear and intense, the issues were on the whole varied and diffuse, ranging from material considerations such as taxes and the price of bread to more purely emotional factors including sexual jealousy. Le Roy Ladurie's account describes the alignment of forces very clearly. The power structure is made up of a coalition of aristocratic and bourgeois elements, concerned above all to defend their position of economic and political advantage. The popular party, on the other hand, consists of peasants and artisans, but also has a significant bourgeois presence. The rebels were fighting for their traditional rights and against a worsening of their situation brought about by new taxes and oppressive regulations. They were also animated by populist and egalitarian sentiments of a relatively novel character. If this episode is a skirmish in the long transition from feudalism to capitalism, it is not always very easy to determine which side was which.

Viewing the events at Romans against the background of popular festive customs in a number of European countries during the Renaissance, Le Roy Ladurie concludes that, although the rebellion and the massacre that followed were an isolated example, the political impulses expressed in and through the Carnival are characteristic of plebeian culture generally.

> Carnival was not merely a satirical and *purely temporary* reversal of the dual social order, finally intended to justify the status quo in an 'objectively' conservative manner. It would be more accurate to say it was a satirical, lyrical, epic-learning experience for highly diversified groups. It was a way to action, perhaps modifying the society as a whole in the direction of social change and *possible progress.*[17]

Le Roy Ladurie emphasizes the purposeful contemporaneity of Carnival, its heuristic and potentially pragmatic and social utility, and suggests that it is grounded in a continuous tradition of plebeian culture that interacts reciprocally with ruling elites by means of this popular festive 'counter-theatre'. Full-scale rebellions are rare, although threats, admonitions and summary justice are relatively common. But Carnival has a sinister side. Plebeian culture is not always generous and progressive, its violence not always directed against injustice and wrongdoing within the power structure. The communal solidarity of the subordinate classes is likely to be achieved through 'displaced abjection', in which feelings of grievance and resentment are redressed at the expense of outsiders such as Jews or foreigners, or of such relatively defenseless substitute victims as prostitutes or actors.[18]

Le Roy Ladurie's study confirms the validity of an inclusive concept of the common people as an aggregate of interlocking constituencies or classes capable of sustained and organized political action against a well-defined ruling elite. It also reinforces the idea of a distinctively plebeian culture with a capacity for reflective inquiry into social conditions and with the means to articulate this reflection in definite semiotic material. The rebels who attempted to overthrow the power structure in Romans, despite their fatal lack of tactical initiative and cunning, had a cogent view of their political situation and a coherent strategy for accomplishing their objectives. The Carnival was an affirmation of the forms of collective life embodied in the festive confraternities themselves, which Le Roy Ladurie has characterized as 'co-operative associations with all members on an equal footing'.[19] It is also a critique of the principle of domination: those who allegedly rule do not provide either material well-being or social peace, and therefore it is left to the crowd to govern itself and to punish those who govern badly.

In a study of 'the meaning of misrule', Natalie Z. Davis shows that confraternities, youth groups and 'abbeys of misrule' were common both in peasant communities and in the towns and cities of early modern Europe.[20] Her analysis of misrule reveals forcefully that 'mere holiday' and 'letting off steam' are among the least important meanings of this extremely pervasive custom. Misrule is in one sense a complete misnomer, since an important purpose of abusive and derisory mimicry is to reinforce community standards of proper decorum and appropriate sexual behaviour. The license, or more accurately the obligation, to deride any and all forms of social transgression has an extensive domain of application: the domestic and personal disorder of privileged households was likely to receive particular attention from the festive crowd, which could ridicule the difficulties and misfortunes of their superiors with impunity. An obvious extension of this function is to criticize the public and political, as well as the private, misrule of established authority. Carnival misrule is overt and deliberate, but, by accurately mimicking the pretensions of ruling families, the covert and possibly willful misrule of constituted authority is exposed.

When there is no longer any distinction to be made between rule and misrule, the possibility of order disappears because the differences that give rise to order have been abolished. Loss of difference gives rise to the terrifying possibility of indiscriminate violence and the permanent loss of social cohesion. Carnival is intended to ward off the crisis of indiscriminate violence, not by means of a purely unselfconscious stylization of a sacrificial murder, but by identifying as a most likely source of danger the ruling elite itself, which more than any other sector of society claims to possess the means for mastering social violence. The deployment of festive misrule is not divisible into two independent functions – protest and surveillance – but is a unified critical activity that seeks to restrain and limit all radicalization from below in the form of individual deviation from socially accepted norms, and all radicalization from above in the form of departures from traditional and customarily tolerated patterns of governance.

Popular festive form reminds the ruling elite that they may actually rule relatively incompletely and ineffectively. Much of the conduct of everyday life, and many of the details of political and economic practice, proceed quite independently of the wishes of the power structure. Carnival is an heuristic instrument of considerable scope and flexibility. Though it is a festive and primarily symbolic activity, it has immediate pragmatic aims, most immediately that of objectifying a collective determination to conserve the authority of the community to set its own standards of behavior and social discipline, and to enforce those standards by appropriate means. At the same time Carnival is a form of resistance to arbitrarily imposed forms of domination, especially when the constraints imposed are perceived as an aggression against the customary norms of surveillance and social control. It is, finally, an idiom of social experimentation, in which utopian fantasies are performed and collective desires for a better life are expressed. These objectives are realized through the characteristic expressive features of Carnival, which include masquerades that take the form of travesty and misrepresentation, stylized conflict and agonistic misrule, and utopian imagery of unlimited material abundance and social peace. But the secular orientation of Carnival should not be regarded as an instance of historical desacralization of practices that initially retained a religious significance. Despite the saturation with temporal concerns, Carnival in early modern Europe belongs to a social world where everything is invested with a sacred character, but only intermittently. Every detail of practical reality has a sacred meaning in that it refers to the existence of that 'moral being' that Durkheim identified with collective life itself. But that 'moral being' is experienced, not as an idealized spirituality, but in the sheer everydayness and crude practicality of social existence.

PART II
THE TEXTS OF CARNIVAL

A LTHOUGH common people in early modern England did not participate in elections, respond to opinion polls or read newspapers, they were nevertheless actively engaged in public life. This engagement was by no means limited to parochial interests but extended to the politics of the wider world, and to the deployment of power and authority on a national and even an international scale. Communication between the centers of power and the people as a whole was accomplished in a number of ways, but spectacle, pageantry and public gatherings in the streets and village squares were of primary importance because they were capable of affecting large numbers of people in a reasonably short time, and because they could leave a memorable impression on their audiences. The traditional scenarios, masks and *dramatis personae* of Carnival and other popular festive forms were the preferred medium of communication for the common people, since these anonymous public forms offered a way to express unauthorized political opinions and suggestions with little risk of penalty.

The artifacts of Carnival are fragile objects made of cheap, impermanent materials. Scenarios, traditional songs, stories and characterizations are transmitted and preserved primarily in oral form, while purely topical, extemporaneous performances are completely ephemeral. The most intangible 'semiotic material' of Carnival is the organization of the festive crowd itself, which gives to its members an experience of a larger human physicality where individual self-consciousness sharply diminishes and identification with the collective 'other' intensifies. Virtually all of this expressive material is entirely evanescent, and indeed it is conceived and designed so as to leave no permanent trace. But, despite the ephemeral character of specific Carnivals, the general shape of popular festive form is preserved in a number of complex analytical, descriptive and parodic texts, for example, *Nashes' Lenten Stuffe*, and *Iacke-a-Lente*. Such works are not 'popular literature' in the strict sense, but then they are certainly not a literature of the elite culture either, and remain to this day in a kind of limbo in respect to the received canon. These texts of Carnival situate themselves exactly at the frontier between elite and popular culture, the zone where reciprocal pressure, contamination, and the diversity of speech types and discursive genres is greatest; and it is precisely in these mongrel or heteroglot texts that the repressed or excluded meanings of popular culture become most intelligible.

These 'repressed' meanings can be organized into three categories. First, there is a general critique of privilege and of the idealization of an hierarchical class system. This critique is accomplished primarily through the use of parodic travesty, the derisory misuse of masks and symbols, and the comprehensive reinterpretation of the political and social world in terms of material life. Second, there is an acknowledgment of conflict and social dissonance as a positive feature of productive life. The battle of Carnival and Lent typifies the stylized conflict of popular festive form, which views social life as a tragicomic struggle in which carefully channeled, limited social violence is salutary and fruitful. Finally, popular festive form is an image of collective desire for enhanced material abundance and freedom from expropriation. These images seem deliberately to confuse a utopian future with a recently past golden age – in Elizabethan England, the 'good old days when Abbeys stood'. In the discussion that follows, each of these themes is discussed in relation to its ideological counterpart within the elite or official culture.

CHAPTER 4
TRAVESTY AND SOCIAL ORDER

OFFICIAL pageantry, which includes the royal progress, religious processions and much civic pageantry, is a display of ranks and categories of the social structure, idealized in mythological, historical or biblical images. Social structure is made visible by allegorical representation. For some observers, a public procession is a central and privileged objectification of what is real and essential in the social order, for it is in this act of public pedagogy that the various ranks and functions of society are fully enumerated, their order of ethical precedence given as an order of deployment in a public space. The court, members of the aristocracy and representatives of the lower orders perform as themselves and as the figural anticipation of more perfect forms to be fulfilled in a providential unfolding of history. Official pageantry makes the ideals of the social order objectively present in the here and now.[1] The prince appears in person, either as a performer or as a uniquely privileged spectator. The procession itself expresses governing concepts of degree and difference, hierarchical plenitude, and social and political harmony.

> And upon the same Saturday, the Queen came forth from the Tower towards Westminster, in goodly array; as hereafter followeth.

She passed the streets first, with certain strangers, their horses trapped with blue silk; and themselves in blue velvet with white feathers, accompanied two and two. Likewise Squires, Knights, Barons, and Baronets, Knights of the Bath clothed in violet garments, edged with ermine like Judges. Then following: The Judges of the Law, and Abbots. . . .

And then followed Bishops, two and two; and the Archbishops of York and Canterbury; the Ambassadors of France and Venice, the Lord Mayor with a mace; Master Garter the King of Heralds, and the King's coat armour upon him, with the Officers of Arms, appointing every estate in their degree. . . .

Then the Master of the Guard, with the guard on both sides of the streets in good array; and all the constables well beseen in velvet and damask coats with white staves in their hand; setting every man in his array and order in the streets.[2]

The project of 'appointing every estate in their degree' and 'setting every man in array and order' is based on the conviction that there is an invisible but nevertheless real and absolute order that exists independently of human artifice. The ideal system is part of a larger, cosmic hierarchy of orderly differentiation, superiority and inferiority, in which every element has a determinate place. The procession, objectively and hierarchically organized in space, is a natural and ideally appropriate image of society. The city streets become a stage, the royal personality occupies the center of a theatrical performance. But this stage is not a locus of transitory illusions: it is a space where the politics of love and reciprocity are fully revealed.

. . . in all her passage she did not only shew her most gracious love towards the people in general; but also privately, if the baser personages had either offered Her grace any flowers or such like, as a signification of their good will; or moved her to any suit, she most gently (to the common rejoicings of all lookers on, and private comfort of the party) stayed her chariot, and heard their requests. So that, if a man should say well, he could not better term the City of London that time, than a Stage wherein was shewed the wonderful Spectacle of a noble hearted Princess towards her most loving people; and the people's exceeding comfort in beholding so worthy a Sovereign, and hearing so prince-like a voice.[3]

Events of this kind are motivated to some degree by partisan or dynastic interest and political expediency. The Tudor kings and queens used the royal entry partly as a political technique to confirm their questionable legitimacy. Behind this pragmatic use of public spectacle is the undoubtedly sincere belief, not only that degree and precedence are essential to social well-being, but also that the display of rank and difference in a magnificent style is a necessary link between ideals and their here-and-now implementation.

Allegory is considerably more than a mere technique or instrument of representation in official pageantry: the nature of the allegorical symbol is an essential part of the truth about nature and society. The social structure is itself a kind of allegory, in that its order is also a sign of other, larger orders that form a chain of significance leading to that which does not signify – the divine Logos. The majesty of the prince, his or her appearance in ceremonial procession, discloses a hidden coordination and sympathy between the temporal order maintained by constituted authority and the providentially ordered domains of nature and history. In spectacles of authority there is 'a kind of mimetic magic, as if, by the sheer force of poetry and spectacle, incipient war and dissolution could be metamorphosed into harmony and peace'.[4] The magic symbols of official spectacle and pageantry ought to be an efficacious technique for promoting social cohesion and social discipline, although in practice never so efficacious as temporal authority might wish. Nevertheless, principles of similitude and hierarchical enumeration supply a cognitive basis for interpreting social conflict and its relation to the idealizations of the social structure.

The image of authority in official pageantry is a political instrument through which the power of a vertically organized social structure may be deployed in order to dispel social dissonance and conflict. The forces of disorder, it is assumed, are transitory delusions, forms of error and spiritual darkness that vanish in the light radiated by the revealed source and agent of order. In the dialectic of official pageantry, princely splendor and magnanimity pursue and defeat discord, because discord has no ontological status. Conflict and social dissonance arise from marginal or subordinated levels of creation that refuse to remain in naturally prescribed positions, but the pretense can never be sustained, because it is a manifestation of that which is excluded and powerless.

De jure power and authority do not openly advocate substantive social change. Instead, authority presents itself as the traditionally sanctioned and therefore naturally elevated agency of changeless, already perfected and complete, reality. The figure of authority is at once distanced from the here and now by self-identification with a mythological and legendary past, and at the same time fulfills and completes the here and now by revealing the underlying harmony of a continuous and durable social structure. In Elizabethan times, the ideology of the monarchy and its clientele, as well as the ideology of its opponents among the elite and privileged community, combines imagery from classical and epic literature, and native legend, with nostalgic imagery of a chivalric past, to create a language in which particular questions of continuity, change, political legitimacy and the allocation of power may be argued. In official pageantry this symbolic language remains at a distance from ordinary citizens, who view these matters of state as deferential and wondering spectators.

The epically distanced and idealized structure of official pageantry represents peace and abundance maintained by a collective acknowledgment of order in the magnanimity of the prince and the respectful obedience of his subjects. The actual processes of material production happen behind the scenes: spiritual and physical well-being are the consequence of a providentially ordained structure. The achievement of prosperity and abundance is not the result of progress, social reform or even the deliberate implementation of ameliorative policy. Instead, abundance is the natural consequence of some higher, more ideal, process of justice embodied in the principle of social hierarchy. The prince, in this context, is represented as the rebirth or return of an earlier and more nearly perfect principle of equity, an idea used in the ideology of power since antiquity and revived with great frequency both in the literature and ceremonial pageantry of the court, and also in the streets of Renaissance cities and towns.

Allegory is a way of representing a coherent order operating through the complexity and apparent disorder of social experience. As a strategy for the interpretation of social reality, allegory is the desire to secure valued meaning from contamination by contingent speech. However, the specific instances of allegory in royal processions and civic pageantry do not all value the same meanings, nor do they represent the unified consciousness of a monolithic ruling elite. The 'official culture' is not a single 'ruling class' but a mobile, shifting pattern of more or less durable alliances and coalitions. The civic pageants often dramatize and draw attention to specific political or economic debts and obligations, or express the intention of consolidating an old alliance or creating a new one. This contingent and instrumental use of allegorical symbols is made possible by a tremendously complex elaboration of alternative allegorical meanings, but the public display of such alternative meanings frustrates and confuses the desire to protect valued symbols from both inadvertent and willful misinterpretation.[5] The proliferation of iconographic and emblematic codes makes allegory self-consciously problematic, self-reflexive and therefore no longer allegorical. As an element of a signifying chain referring ultimately to the Logos, an allegorical symbol is incompatible with mimesis. To display such a symbol in the public square is to invite quotation, and therefore misquotation and abusive mimicry. Despite their elaborate and magnificent splendor, the allegorical displays of official pageantry often reveal the pathos of genuine historical anxiety.

> Any person, any object, any relationship can mean absolutely anything else. With this possibility a destructive, but just verdict is passed on the profane world; it is characterized as a world in which the detail is of no great importance. . . . all of the things which are used to signify derive, from the very fact of their pointing to something else, a power which makes them appear no longer commensurable with profane things, which raises them onto a higher plane, and which can, indeed, sanctify them. Considered in allegorical terms, then, the profane world is both elevated and devalued.[6]

The pathos of allegorical representation derives from the fertility of allegory, its power to generate surplus meanings. But because it is so susceptible to 'demonic' misappropriation, allegorical literature becomes gradually saturated by the melancholy sternness of secular coercion and enforcement.[7]

Elements of social structure, social change and the processes of material production are linked in the pageantry of Carnival, just as they are in official spectacles, but the images of Carnival are not animated by resemblance between a visible sign and an invisible but valuable meaning. Carnival is a travesty; costumes, insignia of rank and identity, and all other symbolic manifestations are mimicked or misappropriated for purposes of aggressive mockery and laughter. In the pageantry of popular festivals, no fixed order may be set forth, because travesty subverts the possibility of orderly setting forth through the monstrous proliferation of differences and identities.

In order to sustain a social structure based on hierarchy, there must be substantial belief in the authority of symbols and in the capacity of a natural system of ideal social ranks to reveal itself in the temporal world. A crown is not just a fancy hat. In Renaissance culture, however, the principle of similitude is no longer an uncontested principle of knowing and representing.[8] Symbols begin to appear more arbitrary and less reliable, the results of this being funny or alarming, depending on the viewpoint of individual writers. One of Ulrich von Hutten's *Letters of Obscure Men* presents the problem in mock-solemn terms:

> I was lately at Frankfort fair, and as I walked along the street with a certain Bachelor, two men met us, who to all outward appearance, were reputable, and they wore black cassocks and great hoods with lappets. Now, heaven be my witness, I took them for two Doctors of Divinity, and I saluted them, taking off my cap. Thereupon the Bachelor nudged me, and said, 'God-a-mercy, what doest thou? These fellows are Jews, and thou uncoveredst to them. . . .' Now seeing that you are a profound theologian, I beg of you earnestly and humbly, that you will deign to resolve this question, and tell me whether this sin is mortal or venial, and mine an ordinary, or an episcopal, or a papal case? Tell me, too, whether it seemeth to you that the citizens of Frankfort do well in having such a custom as to allow Jews to walk abroad in the garb of Doctors of Divinity. It seemeth to me that it is not right, but a great scandal, that no distinction should be made between Jews and the Doctors; it is mockery of holy Theology. And his serene Highness the Emperor ought in no way to countenance it, that a Jew, who is a dog and an enemy of Christ, should strut about like a Doctor of holy Theology.[9]

The fictional writer of this letter believes so uncritically in a symbolically representable world that his inadvertent saluting of two Jews is taken to be a case with deep theological implications. The folly of the writer is in his confusion between the spiritual truth of symbols and their pragmatic reliability in everyday life. In spite of his foolishness, however, the character does see certain relationships quite clearly. To wear another man's clothes or to permit the indiscriminate exchange of garments is to display contempt for the most fundamental values. Temporal authority has the duty to enforce and to regulate expressions of identity in the social integument, for to do otherwise is to fail to observe the difference between, for example, Jew and Christian.

The mockery of 'holy theology' and of every other serious interpretation of the world is the normal state of affairs in every Carnivalesque procession because the basis of popular festive form is precisely the wearing of borrowed and misappropriated costumes to generate rude, foolish, abusive mimicry of everyday social distinctions. Carnival pageantry is antithetical to allegory. Instead of figuring forth an invisible reality, it represents the arbitrary transitoriness of all social forms. Costumes, masks, heraldic insignia and practical objects are all used to confuse the relationship between signifier and signified. Travesty, as the central compositional rule of popular festive masquerade, manifests itself in role- and status-reversal of several different kinds. Identity is made questionable by mixing of attributes – 'code switching' – or by grotesque exaggeration. Guise, that is, the customary, appropriate garb or social integument, is permitted to mingle with *dis*guise and the will to deception.

In contrast to the spectacles of authority, Carnival also eliminates the social boundary or proscenium that separates performer from onlooker.[10] Its participatory masquerades permit people to 'put on' new social roles, to borrow the clothing and the identity of someone else, and to adopt the language and the manners of a different social status. The festive liberty of physical involvement in the street pageantry of Carnival transforms and contradicts the 'truth already established' by official ideology. The chaotic disarray produced by this arrangement does more than express a subversive or unauthorized sentiment: it is also pragmatically threatening and potentially mutinous. The participants in Carnivalesque travesty radically confuse and transgress social space – in Carnival a crown *is* just a funny hat, and a funny hat, or some even more inappropriate object, is a crown. The grotesque inappropriateness and foolishness of the Carnival masquerade displays the impermanence of any relationship between an individual and the social identity claimed by the symbolism of his clothing. This misappropriation of symbols is the occasion for gaiety and derision; for the participants it is also an experience of social solidarity and cohesion within a social space no longer vertically organized into distinct and separate strata.

The parodic travesty of popular festive form provides plebeian culture with an alternative world picture in which the closed ranks and status groups of the social structure no longer constitute the rational norm for discourse and for action. This alternative view of social reality is enacted by a group of special Carnival personae, traditional festive masks and identities deployed each year to preside over festive societies and lead processions. These include Lords of Misrule, fools and clowns, devils and 'black men', and men dressed as women, along with figures of folk drama and mummers' plays. Carnival also includes giants, oversized puppets and effigies carried through the streets. According to Bakhtin, the masks and identities of Carnivalesque pageant life in the squares and market-places embody 'the right to be "other" in this world, the right not to make common cause with any single one of the existing categories that life makes available'.[11] These masks and effigies reappear every year as the simulacra of social 'immortality'. Each of these figures represents a variant on the central pattern of travesty and identity switching.

Giants were among the most popular pageant figures in Renaissance England, especially among plebeian communities. The legendary first inhabitants of Britain were giants; they have been used in literature as an image, both positive and negative, of the British people. The giants of popular pageantry were, however, ambivalent, figures of awe but also figures of fun:

> these midsommer pageants in London, where, to make the people wonder, are set forth great and vglie Gyants marching as if they were aliue, and armed at all points, but within they are stuffed full of browne paper and tow, which the shrewd boyes underpeering do guilefully discouer and turne to a great derision.[12]

By 'underpeering' and revealing the *other*sidedness of the giants impos-ing size and awe-inspiring power, the 'shrewd boys' complete the relationships of travesty. The giant is only an oversized straw man; the ugly monster also has a funny and familiar side. In this gesture exposing the 'browne paper and tow' underneath the imposture of the pageant giant, all social and cognitive distance is cancelled: the giant is able to 'make the people wonder', but that wonder does not exclude 'great derision' and homely familiarity.

The relationship of wonder and derision as well as the disclosure of 'othersidedness' informs all the categories of Carnival's cast of characters. The Lord of Misrule who presides over much regularly occurring festive revelry borrows the gestures and the functions of constituted authority in order to actualize both 'law' and its 'transgression'. The Lord of Misrule does not rule and govern from above: he is immersed in the folly he undertakes to regulate. Transgression becomes law; the rule of abstinence and moderation becomes a rule of unrestricted consumption, the rule of deference and obedience is replaced by a rule of irreverent speech and rude gesture. Law can be replaced by its own violation within a framework of duly sanctioned forms, just as rationality can be displaced by folly. The Lord of Misrule mimics the center of authority and reveals that folly and transgression are the covert reality of rational government. Misrule may himself be a clown, or he may be attended by fools, jesters and other projections of his own asinine majesty. Either way, Carnival personae reveal by a cogent mimicry that both rule and misrule are equivocal, unstable qualities.

Travesty and festive misrule are not merely the disruptive negation of established ideological forms. The indecorousness and symbolic anarchy of Carnival masquerade provide their own order of rules for interpreting social reality, in which the rhythm of production and the celebration of social labor are substituted for idealizations of social order. In popular pageantry, traditional religious and political symbols are combined with humble objects from the kitchen and the workshop, and with images of bodily functions, especially those relating to food and eating. In Breughel's painting *The Battle of Carnival and Lent*, the personification of Carnival rides on a wine barrel instead of a horse, and the combatants brandish cooking utensils instead of weapons. Various figures in Carnival's train wear articles of food or kitchenware on their heads – a kettle, a hat made of waffles – and Carnival himself is crowned with a meat pie that someone has bitten into. The comprehensive rethinking of the social world in terms of common, everyday material and physical experience is central to 'uncrowning' – the fundamental transformation downward of popular festive imagery. In this system, the kettle or meat pie take the place of the crown or helmet as the 'topmost' principle. Carnival brings all knowledge of social reality down to earth and places the body, its needs and its capabilities, at the center of the social process.

In the tradition of popular pageantry, material abundance is represented as a direct relationship between consumption and production. Rank and status, the categories of vertical social structure, are retained, but hierarchical placement is established in accordance with the principles of material life and domestic order.

> . . . if ever a cook be worth the eating it is when Shrove Tuesday is in town . . . they are that day extreme choleric, and too hot for any man to meddle with, being monarchs of the marrow bones, marquesses of the mutton, lords high regents of the spit and the kettle, barons of the gridiron, and sole commanders of the frying pan.[13]

Abundance derives from transformations of matter carried out in work to renew the body. These processes include the agricultural cycle, in which seeds of renewed life and abundance are planted in the dead earth; butchering, cooking and consuming of meat; eating, digesting and defecation. Carnival is 'a monster for feeding' that celebrates quantity and the whole cycle of alimentation. The symbolism of popular pageantry discloses the hidden interconnectedness between living and dead matter. Instead of articulating distinctions, it manifests the continuity between food (slaughtered meat) and living flesh (producers and consumers). Carnival represents a dialectical exchange between life and death, achieved through positive and negative transformations of matter:

> there is a thing called wheaten flour, which the sulphery necromatic cooks do mingle with water, eggs, spice, and other tragical magical enchantments, and then they put it by little and little into a frying pan . . . until at last by the skill of the cook, it is transformed into the form of a flapjack, which in our translation is called a pancake, which ominous cantation the ignorant people do devour very greedily.   (*Iacke-a-Lent*, p. 9)

The mundane art of cooking is a 'travesty' of magic and a positive fulfillment of its claim to provide a genuine satisfaction of needs. The continuous renewal of social life through material abundance is also, paradoxically facilitated by a process of destruction that mimics and parodies productive labor:

> youths armed with cudgels, stones, hammers, rules, trowels, and hand saws, put play houses to the sack, and bawdy houses to the spoil, in the quarrel breaking a thousand quarrels (of glass I mean)

making ambitious brickbats break their necks, tumbling from the tops of lofty chimneys, terribly untiling houses, ripping up the bowels of featherbeds, to the enriching of upholsterers, the profit of plasterers, and dirt daubers, the gain of glaziers, joiners, carpenters, tilers, and bricklayers. And what is worse, to the contempt of justice.   (*Iacke-a-Lent*, p. 10)

As in all Carnival customs, a topsy-turvy principle governs the action: tools are used not for building but for smashing and destroying. Relative privation benefits social life by helping to sustain the livelihood of all the crafts and *métiers*.

Carnival abuse is not confined to violence against property. Youthful celebrants may also engage in violence against persons, in particular against the constables who are commanded to keep the peace:

what avails it for a constable with an army of reverend bill-men to command peace to these beasts, for they with their pockets, instead of pistols, well charged with stone-shot, discharge against the image of authority, whole volleys as thick as hail. . . . Thus by the unmannerly manners of Shrove-Tuesday constables are baffled, bawds are banged, punks are pillaged, panders are plagued. .
                                                              (*Iacke-a-Lent*, p. 11)

The riotous misbehavior of Carnival celebrations indiscriminately attacks both legitimate authority and illicit sexual activity. The abuse of constables and bill-men is obviously an expression of resentment of and resistance to the official surveillance of desire and its satisfaction; the abuse of bawds and panders is an example of 'displaced abjection', in which an oppressed social group acts out its frustration through the victimization of an even more 'abject' or disadvantaged group.[14] In the violence and confusion of festive mummery, the fully contradictory nature of communal feeling is acknowledged. Traditional community standards are enforced, and the rickety, haphazard pattern of social life is affirmed even as its anarchy is disclosed. The abject foolishness of the victim is set against the compensatory aggressive foolishness of the festive crowd. Conflict is not an aberration to be corrected: order is fragile, ephemeral, and its ludicrous pretensions are easily discovered.

Travesty, the comprehensive transgression of signs and symbols, is a general 'refusal of identity'. There is no ideal order to be figured forth by the ceremonial gravity of allegorical forms. Carnival masquerade draws attention to a powerful flow of social energy and to the improvisatory competence of the social group. Identity is never permanent: boys grow into men, apprentices become journeymen, maids become wives and then widows. Furthermore, each individual must work in concert with other men and women directly on the social and material environment, to create the means of life. In this constant bustle of productive activity everything can be changed into something else. The experience of Carnival masquerade and parodic travesty embraces this unlimited exchange between signs and objects as simultaneously comical and tragic.

Society in general is a kind of travesty, and tacit acknowledgment of that condition is essential if there is to be any possibility of orderly social life.

> If anyone seeing a player acting his part on a stage should go about to strip him of his disguise and show him to the people in his true native form, would he not, think you, not only spoil the whole design of the play, but deserve himself to be pelted off with stones as a phantastical fool and one out of his wits. But nothing is more common with them than such changes; the same person one while impersonating a woman, and another while a man; now a youngster, and by and by a grim seigneur; now a king and presently a peasant; now a god and in a trice again an ordinary fellow.[15]

Just as in a stage play, identity is in fact both guise and *dis*guise, a social integument rather than a 'true native form', but it is absolutely necessary to display respect for that integument and to pretend not to notice. Nevertheless, the fact of disguise and deception is never invisible. Every social integument, including the self-display of de jure authority, is absolutely transparent even when the intent to compel obedience is bound to succeed. Theatricality in public life is complicated and requires a complicated response, demanding the critical negation of every allegorical signification in favor of a detached, comprehensive strategy of interpretation and misinterpretation of political power.

The transgressive metaphors of popular festive form are therefore used to interpret actual events. From where the common people stand, many of the episodes of high political life can be seen to decline inadvertently into self-travesty. The tragedy and violence of contingent historical events like the fall of a king are witnessed in the public square as grotesque and bloody self-parody.

> In a stage play all the people know right wel, that he that playeth the sowdayne is percase a sowter. Yet if one should can so lyttle good, to shewe out of seasonne what acquaintance he hath with him, and calle him by his owne name while he standeth in his magestie, one of his tormentors might hap to breake his head, and worthy, for marring of the play. And so they said that these matters bee Kynges games, as it were stage playes, and for the more part plaied upon scafoldes. In which pore men be but lokers on.[16]

The orientation of plebeian culture, both to itself and to the elites that hold political and economic power, is expressed in the form of travesty — literally cross-dressing. These forms facilitate the disclosure of contingency and arbitrariness in the allocation of social identity. The noisy and colorful masquerades of Carnival represent all of social reality, even its most powerful and majestic aspects, as changing and transitory. Political reality is brought into familiar contact with everyday life; its pretensions to grandeur are uncrowned.

CHAPTER 5
BUTCHERS AND FISHMONGERS

MISRULE and masquerade reinterpret hierarchy in terms of material life through ritualized thrashing and parodic travesty. Equally important in the symbolism of Carnival is the rhythm of struggle, perpetual conflict and succession. Conflict and struggle are permanently woven into the texture of social relations as elements of a purposeful and dynamic pattern of social regulation, allocation of resources and communal creativity. Carnival masquerade is a language of resistance for plebeian culture in its relationship to constituted authority and privilege. This resistance may take the form of isolated acts of terrorism, anonymous vandalism, organized riots and even massacres. It is, of course, more usual for resistance to use symbolic violence. In general, plebeian culture uses Carnival and popular festive form as a critical rejection of the technique of hegemonic authority and of the legitimation of all expropriation or radicalization from above.[1] But while the common people may be objectively in conflict with dominant and privileged elites, plebeian culture acknowledges and even seeks to conserve a state of perpetual internal conflict. From the perspectives of everyday life and material culture, all of social experience is seen and represented agonistically. The central and, in the Renaissance, most pervasive festive symbol of that agonistic style is the Battle of Carnival and Lent.

For plebeian culture, the importance of the opposition of Carnival and Lent is precisely the battle, the continual and recurrent strife and reciprocal interchange between two traditional personae. There is, however, a liturgically and spiritually 'correct' understanding of the relationship between these two figures, based on clear differentiation of their respective natures and on the necessary and inevitable victory of Lent. In its simplest form, this differentiation is between sinful and foolish absorption in the pleasures of the flesh, as represented by Carnival, and penitential renunciation of those pleasures in favor of the needs of the spirit, as represented by Lent. In this framework, Carnival is a preliminary and subordinate function of the penitential requirements of the Shrovetide season immediately preceding Lent itself. That function is to objectify unrepented sin, the old ways of fleshy wantonness and excess, so that expiation is made possible through contrition and abstinence. The Battle of Carnival and Lent, understood in this way, is a popular enactment of a universal spiritual drama, in which the soul must choose between flesh and spirit, between worldly and otherwordly desire.

In his discussion of Renaissance drama and the liturgical years, R. C. Hassel has shown that the opposition is never so simple in actual practice. The universal confrontation between flesh and spirit becomes, in the controversial atmosphere of Elizabethan and Jacobean London, a scheme for interpreting more specific forms of religious controversy.[2] Lent becomes assimilated to an image of joyless Puritanism, while Carnival embodies the coarse and even bestial excesses of an archaic pagan past. Hassel maintains that the festive encounter between Carnival and Lent dramatizes a *via media* between the unacceptable alternatives of too much Lenten severity (radical Puritanism) and too much carnality (bestial and sinful paganism and, perhaps by extension, popery). Instead of a conclusive and final victory of the spirit over the world and the flesh, the Battle of Carnival and Lent lends itself to the reconciling of pleasure and virtue through restraint, tolerance and moderation.

> Carnival and Lent are too naturally opposed for frequent or lasting jointure. . . . But occasionally with the unifying spirit of the imagination and the unifying power of love . . . they can coexist in

peace and festivity . . . if precariously jointed through the intervention of love.[3]

This reconciliation of opposites is brought about in the private and domestic sphere, more specifically in the interior space of the great hall or court.

For plebeian culture, the Battle of Carnival and Lent leads to no miraculous transformation from strife to harmony. In its most characteristic popular form, it is not controlled by a 'unifying spirit' of love or imagination, nor is the purpose of the confrontation defined by any final and decisive outcome, whether in the form of a reconciliation of opposite extremes or in the conclusive victory of the Lenten side. Both Carnival and Lent are grotesque and ambivalent figures who exist most decisively for the purpose of their festive agon. In Breughel's *Battle of Carnival and Lent*, the ambivalent and enigmatic ugliness of both figures is evident. The battle is staged in the public square, where everyone is present. It is, moreover, played out in the midst of a range of other activities, including festive games, preparation of food and, on the Lenten side, devotional and charitable acts. Furthermore, though it is the visual and compositional center of the canvas, the battle itself is not the center of the social activity depicted, and no one attends to it except the participants. This is no edifying spectacle: Carnival and Lent themselves are equally grotesque and pathetic, and there is no image of 'wise festivity' to moderate and unify the disparate activities.

The most immediate and pressing concern expressed in the traditional Battle of Carnival and Lent is culinary, for, whatever spiritual significance the season may have, its actualization in material culture takes the form of a shift in cuisine that purports to be a 'fast'. This shift is fasting only in a very limited sense. John Taylor distinguishes the Lenten fast from three common types of actual renunciation: zealous abstinence from any kind of corporeal food, hypocritical or sophistical fasting, and the fast called 'in spite of your teeth'. This last type of fast occurs 'not because there hath wanted meat, but because some have wanted manners, and I have wanted impudence' (*Iacke-a-Lente*, p. 7). The Lenten fast is not, according to this text, an abstinence, 'zealous' or otherwise, from corporeal food, but a change in the daily menu.

Jack-a-Lent's Fast is otherwise than all these, for I am as willing to fast with him as to feast with Shrovetide: for he hath an army of various dishes, an host of divers fishes, with salads, sauces, sweat-meats, wine, ale beer, fruit, roots, raisins, almonds, spices.

(*Iacke-a-Lente*, p. 7)

The Lenten diet does not preclude culinary abundance, since there is a plentiful variety of fish available as a substitute for the prohibited animal meat. The change in menu extends to other foods besides the shift from meat to fish.

The bakers metamorphose their trade from one shape to another, his round, half-penny loaves are transformed into square wigs, (which wigs like drunkards are drowned in their ale) the rolls are turned to simnels, in the shape of bread-pies, and the light puffed-up four-cornered bun, doth show that the knavery of the baker is universal, in Asia, Europe, Africa, and America.

(*Iacke-a-Lente*, p. 18)

Similar kinds of culinary opposition are represented in the Breughel painting, not only in the contrast of pork and cod, but also in the Carnival waffles and the pretzels of Lent.

Despite Taylor's professed enthusiasm for the fishy abundance offered by Jack-a-Lent's fast, there was evidently some resistance, at least in England, to the Lenten renunciation of meat. Thomas Nashe, in *Pierce Penniless*, suggests that a strong preference for meat is the characteristic English form of gluttony.

It is not for nothing that other countries, whom we upbraid with drunkenness, call us bursten-bellied gluttons for we make our greedy paunches powdering-tubs of beef, and eat more meat at one meal than the Spaniard or Italian in a month. Good thrifty men, they draw out a dinner with sallets, like a Swart-rutters suit, and make Madonna Nature their best caterer. We must have our tables furnished like poulters stalls, or as though we were to victual Noah's ark.[4]

To the extent that such a preference existed, it would tend to favor butchers, and in *Lenten Stuffe* Nashe suggests that Lent is a useful institution because of the protection it affords to the rival trade of fishmonger and the limits it places on the increased flow of wealth and authority to butchers that would result from the elimination of traditional constraints on the operation of the market.

> If it wer not for [the red herring] . . . Lent might be clean sponged
> out of the calendar, with rogation weeks, saints eves, and the whole
> ragmans rule of fasting days; and fishmongers might keep Christmas all the year for any overlavish takings they should have of
> clowns and clouted shoes, and the rubbish menialty, their best
> customers; and their bloody adversaries, the butchers, would never
> leave cleaving it out in the whole chines, till they had got a Lord
> Mayor of their company as well as they.[5]

The pattern of abstinence from meat and the shift to a diet of fish during Lent is, in the liturgically authorized framework of the church, a religious and spiritual discipline, a renunciation of the flesh as part of a purification that prepares the soul for Easter. As the passages from John Taylor and Thomas Nashe suggest, however, there is an overriding material and economic basis for the culinary shift as well. In these terms, the Battle of Carnival and Lent can be understood as a permanent rivalry and competition between butchers and fishmongers that conserves both companies but limits the ascendancy of either.

The conflict between butchers and fishmongers arises from their competition for a favorable share of the market; but both companies are equally vital and productive elements of the community. 'Friendly, frolic, frank, free-hearted, famous flourishing Fishmongers, and brave, bold, battering, beef-braining butchers, to both your companies in general I wish health and happiness' (*Iacke-a-Lente*, p. 2). The friction between these two trades is no illusion; their conflicted interrelationship is never resolved, though it is moderated by customary practices that correspond to the seasonal rhythm of agricultural labor. For much of the year butchers are permitted to carry out unrestricted trade, slaughtering cattle as they come to the market and offering a variety of meat to a general clientele. Evidently the supply of cattle is not steady throughout the year, however. Surplus cattle that cannot be economically carried through the winter are slaughtered and the meat salted. Some time in late winter, when the supplies of preserved meat are scarce, the butchers may close up shop for a brief period. During this seasonal interval, fishmongers enjoy a dominant share of market activity, while with the establishing of Lent's government, the butchers suffer temporary eclipse and '(like silenced schismatics) are dispersed, some riding into the country to buy oxen, kine, calves, sheep and lambs, leaving their wives, men and maids, to make provision of pricks for the whole year in their absence' (*Iacke-a-Lente*, p. 12).

While the butchers are uncrowned and cuckolded, their rivals enjoy prosperity, and their victims peace and a respite from violence and slaughter.

> The cut-throat butchers, wanting throats to cut
> At Lent's approach, their bloody shambles shut:
> For forty days their tyranny doth cease,
> And men and beasts take truce and live in peace.
>
> *Iacke-a-Lente*, p. 13

In due course, however, the seasons change, the butchers are restored to dominance, and Lent in his turn is driven out of the country. Slaughter returns, which for some brings rejoicing.

> It is a thing worthy to be noted, to see how all the dogs in the town do wag their tails for joy, when they see such provision to drive away Lent, (for a dog, a butcher, and a puritan, are the greatest enemies he hath). (*Iacke-a-Lente*, p. 19)

Taylor's jesting inclusion of Puritans among the 'enemies' of Lent is part of his satiric denunciation of them as mere hypocrites, who oppose Lenten observances while claiming to uphold a high standard of abstemious conduct. Butchers oppose Lent for more obvious mundane economic reasons.

Just as butchers and fishmongers each have their customary seasons of prosperity and of economic distress, so the festive personae of Carnival and Lent have alternate periods of ascendancy followed by ritualized thrashing and expulsion. They belong together, and their agonistic relationship may be seen as the comprehensive model of economic practice interpreted from the point of view of traditionally organized, productive life. The fat-bellied, cheerfully gluttonous figure of Carnival represents the 'abundance of the material principle' generated by social labor – production, destruction or consumption, and reproduction. But Carnival has an abstract and orderly aspect as well, the imagery of production implying principles of social discipline and the regulation of social conduct. Thrashing constables and sacking bawdy houses is a basic function of Carnivalesque misrule. The severe and abstemious figure of Lent is, on the other hand, primarily an image of social discipline and regulation, the embodiment of rules of abstention and the prohibition of physical pleasure. But, like Carnival, Lent is 'two-sided', the other side being an alternative principle of material abundance based not on the slaughter of animals but on the harvesting of the sea and its creatures.

Once the 'bloody butchers' have been driven out of town and a certain peace has been established, the 'violence' of Lent reveals itself.

> The wet fishmongers all this while (like so many executioners) unkennel the salt eels from their briny ambuscadoes, and with marshall law hang them up: the stock-fish having tried a terrible action of battery is condemned to be drowned.
>
> (*Iacke-a-Lente*, p. 15)

Although the battle of Carnival and Lent does make use of a number of simple binary oppositions – fat and thin, butcher and fishmonger, beef and herring, colorful clothing and black clothing – the formal rule relating the two terms is not a juxtaposition of mutually exclusive categories. The battle is between two equally 'full' and complete images of material life. Communal well-being depends on observing the rhythm of alternation, by which Carnival is driven out by Lent and in due course Lent is driven out by the return of the Carnival butchers with their flocks and herds.

Observance of the Carnival-Lent distinction is not exclusively or even mainly a religious prepoccupation. In Elizabethan England an over-strict enforcement of observance and over-literal interpretation of Lent may be construed as either too puritanical or too papist; the institution of Lent is most tactfully sustained on secular grounds: 'Lent would very feign take up his lodging here with religion, but religion will not be acquainted with him, and therefore civil policy hath the managing of the business' (*Iacke-a-Lente*, p. 12). The transfer of Lent to the jurisdiction of civil policy and secular authority is undertaken to preserve the social, ethical and disciplinary value of Lent, together with its importance in the political economy, without retaining any 'idolatrous' over-concern with the externals of the Lenten diet.

I am persuaded that a man may go to heaven as well with a leg of a capon as with a red herring. But seeing Lent is ordained to a good intent, for the increase and preservation of calves, lambs, swine, and all kind of beast, and birds whatsoever, whereby the breeding and multiplicity of these creatures makes our land the terrestrial paradise of plenty, and so is . . . able to maintain herself.

(*Iacke-a-Lente*, p. 22)

Because the imperative economic criterion is to sustain diversity and an abundant level of subsistence, it is impermissible to 'let the market decide'. A land of terrestrial plenty requires full and positive acknowledgement of alternative forces of production, Carnival *and* Lent, as well as the successive rejection, expulsion and execution of each.

The opposition between butchers and fishmongers reflects a complex division of labor; each trade is integrated into the overall economic pattern in distinct ways. Fishmongers do not depend on the agricultural sector, and in fact their success diminishes the economic importance of land as a resource. In addition, fishmongers, unlike butchers, are not subject to direct market regulation.

For all the Butcher curseth our fasting dayes, yet shall your gettings be good: and if he grudge that you should be permitted to sell all the yeere, and his shops shut up in Quadragesima, you shall tell him that Lent is the Fish-mongers harvest, though it bee the Butchers spring.[6]

This privilege may reflect a degree of royal favor and traditional recognition for the Fishmongers' Company. In a pageant written for them by Anthony Munday, the central dramatic persona is one William Walworth, a fishmonger knighted in the field for his personal defense of King Richard II.[7] In any case, it is evident from innumerable annual proclamations prohibiting the slaughter and the sale of meat during Lent that the Crown gave active support to the fishmongers' traditional privilege.

Butchers, by contrast, are directly integrated into the rural economy and their trade must follow the seasonal rhythms of agricultural production. They constitute a 'basic industry' as the suppliers of raw materials to a number of other traditional trades and production processes.

Keep your owne counsell, set a smooth face and a round face upon it, and then there is never a steward that sharkes in your shambles will smell out the putrefaction. The tanners will prevent the worst, and ply you with pledges aforehand for your hides, but keepe not backe the hornes in any case for thats ominous. Furriers and Glovers will put money into your handes as warme as wooll for your sheepe skinnes, but for the love of a chitterlin fee you hold your beasts entrails at a clean price, and make the Tripe-wives pay sweetly for them, or I protest in the pretense of an hogges countenance ile never feede more on them. The countrey-farmers wives will swappe with you quickly for their calves, because they draw away their milke, and marre their good markets. And the Graziers will send you their bigge bon'd beeves upon trust if you pay them largely, and keep your day truly.[8]

Butchers are a pivotal exchange point in a complex chain of commodities and this advantage offsets the de jure protection afforded fishmongers. They are supplied both by traditional small-scale agricultural producers ('countrey-farmers wives') and by capitalist farmers ('graziers'). In addition, their by-products form the intermediate link between rural production and urban manufacture. Because of this strategically advantageous situation, however, butchers are visibly implicated in the large and disruptive changes taking place in the social and economic organization of agricultural production.

Fishmongers were no doubt involved in complex economic networks and, therefore, equally implicated in the widely criticized forms of social change. But to observers concerned with the adverse social consequences of a rapidly advancing capitalist agriculture – and they were numerous in Elizabethan times – the butchers were much more obviously implicated in these changes than the fishmongers. Butchers were the object of direct social pressure to restore traditional subsistence agriculture, primarily because of their direct and open involvement with speculative grazing. The 'civil policy' to which Lent becomes assimilated is, outwardly at least, an effort to preserve and to restore traditions of rural 'hospitality' by limiting the ultimate market for slaughtered cattle. For the Crown this policy is justified for several reasons of national interest.

The annual proclamations of the Privy Council for the restraint of killing and eating of flesh in Lent are mainly concerned with routine administrative matters. Fishmongers are not to raise their prices.

Butchers are to close their shops. A strictly limited number of butchers are licenced to slaughter meat to supply the needs of the sick and to provision ships, subject to strict audit. Occasionally the proclamation may include a brief expression of scandalized official piety.

> And forasmuch as the use and libertie now taken, is so farre declined from the abstinence and moderation of former times, as instead of fasting, and forswearing suppers on Fridayes both in Lent, and other times, which heretofore was duly observed, there is now nothing more usuall, then to make speciall choice of Friday nights for Suppers and entertainment and to mark out those days for riot and excesses, to the great offence and scandal of Government.[9]

The civil policy of Lent and the regulation of the cattle market receive a much more elaborate justification in a Privy Council document in broadsheet of 1595, called 'A briefe note of the benefits that grow to this Realme, by the observation of Fishe-daies with a reason and cause wherefore the lawe in their behalfe made, is ordained.' This document enumerates three reasons for limiting the sale and consumption of meat. First, the law contributes to the maintenance of the navy by encouraging fishing, the training of seamen, and the building and repair of ships. Second, it helps to repair the decay of coastal towns. Finally, it contributes to reversing the decay of the mixed agricultural economy by indirectly resisting the conversion of land to cash-crop grazing of cattle.

> Furthermore, it is to be considered, that the trade for grazing of cattell, through the unlawfull expence of flesh is so much increased, that many farme houses and villages, wherein were maintained great numbers of people, and by them the markets plentifully served with corne and other victuals, is now utterly decayed and put down, for the feeding or grazing of Beefes and Muttons onely, by means whereof, the people which in such places were maintained are not only made vagrant, but also, Calves, Hogs, Pigs, Geese, Hennes, Chickens, Capons, Egges, Butter, Cheese, and such like thinges, doth become exceeding scarce and deare by want of their increase in those places, so that the Markets are not, nor cannot be served as in times past they have been.[10]

The civil policy of Lent is an attempt to address the most sweeping and disruptive processes of social change, specifically the transfer of resources from traditional mixed farming, with customary redistributive allocation of varied products, to newer forms of speculative, single-crop agriculture. The document quoted does not reveal the extent to which the Privy Council was able to make a coherent analysis of the problem or to respond with an effective policy. Still less does it reveal the real purpose of any such secular policy or the specific social interests it may have served. Nevertheless, the text does show the complex interpenetration of religious and secular concerns, and the intimate saturation of those concerns with the most humble details of everyday life. The Privy Council's law respecting fish-days has everything to do, not only with the welfare of a primary national asset like the navy, but also with the price of eggs and of other household commodities.

The Privy Council's 'briefe note' represents the Crown as making common cause with fishmongering, as well as with mixed farming. This perhaps incongruous coalition of interests sets itself against engrossing landlords, against commercial speculators and, as well, against butchers and their 'overlavish' clientele, both rural and urban. The moral basis for this is not the abstract authority of the monarch or the obedience owed by subjects; it is, instead, the image of communal life hinted at in the long list of agricultural products – calves, hogs, pigs, geese, hens, chickens, capons, eggs, butter, cheese – all of which have become scarce and expensive as a result of the decay of hospitality.

There was considerable difference of opinion in Renaissance England as to who was to bear the blame for enclosure, dispossession and vagrancy, and as much difference of opinion as to what social groups continued to uphold the tradition of hospitality. However, if there is an idea about which Elizabethans professed unanimity, it is the image of an idyllic country hospitality rather than philosophical abstractions of hierarchy and the chain of being.

Although it certainly entails periodic festivity, the concept of hospitality is something very different from the art of gracious living. Hospitality refers to a comprehensive pattern of social welfare that requires a fraction of production to be held in reserve for reallocation to the poor, the disabled and the dispossessed. Any alternative allocation of available resources that deprives those in need violates the mutual social bond of each to all.

[Those gentrie] that ancientlie did entertaine hospitalitie, their servants and retainers, welcomed their friends, and were helpful to such of them as stood in neede, are now come into cities, where . . . they spend that formerly did maintained so many. . . . From such devourers of estates, doth arise the improving of Lands, racking of Rents, destruction of ancient hospitalitie, and oppression of poor Farmers and tenants . . . the Gentrie having ever thought it their greatest treasure, to have their Farmers and Tenants able at home and abroade, in good fashion to attend their service: but now if a Farmer, by multitude of Children, great charge, death of Cattell, or other accidents (to which human affaires are subiect) become poore, straight comes some rich Grazier, or remorseless Usurer, offers more for his Farme then it is worth; and being no sooner accepted, the poore tenant is thrust out of doors.[11]

Lavish banquets and artfully designed entertainments may actually violate the principle of sustained and conscientious social generosity implied by the image of true hospitality.

In *Summer's Last Will and Testament*, Summer suggests that 'Christmas is god of hospitality'. In a comic reversal of expectation, however, the character named Christmas is a miser who asserts that hospitality is grown out of fashion. To justify his miserliness, Christmas maintains:

A man's belly was not made for a powdering-beef tub. To feed the poor twelve days and let them starve all the year after would but stretch out the guts wider than they should be, and so make famine a bigger den in their bellies than he had before.[12]

Christmas is not really concerned for the needs of the poor, however. From this unexceptionable premise he draws the inference that hospitality in its entirety ought to be discarded, because it encourages idleness and arrogance among vagabonds and beggars. Christmas would abolish all forms of festivity, rejecting its charitable forms of social redistribution as well as ostentatious luxury. Summer's reply recuperates the tradition of hospitality as a function proper to the nobility.

SUMMER. Christmas, I tell thee plain, thou art a snudge,
    And wert not that we love thy father well,
    Thou should have felt what 'longs to avarice.
    It is the honor of nobility
    To keep high days and solemn festivals,
    Then, to set their magnificence to view
    To frolic open with their favorites,
    And use their neighbours with all courtesy.[13]

Festive generosity is legitimated, as is the unequal allocation of wealth that makes magnanimity a virtue, but only against a critical background that reiterates themes of the transience of life and of the vulnerability of the poor and dispossessed. Even the miserly Christmas contributes to the critical spirit and tendency of the work: 'Our feet must have wherewithal to fend the stone; our backs, walls of wool to keep out the cold that besiegeth our warm blood; our doors must have bars, our doublets must have buttons.'[14] The hospitality that Christmas would reject, and that Summer defends as the exclusive prerogative of gentry and nobility, is directed to exactly these social exigencies. However, though Nashe in this text suggests that the nobility have the honor of preserving this pattern of festivity, there are others who suggest that hospitality is in fact best served by other sectors within the community.

The Complainte of Christmas depicts a journey by the spirit of Christmas to various countries of Europe, in all of which Christmas finds severe defects in the practice of hospitality. In England, Christmas first visits the house of a lord of the manor where he finds no suitable entertainment because the young master has gone up to the city to spend his wealth. True hospitality is found in the humbler environment of the small farms.

At last the Bels began to ring, every householder began to bestirre himself, the maid servants we saw run hurrying to the Cookes shops with Pies and the Iacks went as nimbly as any of the wives tongues. And before we were aware, whole Parishes of people came to invite us to Dinner. Some tooke me by the hands and would have me his guest, another took Saint Stephen, a third, Saint Iohn, a fourth, Childermasse.[15]

Christmas hospitality is, in this text, a collective and anonymous shared abundance. The withdrawal from the practice of hospitality by the 'young master' of the great hall is the end result of a gradual displacement of traditional forms of the division of labor by new, economically efficient techniques. This process is particularized for Taylor in the device of the smoke-jack, a mechanism that uses heated air rising in the chimney to turn the spit.

> The Iacke, which in former times did rule the roast, and hindered many poore mens children from the warm office of turne-broches. It never was a bountifull time since a Dogge in the wheele and the Iacke in the Mantletree began to turne the spit, for they began first to turne hospitality out of doors.[16]

But even though the gentry abdicate from their duties towards hospitality, the practice of cooperative reallocation is nevertheless sustained by common people.

Nashe, Taylor and even the Privy Council are in agreement in the appeal to hospitality both as the norm of harmonious social practice and as the temporal horizon toward which purposeful social action is to be directed. Responsibility for the 'decay of hospitality', or in other words the destruction of traditional society, is attributed to various parties. The question of assigning responsibility for the breakup of the traditional pattern was a contentious issue at the time, and it remains a matter of acrimonious controversy in present-day scholarship. To those who experienced disruptive changes in a traditional way of life it was not yet possible to speak of a transition from manorial production to capitalism. The distinctive practice of capitalism had not, at the end of the sixteenth century, emerged sufficiently clearly to have produced an ideological discourse of its own, let alone a coherent defense of itself. No one was yet prepared to argue that the market is natural or that the drive towards accumulation is socially self-justifying. No one was prepared to defend an ethos based on accumulation through such practices as enclosure, though many powerful families were to benefit by such an ethos and eventually to seek its legitimation.

The controversy over the 'decay of hospitality' is conducted in part through festive activities. Festive customs take up this long-term structural conflict, along with many local forms of social rivalry and opposition. Celebratory practice, in all its forms, including the Battle of

Carnival and Lent, cannot be adequately grasped as an exceptional 'saturnalian' departure from everyday life. On the contrary, it is evident that festivity is the intensification and the fulfillment of everyday life and material culture. In the distinctively popular festive forms of plebeian culture, moreover, the importance of local and immediate social conflict and struggle to the overall maintenance of a 'bountiful' way of life is continually emphasized.

The Battle of Carnival and Lent is the stylized form of real structural ambiguity and tension. It corresponds in particular to the paradigmatic and exemplary chronic dissonance between butchers and fishmongers. In this context, however, conflict has a positive meaning and function. Carnival concerns itself with strongly felt attitudes about economic security and abundance, and with the traditional and customary right of individual producers to retain the social wealth they actually produce. These concerns imply a complex distribution of secular authority into widely diffused, decentralized centers of local custom and practice.

> We finde it necessarie in all common wealthes, for subjects to live under the direction of lawes, constitutions or customes publickly knowne and received, and not to depende only upon the commandement and pleasure of the governor, be the same never so just or sincere in life and consideration.[17]

The public character of law and custom takes precedence over the mystical or charismatic authority of the prince.

But there is a further distinction made in this text between law and custom.

> Custome taketh his force by degrees of time, and consent of a certaine people, or the better part thereof, but a lawe springeth up in an instant and receiveth life from him that is of sovereigne authorite to command. A custome enlargeth itselfe by plausible entertainment and acceptable circumstances of time and occassion, with general liking and allowance, whereas a law is commanded and published by power and received by dutifull constraint, and that often against the goodwill of them that are bound by it.[18]

As against the arbitrary authority of the sovereign, and the textualized authority of law, this writer unequivocally favors the anonymous and collective authority of custom, defined as a flexible, evolving, orally transmitted pattern of social practice. As with any traditional authority, customs have limited, local provenance.

> A custome is applyed to the commoditie of some one province, circuite or citie, and grounded upon a speciall reason of convenien-cie or commodietie, for those persons or place where it is observed . . . so that in customes the estate or condition of the people are to be respected.[19]

By grounding secular authority in custom and insisting that custom take precedence, not only over charismatic personal rule, but also over law and constitution, the writer of this 'breefe discourse' describes the social fabric as an unsystematic aggregate of local practices. Oral and practical communicative activities dominate the written word; society consists of semi-independent groupings of small communities that are empathetic and, at the same time, habitually agonistic in their relationship to each other. This agonistic clash of local customs and particular communities is objectified in popular-festive performance scenarios: occasional brawls and feuding may occur as the extension of symbolically acted-out animosity. However, plebeian culture does not look to a superordinate, de jure authority to resolve conflict, because one of the primary strategic aims of all agonistic expression is to hinder and resist any exclusive concentration of secular authority and the growth of any smoothly functioning administrative apparatus, including the civil state. Social conflict is a salutary force, which conserves the diffuse, implicit author-ity of the local community and, equally, contributes to the tradition of mutual and reciprocal responsibility for sustaining collective subsistence.

CHAPTER 6
A COMPLETE EXIT FROM THE PRESENT ORDER OF LIFE'

Popular festive form celebrates and briefly actualizes a collective desire for a freer and more abundant way of life. This desire is at once a forward-looking hopefulness and a memory of better times. Recollection of a golden age was an important element in the Roman Saturnalia, a winter festival during which masters served their slaves, in celebration of the reign of Saturn. In these celebrations Saturn is recognized as a working god who presides over various agricultural tasks, especially the manuring of the fields and other activities connected with the sowing of grain. His feast anticipates the growing, harvesting and eventual consuming of agricultural production, and the renewal of human life. The 'reign of Saturn' commemorates a time in which an undivided human collectivity enjoyed the riches of the earth without exploitation or struggle.[1]

This utopian understanding of Saturnalia is preserved in early modern Europe in legends of Lubberland and the Land of Cokaygne, and also in the characteristic idiomatic language and imagery of Shrovetide feasting.[2] Though it has been characterized as nothing more than a fool's paradise, this image of easy gratification and the abolition of invidious

social distinctions is the cogent expression of the hopeful desires of
unprivileged men and women.

> CADE. There shall be in England seven half-penny loaves sold for a
> penny. The three-hooped pot shall have ten hoops, and I will make
> it felony to drink small beer. All the realm shall be in common, and
> in Cheapside shall my palfrey to grass. And when I am King, as
> King I will be . . . there shall be no money. All shall eat and drink
> on my score, and I will apparel them all in one livery, that they may
> agree like brothers, and worship me their lord.
>
> (2 *Henry VI*, IV. ii. 70–82)

The substance of Jack Cade's political agenda is in sympathy with the
popular utopian wishes of peasant revolutionary movements of the early
modern period. Material abundance will be achieved for all, the money
economy will be abolished, and social equality will displace exploitative
class distinction. According to conventional historicist criticism, the
structure of Shakespeare's play contains an unambiguously inscribed
political ideology which enables the audience member or reader to
understand Jack Cade as a pathetic, ludicrous and potentially vicious
aberration.[3] This view draws attention to Cade's ideological inconsisten-
cy and to the logically self-contradictory substance of his wishes,
specifically in examples such as the seven halfpenny loaves to be sold for
a penny. Cade's folly is identified with rebellious intentions, with the
consequence that he is exposed to ridicule, expelled and executed.

Despite these strategies of ideological containment, however, the
speeches of Cade and his followers constitute a powerful political and
discursive indiscretion. The feelings of the characters are those of class
resentment, bitterness, and a specific sense of historical inequity and
injustice. In addition, utopian wishes for cheaper bread reveal that, after
all, a halfpenny loaf is not an absolute unit of measure but rather a
fluctuating quantity subject to capricious change in the market. 'Seven
halfpenny loaves for a penny' reflects a contemporary desire for a general
disinflation of the price of commodities, which had been rising more or
less steeply for decades.[4] Jack Cade's anachronistic and confused reference to the inflationary situation of sixteenth-century England is, like a
great deal of popular utopian language, an example of 'matter and
impertinency mix'd'. This transgressive and illogical discourse enables
Cade to propose two mutually contradictory remedies for price inflation

– lowering the price of bread by the overthrow of the existing power structure, and – equally desirable – abolishing the money economy altogether. Underlying all of this is persistent social antagonism, and the wish to destroy class society by violent means. 'We will not leave one lord, one gentleman. Spare none but such as go in clouted shoon' (2 *Henry VI*, IV, ii, 194–5). Shakespeare's play presents the audience with scenes of official retribution, but the expression of popular resentment nevertheless escapes being totally repressed.

Utopia, in both idiomatic popular expression and formal literary presentation, is a place in which men and women live together according to new and better principles of social and political justice. Even in relatively static and rigidly determined societies, stories of a new beginning elsewhere reflect an awareness that existing conditions and established social hierarchies have not always existed and are not inevitable, natural or providential.

> When I consider and turn over in my mind the state of the commonwealths flourishing anywhere today, so help me God, I can see nothing else than a kind of conspiracy of the rich, who are aiming at their own interests under the name and title of the commonwealth.[5]

More's *Utopia* is a critique of the authorized history of his society and of the haphazard social arrangements that lead to dispossession and suffering. It is also an alternative to actual history based on recollection of the original human purposes underlying particular institutional forms.

Because *Utopia* is written in seriocomic form, it has not always been easy to decide what is said in jest and what in earnest. Nevertheless, there is a critical and scholarly consensus that More's real views of social organization are conservative and essentially authoritarian. According to Professor J.H. Hexter, the overriding strategy of *Utopia* is a criticism of historically specific abuses and aberrations against a background of traditional institutions that are the precondition for any possible social harmony. Hexter identifies the partriarchal family as the governing form of social authority.

> At any given time about half the Utopians are farmers and half city folk. To use current terminology, the agricultural units are not

collectives or state farms. They are family farms, although the farm family is somewhat extended, consisting of forty adult members. And the industrial activity of the towns seems to be organized in family units, too, with son ordinarily succeeding father in the family trade, and the women working in the house on the wool for the simple gray cloth in which all Utopians dress.[6]

As Hexter points out, this micro-organization of social life in Utopia corresponds rather strikingly to a similar pattern of micro-organization in late medieval and early modern England.

> The place of the patriarchal family in the habits of mind and patterns of action of More and his contemporaries helps to explain a peculiarity in the way they thought. . . . For most people, living and earning a living, unlike war, schooling, worship, and politics, went on in the same place – the family. In the country almost everybody lived with his family and in his family's house or hovel, and lived from his family holding.[7]

Hexter maintains that, in the imaginary utopian community, the family and the administrative state are the only permitted forms of collective life. The happiness of citizens of Utopia flows from the strengthening of these fundamental institutional bonds and the elimination of conflicting forms of loyalty.

A similar view has been articulated by Raymond Williams in *The Country and the City*. Williams describes More as equally animated by resentment of powerful 'great' landowners and of the 'idle and luxurious poor' – that is of tenant farmers and agricultural laborers. Book 1 is a fairly traditional complaint over the 'decay of hospitality' brought about by the decline of small-scale agriculture by the process of enclosure. The utopian agenda in Book 2 is an expression of nostalgic longing for the restoration to small owners of their traditionally privileged and advantageous situation.

> The social experience behind this is clear. An upper peasantry, which had established itself in the break-up of the strict feudal order, and which had ideas and illusions about freedom and independence from the experience of a few generations, was being pressed and expropriated by the great landowners, the most

successful of just these new men, in the changes of the market and of agricultural techniques brought by the growth of the wool trade. . . . Its ideal of local paternal care, and of national legislation to protect certain recent forms of ownership and labour, seems to draw almost equally on a rejection of the arbitrariness of feudalism, a deeply felt rejection of the new arbitrariness of money, and an attempted stabilisation of a transitory order, in which small men are to be protected against enclosures but also against the idleness of laborers. [8]

The Utopian design is an attempt to combine the archaic repression of the patriarchal family with the administrative surveillance of the modern state, in order to benefit a small class of owners whose way of organizing land and labor represents the optimum social and ethical choice for all society.

If these views are correct, it is hard to imagine how any significant connection could exist between More's *Utopia* and either popular utopian legends or saturnalian festivity. Texts such as *Utopia* can none the less be read, not only in the light of their historically limited intentions and the contingent circumstances they address, but also in the light of the tendencies they give rise to, and the license they provide for others to reveal more fully the emancipatory potentiality of traditional ideas. [9]

Despite, or perhaps because of, its socially and politically conservative ideological constraints, the text of *Utopia* is able to propose a radically transformed economic organization. This economic pattern should be described, not negatively, as the abolition of private property, but positively, as collective ownership and collectivized labor. The radical and emancipatory meanings implicit in *Utopia* rest in the ethical as opposed to the political or administrative implications of collectivized human effort. *Utopia* restores to labor its decisive significance. Social relations as well as culture flow from productive rather than from proprietary relationships. Although Utopians practice some division of labor, particularly with respect to gender, there is little specialization. Every citizen does his share of repetitious toil, both in agriculture and in manufacture, and also participates in public life and in contemplative activity. Because collective ownership and collective labor are the exclusive forms of economic activity, there is no separation of production from consumption. There is a distribution of goods, but, because only production for more or less immediate use is ever undertaken, there can be no system of profitable exchange and therefore no accumulation of wealth or transfer of 'surplus'.

The political constitution of Utopia is the imaginative form of what More considers the founding purpose and ideal of every social organization. That ideal is an unbroken continuity of collective life. The question as to how an individual might live or what an individual must believe finds its answer in knowing what a given community has always done. Even in his most ideologically tendentious and indeed persecutory writing, that essential utopian conception reveals itself as an operative norm and pattern of desire. More argues in his *Apology* that people should stick to 'the old faith' even if it is contradicted by an angel from heaven.

> [It is] such fayth as by your self, and your fathers and your grandfathers you have knowen to be beleved and have over that lernde by them that the contrary was the tymes of theyr fathers and theyr grandefathers also, taken even more for heresy.[10]

The authority of the community and its collective, unwritten memory takes precedence over any written text, and over any formal doctrine. More's position is a social or collective form of the ancient virtue of *pietas*. This is the virtue of trusting and preserving the way of life lived by parents, grandparents and ancestral relatives.

More's text shares certain formal characteristics with the popular utopian tradition – specifically the use of seriocomic discourse to express the most significant social and political concerns. It also shares with popular utopian forms the image of an initially undivided community of equals as the central criterion of social well-being and as the alternative myth of origin, a myth, not of fall and expulsion from Eden, but of the perpetual return of *Saturnia Regna*. More's *Utopia* gives formal literary embodiment to the more ephemeral popular image of primitive communism. That image began to haunt European consciousness long before it was taken up by the labor movement in the nineteenth century and was identified by Marx as a ubiquitous and terrifying specter. In the later sixteenth century, 'Utopia' as a political term has become common linguistic property and reentered plebeian culture.

Jack-a-Lent hath no society, affinity or propinquity with flesh and blood, and by reason of his leanness (As Nymshag an ancient Utopian philosopher declares in his treatise on the antiquity of ginger-bread, Lib. 7 Pag. 30000.) he should have been a footman to a prince of that empire named Lurguash Haddernot; but Lent showed him the trick of a right footman, and ran away from him faster than an Irish lackey, and from that time to this was never seen in Utopia.   (*Iacke-a-Lent*, p. 5)

Taylor's biographical sketch of Jack-a-Lent reveals a typically plebeian or artisan identity. The festive persona is a runaway servant, a fugitive from the aristocratic regime of Utopia. His visit to England turns both the fictional space-time and the conservative ideology of More's *Utopia* upside-down. Jack-a-Lent's freedom from socially coercive bonds is achieved by coming back to the here and now of London, where the archaic claims of manorial service inscribed in Utopia's constitution are suspended. Utopian desire and hope are separated from the administrative and patriarchal constraints of Utopian social order.

The linking of a festive persona with the literary conception of Utopia, and with the pragmatic conception of the freedom of a runaway servant, is a jesting reference to political and social ideas that find more formal and more fully elaborated expression in other texts. The ideology implicit in *Iacke-a-Lent* is defined by the experience of the city, by its hopes and expectations as well as by its traditions. This experience, in the late sixteenth century, is based on a considerable degree of relative political autonomy and by the strong consciousness that the city represents a distinctive pattern of social life: '. . . what is a citie but a manifold and ioynt society consisting of many householdes, and living under the same Lawes, freedoms, and franchises.'[11] London, as it is described in *A Breefe Discourse*, is a network of relationships, the totality of the ways its people, organized into households, live together. Urban culture is, furthermore, not only distinct from the social and ethical practice of manorial life, but undoubtedly corrosive in its effects on the social bonds that prevail in the agricultural community.

. . . in the vii year of Henry the vi, that in a *nativo habendo* brought by a Lorde to recover his villen, it was adiudged a good return made by the Shiriffe of London that such was the Custome of London, that a villen having remained there the space of one whole yeare and a day, could not be fetched or removed out thence. For so great is the prerogative of that place, that it giveth protection to the villen or bondman against his lord while the saide bondman shall be resiant [i.e. resident] there.[12]

This custom or prerogative is of sufficient authority to challenge the power of a lord over his dependents. It is not, however, the main focus of the argument pursued in this text.

The particular custom defended at elaborate length in *A Breefe Discourse* concerns the distribution of a man's property upon his death. The writer maintains that, among Londoners, a venerable and worthy custom requires that a man's earthly goods be divided into equal thirds, with one-third allocated to the wife, one-third to the surviving children, and the remaining third left to the discretion of the deceased to distribute as he wishes. This custom would overturn several widely observed laws of property. To begin with, the argument claims for women a right to inherit wealth equal to that of men. Such an arrangement diminishes the force of patriarchal authority and provides women with a degree of economic independence that corresponds to their active role in the productive process. Secondly, the custom opposes the rule of inheritance by primogeniture. The children receive a joint distribution; the pattern of dependency on the heir and the conflicts to which this gives rise are thus avoided. This custom, if actually put into practice, would substantially transform the pattern of social and economic life. In effect, the members of the community engage in a mutual social strategy for the distribution and redistribution of wealth. Under the regime of primogeniture and dynastic marriage, large monopolies of wealth and property can in time be assembled. Under the regime described in *A Breefe Discourse*, there would be a tendency instead to maintain an approximate social and economic equality, not, perhaps, among individuals but certainly among households, which constitute the social units of urban life.

The most complex and ingenious popular-festive, utopian text from a literary point of view is *Nashes Lenten Stuffe*. Nashe objectifies his counter-model of political and social life in two elaborately detailed symbols – the description of the town of Great Yarmouth in Norfolk and the figure of the Red Herring. The text is a parodic mimicking of a journey to an outlandish society. Nashe presents himself as a returning exile who has seen a vital, prosperous and harmonious community that is both counter-model and accurate memory of more satisfactory social arrangements. The text is addressed to various unprivileged and unlearned groups within the social milieu. Nashe, proscribed and a fugitive from arrest, identifies with other disadvantaged and struggling groups, though his outlook remains cheerful, irreverent and hopeful.

> . . . in my exile and irkesome discontened abandonment, the silliest miller's thombe or contemptible stickle-banck of my enemies is a busie nibbling about my fame as if I were a deade man throwne amongest them to feede upon. So I am, I confesse, in the worlde's outwarde apparance, though perhappes I may prove a cunninger diver than they are aware, which if it so happen, as I am partely assured, and that I plunge above water once againe, let them looke to it, for I will put them in bryne, or a piteous pickle, every one. [13]

Like everything else in the text, this self-characterization is saturated with inversive or topsy-turvy images. The diver, or loon, seeks its food by diving under water, where it is able to remain for a long time, often reappearing at an unexpected spot. Nashe is himself a 'cunninger diver' whose 'plunge above water' suggests both a successful pursuit of sexual gratification and an equally gratifying revenge against his enemies.

Both Nashe, the 'cunninger diver', and Humfrey King, the 'diminutive excelsitude', belong to a community defined by customs of good fellowship, or, as Bakhtin characterizes it, 'prandial libertinism'. [14] They belong to an excluded or marginal social group that is not 'rich, noble, right worshipful or worshipful, or spiritual or temporal'. Their 'fellowship' unites the pleasure of food and drink with the pleasure of free philosophical inquiry and linguistic inventiveness. In the spirit of prandial libertinism, the text is offered as a contribution to both visceral and discursive banqueting.

> Here I bring you a redde herring; if you will finde drinke to it, there an ende, no other detriments will I putte you to. Let the Kanne of strong ale, your constable, with the toaste, his browne bill, and sugar and nutmegs, his watchmen, stand in a readinesse, to entertaine me every time I come by your lodging. In Ruscia there are no presents but of meate or drinke; I present you with meate, and you, in honourable courtesie to requite mee, can do no lesse

than present mee with the best morning's draught of merry-go-downe in your quarters: and so I kisse the shadow of your feet's shadow, amiable Donsell, expecting your sacred Poeme of the Hermites Tale, that will restore the golden age amonst us.

(*Lenten Stuffe*, pp. 179–80)

It is, however, Nashe himself who provides the imaginary re-creation of the golden age in his description of the town of Great Yarmouth.

Nashe undertakes the praise of Great Yarmouth to repay his indebtedness to the citizens of that town for affording him protection and hospitality during his exile after the banning of *The Isle of Dogs*. Yarmouth is noted as a center of the herring fishery; Nashe describes it as a considerable cosmopolitan center rather than as a quiet fishing village.

But how Yarmouth, of it selfe so innumerable populous and replenished, and in so barraine a plot seated, should not onely supply her inhabitants with plentifull purveyance of sustenance, but prouant and victuall moreover this monstrous army of strangers, was a matter that egregiously bepuzled and entranced my apprehension. Hollanders, Zelanders, Scots, French, Westerne men, Northren men, besides all the hundreds and wapentakes nine miles compasse, fetch the best of their viands and mangery from her market. For ten weeks together this rabble rout of outlandishers are billetted with her; yet in all that while the rate of no kinde of food is raised, nor the plenty of their markets one pinte of butter rebated, and at the ten weeks end, when the campe is broken up, no impression of my dearth left, but rather more store than before. Some of the town dwellers have so large an opinion of their setled provision, that, if all her Maiesties fleet at once should put into their bay, within twelue dayes warning with so much double beere, beefe, fish, and bisket they would bulke them as they could wallow away with.
(*Lenten Stuffe*, p. 158)

The abundance created at Yarmouth is a 'feast for all the world'; it flows endlessly from the efforts of the town and its surrounding countryside. As Nashe represents it, this abundance does not follow the capricious fluctuations of the market but is sustained at the same fair price even during the period of maximum demand. It is, moreover, a general rather than a single-commodity abundance, consisting of beer, beef, fish and biscuit, even though Yarmouth's primary industry is herring. Yarmouth is a living embodiment of popular utopian memory, when food was both cheap and abundant.

> It were to be wished that other coasters were so industrious as the Yarmouth, in winning the treaure of fish out of those profundities, and then we should have twentie egges a pennie, and it would be as plentifull a world as when Abbies stoode; and now, if there be any plentifull world, it is in Yarmouth. (*Lenten Stuffe*, p. 171)

This is, of course, the nostalgic recollection of peace and plenty so characteristic of popular utopian imagery, with its twenty eggs for a penny, but Nashe, in his journey of exile, has found in Yarmouth that the 'good old days' have not ended.

The material abundance of Yarmouth corresponds to a particular political economy, in which the collective wealth is more or less equitably shared.

> All Common wealths assure their prenominations of their common divided weale, as where one man hath not too much riches, and another man too much povertie. Such was Plato's communitie, and Licurgus and the olde Romans lawes of measuring out their fields, their meads, their pastures and houses, and meating out to every one his childes portion. To this *Commune bonum* (or every horse his loaf) Yarmouth in propinquity is as the buckle to the thong, and the next finger to the thumbe; Not that it is sibbe or cater-cousins to any moungrel Democratia, in which one is all, and all is one, but that in her, as they are not all one, so one or two there pockets not up all the pieces. (*Lenten Stuffe*, p. 168)

It is the proximity of Yarmouth, and the continuity of its collective social practice that recommend it as an image of utopian transformation. It is, furthermore, only relatively utopian. It is only approximately equitable in its distribution of wealth, but accomplishes its social and economic purposes with relatively little formal administration and surveillance.

In *Lenten Stuffe*, Nashe recreates the utopian 'other world' in his image of the more mundane utopian possibilities of Yarmouth. This image is the popular festive version of the ideal city, the energy and the vitality of these social forms flowing not from the majesty of a prince but from the ambivalent splendor of the Red Herring.

> Small thinges we may expresse by great, and great by small, though the greatness of the redde herring be not small (as small a hoppe on my thumbe as hee seemeth). It is with him as with great personages, which from their high estate and not their high statures propagate the eleuaute titles of their Gogmagognes.
>
> (*Lenten Stuffe*, pp. 185–6)

The herring, the humblest of fish, is nevertheless a figure of greatness. This ambivalence is expressed in very cheerful and positive language, but it is a corrosive ambivalence that confuses and makes relative the language of social comparison and discrimination. The Red Herring is himself both singular and collective, great though small, savory yet offensive. As a festive persona and as a seasonal and traditional food, he makes a ceremonial entry into the cities and towns like some great lord or royal personage.

> For our English Mikrokosmos or Phenician Didos hide of grounde, no shire, county, count palatine, or quarter of it, but rigs out some oken squadron or other to waft him along Cleopatraean Olimplick-ly, and not the diminutivest nooke or crevise of them but is parturient of the like superofficiousness. . . . Citty, towne, cuntry, Robin hoode and little Iohn, and who not, are as industrious and carefull to squire and safe conduct him in, but in ushering him in, next to the balies of Yarmoth, they trot all before, and play the provost marshals, helping to keep good rule the first three weeks of his ingresse. (*Lenten Stuffe*, pp. 186–7)

The procession of the Red Herring receives as much deferential respect and attention as that accorded to a real king or queen, but this respect is a cogent acknowledgment of the social and political importance of the fish as a commodity and of fishing as a basic industry. The inversive imagery turns the social world right side up, and reveals the material basis for civic and national well-being. The herring is found everywhere; he contributes to every sphere of life. He is 'a legate of peace' and at the same time 'such a hot stirring meate [that he] is enough to make the crauenest dastard proclaime fire and sword against Spaine' (*Lenten*

Stuffe, p. 191). This embodying of social wealth is both a positive image of abundance and a powerful negative dialectic of uncrowning. Wherever the herring appears, he takes part in the cheerful and abusive overthrow of sterile and tyrannical authority.

There are numerous embedded tales in *Lenten Stuffe* that show the Red Herring in the role of mute, humble, sometimes clownish agent of the uncrowning and mockery of secular and ecclesiastical princes. Nashe interprets several stories derived from classical literature as herring allegories, as, for example, the story of the tyrant Dionysus and the stripping of the golden coat from the statue of Jupiter. Nashe identifies Jupiter himself as none other than the Red Herring in his golden coat, worshipped by the people as one of the shapes taken by the god. This golden image is overthrown by Dionysus, 'a good wise fellow' but also an irreverent one 'who spit in Aristippus the Philosophers face many a time' (*Lenten Stuffe*, p. 194). Dionysus enters the temple, abruptly seizes the herring, strips off its skin and eats it. Thus the god is turned back into a mere fish, brought down to earth, 'thruste downe his pudding house at a gobbe'. This uncrowning is, however, only one event in a cycle, since Dionysus is himself overturned by the herring-Jupiter.

> . . . yet long it prospered not with him, (so revengefull a iust Iupiter is the red Herring), for as he tare him from his throne, and uncased him of his habiliments, so, in small devolution of yeres, from his throne was he chaced and cleane stript out of his royalty.
> (*Lenten Stuffe*, p. 194)

The general pattern of uncrowning and renewal is cyclical and reversible: fish are gods, gods are fish – an idol can be worshipped or eaten for lunch – and Dionysus is a good, wise king, but perhaps better suited to being a schoolmaster.

This general politics of uncrowning is developed in more particularity in two additional tales, that of 'how the herring rose up to be king of the fishes' and the story of the fisherman of Yarmouth who accidentally learned to smoke herrings. In the first of these stories, the fish convene a general council or parliament for the purpose of choosing a king to lead them in their war against the birds. This war is provoked when a falcon, accidentally let loose by a falconer, mistakes a fish for a partridge and, in attempting to seize it as prey, is eaten by a shark. The birds initiate a vengeful war of the high against the low, of the heraldic falcon and goshawk, aided by titmouse and swallow, against the lowest and most undistinguished of creatures. The herring is chosen to be the king of the fishes because he will be easily deposed. Once his limited and temporary military function has been achieved, the fish can return to the ordinary course of their daily lives. 'No rauening fish they would putte in armes, for feare after he had everted their foes, and flesht himselfe in bloud, for interchange of diet, hee woulde rauen up them' (*Lenten Stuffe*, p. 203).

The canny fisherman of Yarmouth discovers the process of smoking fish inadvertently, but he is able to gain extraordinary advantage from his discovery. He eventually makes his way to the pope's palace, where he offers to sell 'the king of the fishes' to His Holiness. 'Is it the king of fishes? . . . and is any man to have him but I that am king of kings and lord of lords?' After some extended negotiation with the pope's caterer, the fisherman succeeds in selling a single smoked herring for 300 ducats. The preparation of the herring in the pope's kitchen is an elaborate and unseemly farce, which reaches its climax as the foul odor of rotten herring pervades the pope's chambers.

> The busie epistasis of the commedy was when the dishes were uncovered and the swarthrutter sowre tooke ayre: for then hee made such an ayre, as Alcides himself that clensed the stables of Agaeus nor any hostler was able to endure. (*Lenten Stuffe*, p. 209)

In these stories, a general pattern of uncrowning is given more historically specific focus. The herring is a 'king' who leads a general resistance to vindictive and arrogant expropriations of 'land foules', whose preparations for war suggest the chivalric codes and social purposes of a land-based feudal and manorial culture. In the tale of the pope and the smoked herring, the pride and avarice of a corrupt and worldly religious institution is unmasked and subjected to comic humiliation. In all of these tales the Red Herring is an emancipatory figure, the instrument by means of which moribund and arbitrary authority is overthrown. This utopian hopefulness is actualized in the obviously unheroic form of a smoked fish, but the herring emancipates precisely because of his humble and ambivalent characteristics. He is kingly, not because of his magnificence, but because he lacks magnificence; he is a nourisher, the embodiment of an anonymous collectivity, and a creature of multiple disguises and transformations – a golden and shining image of wealth, as well as an unbearable and overpowering stench.

Lenten Stuffe is a travesty of a formal, literary Utopia, and its politics are proposed both in jest and in earnest. The structure parodies and reverses the more sober presentation of utopian form originated by More. The 'praise of the Red Herring' is *Utopia* carnivalized. The saturnalian possibilities of material abundance created by collective labor are reunited with the anarchic and prolifically creative language of everyday life. Everything is treated as laughing matter, even the central utopian hope itself. The utopian reality is reached by a journey, but that reality is not represented as a distant and exotic social horizon. The golden age was not long ago, but right now. Nashe finds Utopia at Yarmouth; he finds the economic, material and symbolic instrument of utopian transformation in the Red Herring. His exile turns out to be a liberating journey, an exit or strategic retreat from London and from the various presumptive claims of a hegemonic center. More imagined the subversive possibility of collective ownership and secured that possibility by placing it at an indefinite distance from the here and now, and by containing it within a traditional ideology. Nashe discovers an utopian form close at hand, where abundance and equality already exist without any formal elaboration of secular authority. For Nashe, social life is a haphazard arrangement of old and new customs, and patterns of interaction. His politics, like that of the writer of *A Breefe Discourse*, is conservative in its determination to maintain a well-established social practice relatively effective in achieving a satisfactory level of social wealth. Nashe's 'conservative' position is, however, precisely the oppositional and subversive position, not only vis-à-vis the radically increasing administrative authority of London, but also in relation to entrenched power and authority in both its traditional and its emergent form.

The transgressive and topsy-turvy imagery of *Lenten Stuffe* is completed in the powerfully ambivalent figures of Jack Cade and Jack Straw.

> The rebel Iacke Cade was the first that devised to put redde herrings in cades, and from hym they have their name. Nowe as wee call it the swinging of herrings when wee cade them, so in a halter was hee swung, and trussed up as hard and round as any cade of herring he trussed uppe in his tyme, and perhappes of his being so swung and trussed up, havyng first found out the tricke to cade herring, they woulde so much honour him in his death, as not onely to call it swinging, but cading of herring also. (*Lenten Stuffe*, p. 221)

The rebellious Cade is jestingly rehabilitated; he is recalled, not as a negative and disruptive figure, but as a hero of productive life. His execution and punishment are transformed into posthumous honoring; even the trajectory of the gallows receives an inverted meaning as the swinging up of the victim is depicted as a social elevation. Cade reappears as a full barrel of herring, and his name is preserved as part of the humble vocabulary of fishermen. Jacke Straw was 'the first that putte the redde herring in straw ouer head and eares like beggars'. A rebel like Jack Cade, Jack Straw 'hadde no wit nor wealthe but what hee got by the warme wrapping up of herring, raised this Prouerbe of him Gentleman Iacke Herring that puts his breeches on his head for want of wearing' (*Lenten Stuffe*, p. 221). The historical impulse to rebel against entrenched and established authority is remembered and preserved in these figures, who reappear in proverbs, in punning use of the language of work and in festive personae.

In *Lenten Stuffe*, Nashe organizes this complex language of popular utopian memory into an alternative 'political economy of the Red Herring'. In this alternative economy, social wealth is generated by labor rather than by land. The Red Herring is a jesting, emancipatory figure who shows society a way to achieve independence from land as the exclusive source of subsistence and thus to break the hegemony of proprietary ownership, both in its archaic, feudal forms of redistributive subsistence farming and in the newer, capital-accumulating forms of grazing and wool-production.

Part III
Theater and the Structure of Authority

THE NATURE and purpose of theater as a social institution was an energetically contested issue in the cultural and political life of London throughout the late Elizabethan and the Jacobean period. Despite the visible success of the public playhouses as a new communications industry, the theater did not enjoy universal acceptance and support. On the contrary, the relationship of the theater to cultural life as a whole was undecided and gave rise to acrimonious public debate.[1] The playhouses were subjected to a virtually constant stream of criticism and official interference from various social and ideological communities. Officers of the Crown conducted an uneasy surveillance of theatrical activity and were obliged to suppress performances from time to time out of an evident fear of seditious utterance. The municipal authorities complained about crime, about contagion, and about the adverse effect of theatergoing on prevailing standards of social discipline, especially among the subordinate classes. Puritans and other moralists were concerned with blasphemy, immoral behaviour and especially with the power of dramatic images to influence the social conduct of the members of the audience.

... if you will learn how to be false, and deceive your husbands, or husbands their wives . . . how to ravish, how to beguile, how to betray, to flatter, lie, swear, foreswear, how to allure to whoredom, how to murther, how to poison . . . shall you not learn then at such interludes how to practise them?[2]

This description of theater as the center of a black or diabolical pedagogy suggests how seriously some observers regarded the social impact of 'playing'. Anecdotal material of this kind indicates that theaters were not politically innocuous, and that people visited playhouses for reasons other than the private and highly specialized experience of enjoying worthwhile dramatic art.

The prevailing view of this controversy among contemporary scholars has been that opponents of theater were a vocal minority whose objections had little effect on the popularity of playhouses among a diverse and heterogeneous audience. The mingling of rich and poor, of gentlefolk and common people, contributed to the complex elaboration of dramatic form. Thus the playhouse 'had room for the groundlings [and] there was something for everybody'. Pluralism and 'free enterprise', according to this view, account for the immediate success of the playhouses and for the controversy surrounding that success.[3] But this populist description often fails to appreciate the cogency of the arguments against the theater, or the ideological and political issues underlying the conflict. The implication that theater might actually be a form of diabolical mis-education, capable of substantive disruption in the prevailing organization of social life, is dismissed as a narrow-minded opinion outside the social consensus that understands and supports the value of dramatic art. The antitheatrical literature thus represents a fundamental misunderstanding of the reconciliatory capacity of a pluralistic theater. The general view that the audience represented a wide range of social groups has been supported by scholars with quite divergent ideological points of view, including, for example, Robert Weimann, who asserts that it was 'made up of every rank and class of society', and J.H. Hexter, who maintains that 'Shakespeare was expecting a large number of plain folk . . . to share . . . express primary concern for the sanctity of property'.[4]

Despite the catholicity of its appeal, the populist and pluralistic conception of a theater offering something different for every member of a heterogeneous audience has recently been challenged. A much more elitist description of the sociology of the theater has been proposed by Professor Ann Cook in her discussion of 'the privileged playgoers'. This argument rejects the ideas of heterogeneity in favor of a view of theater as a manifestation of cultural domination that exists primarily for the benefit and the enjoyment of an affluent and powerful elite. 'London's large and lively privileged set ruled the playgoing world quite as firmly as they ruled the political world, the mercantile world, and the rest of the cultural world.'[5] Cook argues that theater was an expensive luxury available only to that very small minority of men and women in any age who make up a community of taste and common interest and are designated 'the privileged'.

In fact, as Cook's study acknowledges, the evidence does not support the contention that the theater existed exclusively, or even mainly, for the privileged playgoer. In addition to the sort of people who were used to seeing companies of players perform 'in their own mansions', the audience also included upwardly mobile craftsmen, downwardly mobile 'younger sons of good family' with disposable income, together with a visible minority of apprentices, journeymen, sailors and other ordinary commoners. The theory of a privileged playgoer is, however, defended by means of a number of auxiliary hypotheses. The 'poorer sort' are, according to Cook, present only in small numbers, and they are likely to attend plays much less frequently than their wealthier neighbors. And those of lesser means who *did* attend are described as either 'irresponsible', because the theater was a luxury poor people couldn't afford, or 'disreputable', because those common people who *were* able to afford the luxury could do so only as the result of ill-gotten gains. The most striking fact – that common people were present in open defiance of local authority and elementary fiscal prudence – is thus dismissed as a mere aberration. In adopting such an auxiliary hypothesis, Cook has shifted her argument from sociological description to advocacy for a particular etiquette of reception and for a particular definition of the political and social function of the theater.

The rejection of the 'populist' view that theater might appeal to a diverse 'market' is also a rejection of the view that it has a significant political function. If only a privileged minority enjoys the theater, then it has no conceivable purpose in the reconciliation of differences or even in the ideological mobilization of common people, to say nothing of its possibilities for critical representation and dissent. The exclusive and overriding purpose of the theater is the consumption of art. The 'elitist' view represented by Cook correctly identifies this highly specialized function with wealth and privilege, while refusing to acknowledge that there ever could have been any other purpose implied by the existence of the public playhouses. From this viewpoint, the antitheatrical literature and other evidence of historical controversy can be accounted for by explaining how the authors of the various polemics failed to understand the value of art. In this respect Cook's strategy is similar to that of the 'populist' theorists, who also refuse to take seriously any implication that theater may have been socially dangerous. However, if it is regarded as a social institution with its origins in more diffuse forms of public life, then theater might indeed be anomalous and therefore threatening to certain ideas of public order. The controversy about the public playhouses and related forms of theatrical activity was not a dispute about who attended performances, or about who should attend performances, or even about the permissible content of dramatic literature. It is a controversy about the structure and the allocation of authority. To its opponents, and even to some of its supporters, the theater represents a genuine rupture in the fabric of social authority. Because the subsequent legitimation of the theater derives to a substantial degree from the effort to address precisely those issues of authority raised by its opponents, it is important to analyze those issues without prejudging the motives of authors who question the existence of the theater, and its relationship to the structure of political power and its availability for opposing forms of social initiative.

CHAPTER 7
AUTHORITY AND THE AUTHOR FUNCTION

I N A THEATRICAL performance, writing appears in the guise of speech. An actor recites his lines in a manner that suggests that his words are spontaneous, unrehearsed and immediate. In the conditions of performance, a text recuperates the qualities of spoken utterance. Writing is reconcretized as sound; the speech is addressed to auditors who are present at the moment of utterance. The communicative space in which this activity occurs is not, moreover, an empty or uncluttered space in which a message is disseminated without interference. On the contrary, it is already full of sound and of other socially significant semiotic material. In such a state of affairs, a serious dislocation of authority is not only possible but likely, and several questions must therefore be raised. Where does this writing come from? How has it been produced? On whose authority is it reconcretized here and now as audible speech and visible gesture? The theater as an institution does not in general provide a definitive or particularly reassuring answer to these questions. And in the specific institutional and cultural setting of Elizabethan England, the theater existed in a particularly intense situation of unresolved structural ambiguity.

Theater creates an ambiguous temporal situation outside the

schedules of work and religious devotion. The time of performance is a festive time in which play and mimesis replace productive labor. While 'amateur' performances that actually coincide with holidays may be tolerable, a public playhouse that offers to provide a holiday experience without a formal liturgical sanction is clearly a 'resort of idleness'. In the playhouse, an audience has an experience that provides an alternative to regular social discipline: between periods of authorized activity an 'interlude' provides an escape from supervision and from surveillance of attitude, feeling and expression. Theater also disrupts time by means of its capacity to represent anachronism. Narrative time contradicts the authority of the calendar and brings the past into immediate juxtaposition with the present. Although such a juxtaposition could be useful as an instrument of political legitimation, in the theater it is a treacherous resource. A pragmatically illicit or unauthorized use of time (idleness) coincides with an altered representation of time (anachronism), leaving open the possibility of revisionary and therefore seditious misinterpretations of both past and present.

The untimeliness of a theatrical performance is compounded by the location of theaters in a complex social space. The public playhouses were 'extra-mural' and therefore exempted from the formal jurisdiction of the city authorities, although they were a de facto element in the economic and social life of London. Their social location was perhaps even more ambiguous than their geographical situation. On a day-to-day basis, the professional companies conducted their affairs as a commercial enterprise. Unlike the established trades and craft guilds, however, the players had no long tradition of practice to legitimize their right to earn a livelihood by presenting their skills to a paying audience. In order to overcome this difficulty, the earliest companies were founded on the basis of the legal fiction that the performers were household servants of high court officials. The social position of the players and of their work was based on two contradictory presuppositions – that they were engaged in a business or industry, and that they were engaged in 'service' to their aristocratic patrons. This ambiguity was, to some elements of the community, highly objectionable, since the players were, like vagabonds and itinerant peddlers, at the bottom of the social ladder and yet had somehow become affiliated with its highest and most privileged spheres.

Even more troubling than the peculiar and anomalous situation of the theater in relation to time and space, however, is the relationship of the player to language and to the text he recites. An actor's work is not at all like work in the usual sense – it is a professional and remunerative play, mimicry and experimentation. An actor earns a livelihood by representing or mimicking the language and gestures of other men and women. The appropriation and misappropriation of the speech of another is the very raison d'être of acting and of the audience's interest in what an actor does. Thus an actor is permitted to *dis*guise himself, that is to arbitrarily copy the *guise* or appropriate social integument of another man or woman. And the actor is also the disseminator of indirect discourse, the image of language that belongs to someone else. These relationships are parodic, forms of discursive and semiotic misrule that saturate all performance. They also necessarily embody the will to deception. Acting, or playing, is thus a disturbing and disquieting activity that engages real feeling in the absence of any occasion for it. 'What's Hecuba to him or he to Hecuba that he should weep for her?' (*Hamlet*, II. ii. 585). Unlike the consecrated minister of God's word or the political orator, an actor is a man whose public utterance does not represent what he feels or thinks, although it is said with full conviction and the sound of authority. An actor is not just someone whose speech is 'dissembling': the deeper problem is that he is most valued for his ability to dissemble convincingly. Because of this, the theater may indeed be the site of a diabolical pedagogy, a 'school of abuse' or at least a setting in which authority may be radically interrogated. The late sixteenth-century polemic against the stage actually takes account of this radical potentiality of the theater, by focusing attention not on texts but on players and their ambiguous relationship to all authority. The much weaker humanistic defenses of the theater overlook this radical potential, concentrating instead on making a case for literature and the literary artist as the reason for the playhouse's existence.

The professionalization of writing for the stage developed in the years from approximately 1590 to 1610, a period noted for the completion of many memorable works of dramatic literature.[1] However, the theater as an institution housing players and their audiences already existed before that time. The notorious antitheatrical polemics of Phillip Stubbes and John Northbrooke were written at a time when the patterns of literary authorship or playwriting were weakly defined and very timidly defended. But the attack on the theater is not primarily directed against literature. The attack on the players is part of a larger critique of popular culture, its disperson of authority, and its pervasive and tacit sanction of misrule in all the patterns of everyday life.

Anatomie of Abuses is a comprehensive denunciation of a wide range of activities, a few of which are readily characterized as crimes, for example prostitution. But a significant portion of this text is concerned with 'abuse' in the choice of wearing apparel, and in eating and drinking. These activities are not, of course, private matters, but rather aspects of each person's social integument or guise, significant expressions of *métier* and social position. There is a 'lawful' display of rich apparel appropriate for certain members of society.

> I wold not be so understood, as though my speaches extended, to any either noble, honorable, or worshipful: for, I am so farre from once thinking that any kind of sumptuousness, or gorgeous attire is not to be worn of any of them, as I suppose them rather Ornaments in them, than otherwise.
>
> And that they both may, and for some respects, ought to were such attire (their birthes, callings, functions and estats requiring the same) for causes in this my Booke laid downe, as maye appeare, and for the distinction of them from the inferiour sorte, it is provable both by the word of God, Ancient Writers, and common practise of all ages.[2]

'Gorgeous attire' signifies rank, excellence, dignity; its usage is governed by divine and secular authority. The 'abuse' of such attire is not ostentation or magnificence as such, but the use of such significant manifestations by the inferior sort that results in the effacement of social distinction.

Stubbes's denunciation of the abuses of 'gorgeous attire' and of 'overlavish diet' is minutely detailed. He enumerates at length types of fabric, sewing and tailoring techniques, and gives precise descriptions of recipes and methods of cooking. The discussion reveals that he is conversant with the diverse speech types and technical vocabularies of the productive sphere, and that it is the plenitude of these social languages that constitutes the most fundamental basis for all other abuses. The disguisings of everyday life may be abuses, but they are hardly isolated instances of waywardness or disobedience. The plenitude of speech types corresponds to a dispersion of all other forms of semiotic material, and what makes this so alarming is that the diversity of language objectifies a comprehensive knowledge of productive life – therefore it is already everywhere. Abuses cannot be isolated and excluded by secular authority, because the initiative for these public misstatements of identity is already widely dispersed among the 'inferior sort'.

Stubbes's attack on playing and on players must be understood against this general background of abuses in everyday life. Mimicry, disguise and the dispersion of authority have become pervasive; discriminations of rank, of status and even of gender become unintelligible. This is the basis for the polemic against the stage, and for the linking of plays and interludes with a comprehensive view of the disintegration of the social fabric. There is a 'lawful' form of ceremonial pageantry and theatrical display, which, like 'gorgeous attire', are permitted – in fact required – as signs of excellence and superiority. But plays and interludes become an abuse insofar as they are produced by the 'inferior sort' as the expression of their own knowledge of social and spiritual life. Theatrical activity compounds and intensifies the practice of mimicry and disguise, by creating a space in which even divine authority is ridiculed and debased.

> All stage-playes, Enterluds and Commedies, are either of divyne, or prophane matter: If they be of divine matter, then are they most intollerable, or rather Sacrilegious, for that the blessed word of God, is to be handled, reverently, gravely, and sagely, with veneration . . . not given, to be derided, and iested at as they be in these filthie playes, and enterludes on stages and scaffolds, or to be mixt and interlaced with bawdry, wanton shewes and uncomely gesture. . . . For at no hand, it is not lawfull, to mixe scurilitie with divinitie, nor divinitie with scurrilitie.[3]

Playing is most intolerable when it represents divine matters. The defense of theater therefore could not possibly rest on the presence of any ideologically authorized interpretive norms, chaste ideas inscribed in the dramatic text or exemplary punishments meted out to wrongdoers. In fact, this would only make matters worse. The theater is not the proper place for any such pedagogical good intentions; it is not a pulpit, a school or a courtroom; it can only mimic and therefore diminish the authority properly allocated to such institutions. And further, the theater is a site for promiscuity – it permits the mixing of distinct and exclusive speech types, and above all of jest and earnest. 'Scurillitie' is intrinsic to playing, which is finally nothing less than the will to deception itself.

> Who will call him a wiseman that plaieth the part of a foole and a vice: who can call him a Christian, who playeth the parte of a devil, the sworne enemie of Christe: who can call him a just man, that playeth the part of a dissembling hypocrite: And to be brief, who can call him a straight deling man, who playeth a Cosener's trick.[4]

The 'cosener's trick' is not simply a part of the narrative fiction represented on the stage. Theatrical performance is a cosenage in the most circumstantial and material sense, because money changes hands but no authentic goods are received.

Stubbes's position is based on the conviction that there is a Word fully identified with God. This divine Word is absolute in meaning and in value: it has always been true, it always will be true.

> In the first of John we are taught, that the word is God and God is the word. Wherefore, who so ever abuseth this word of our God on stages in playes and enterludes, abuseth the Maiesty of GOD in the same, Maketh a mocking stock of him, and purchaseth to himselfe eternal damnation.[5]

Stubbes sees that in theater this sacred Word may be suffered to reappear within the sphere of contingent utterance, where it will become a word just like any other. The theatrical miming of a sacred discourse diminishes it to the status of a speech type – a mere technical language, the shoptalk of the religion trade. And the more reverently the word is pronounced from the stage, the more it is derided, because it emanates not from an ordained minister of the Word but from a professional dissembler and 'corrupter of words'.

Anatomie of Abuses appeared at a time when there was considerable theatrical activity but relatively little dramatic literature. In Stubbes's view, 'playing' is most closely connected with such popular festive customs as wakes, maypoles and Lords of Misrule; it has relatively little to do with literature. The denunciation of theater addresses a situation in which playing has precedence over serious writing. The players are not 'actors' – they are the immediate creators of the performances and interludes. Their creativity relies on their capacity to extemporize dramatic texts out of 'secondhand' or 'used' plays combined with other materials, including literary and folk narrative, by their own improvisatory skill. This is a form of creativity that favors contingent and ephemeral manifestations over the finished text or work of art. The resulting aesthetics of heterogeneity, crude sensation and parodic mimicry create a situation of maximum intellectual and affective openness, but minimum accountability. In Stubbes's view, the player is able to say forbidden things with impunity, and only one political and administrative response to this is possible – the complete abolition of playing and the proscription of players.

The proposal to abolish playing is part of a larger program to restore the structure of authority by subjecting popular culture to vigilant surveillance and coercive restraint. As far as the theater itself is concerned, however, there is an alternative to abolition, that is to reinvent the institution so as to provide it with a well-defined and carefully limited social function. The project of legitimation seeks to diminish the dispersed, anonymous authority of 'players' in favor of a well-defined author function that allows for the ownership of texts and, just as important, for lines of accountability to de jure authority. The most energetic and articulate advocate for this program of legitimation is Ben Jonson, who proposes a number of ingenious solutions to the kinds of problems raised by Phillip Stubbes. But it would be only partly true to suggest that Stubbes and Jonson are on opposite sides in the controversy over the theater. Both projects – abolition and legitimation – proceed from the same critique of popular culture, and from the same anxiety and resentment over the dispersion of authority in the intensified public life of the playhouses.

Kind-Hartes Dreame by Henrie Chettle describes this process of legitimation by means of a dream image in which Tarlton, the exemplary figure of the extemporizing player, returns from the dead to denounce the 'unprofitable recreation of Stage playeing'. The denunciation incorporates the familiar themes of idleness and immorality.

> Fie uppon following plaies, the expence is wondrous; upon players speeches, their wordes are full of wyles uppon their gestures, that are altogether wanton. Is it not lamentable that a man shoulde spende his two pence on them in an after-noone, heare covetousnes amongst them daily quipt at, being one of the commonest occupations in the countrey; and in liuevly gesture see trecherie set out,

with which every man now adaies useth to intrap his brother. Byr lady, this would be lookt into: if these be the fruites of playing, tis time the practisers were expeld.[6]

The harm done by playing stems from its highly public character, and from the 'vulgar' conversation and contempt for authority encouraged by the abuse of 'honest recreation'. Notwithstanding such abuse, Tarlton maintains that there is a proper use of playing.

> In plaies it fares as in bookes, vice cannot be reproued, except it be discouered: neither is it in any play discouered, but there followes in the same an example of the punishment: now he that at a play will be delighted in the one, and not warned by the other, is like him that reads in a booke the description of sinne, and will not looke over the leafe for the reward.[7]

Plays and playgoing can be legitimated on the basis of a correspondence with books and with careful, attentive reading informed by prior knowledge of moral imperatives.

The reinvention of the theater in conformity with the models of literature and of pedagogy is fully elaborated by Jonson in a series of prologues to his plays. In *Bartholomew Faire*, a series of articles are read to the audience enumerating the terms of a contractual relationship between the author and each of its members. Prior to this, however, the 'stage-keeper' appears to complain of the presumption of the author and to recall an earlier form of theatrical creativity.

> I kept the stage in Master Tarltons time, I thank my stars. Ho! you should ha' seen him ha' come in and ha' beene coozened i' the Cloath-quarter so finely! And Adams the Rogue, ha' leap'd and caper'd upon him, and Ha' dealt his vermine about as though they had cost him nothing. And then a substantiall watch to ha' stolne in upon 'hem, and taken 'hem away, with mistaking words, as the fashion is, in the Stage-practise.[8]

In Master Tarlton's time, 'Stage-practise' featured slapstick, leaping, capering, thrashing and mistaking words. But the 'stage-keeper', with his fond memories of Tarlton, is driven off the stage by the 'booke-holder', who speaks for a radically transformed social and communicative relationship in the theater. The 'stage-keeper's' function is now diminished to performing menial tasks. Farcical improvisation gives way to dramatic literature. Players are reduced to the status of servants of the author and his master-text. The dramatic expulsion of the 'stage-keeper' objectifies the displacement of a popular, improvisatory and extra-official participatory tradition by a legally sanctioned sequence of creation, transmission and 'purchase' of a finished literary product.[9] The contractual articles specify the respective functions of the audience members and of the author. In consideration of the price paid for admission, the individual auditor is entitled to his or her own private interpretation; but there is to be no public dissemination or exchange of interpretation. Interpretive consultation is forbidden – and not just in order to discourage misinterpretation. All interpretation, even correct interpretation (whatever that might be) is in principle not permitted because it proceeds from the conviction that there is something further to be said. And this conviction specifically contradicts the principle that discursive sovereignty over the 'matter' or text of the theatrical event be allocated exclusively to the author.

In place of the dispersed authority of 'playing', Jonson proposes to establish the playwright as the individual center of production, fully responsible for the creation of a dramatic text to be presented to a consuming public as a complete, integral work. His sense of artistic integrity and self-sufficiency is expressed jestingly in the induction to *Bartholomew Faire*, but it is even more forcefully objectified in his pragmatic determination to see that the publication of his plays was completed in accordance with his own wishes. This careful attention to the details of publication reveals a desire to retain as far as possible all benefits deriving from his work – in other words, to own that work. But Jonson's proprietary claim is best defended when there is a corresponding assumption of accountability. In order to own his work, he agrees to be punished if it should be judged 'criminal'.

> Your maiesty hath seene the Play, and you
>   can best allow it from your eare, and view.
> You know the scope of Writers, and what store
>   of leaue is giuen them, if they take not more,
> And turne it into licence: you can tell
>   if we have us'd that leave you gaue us, well.
>   (*Bartholomew Faire*, Epilogue, ll. 1–6)

Jonson was able to create a profession for himself only by devising and codifying a complete structure of authority for the theater, together with an etiquette of reception that takes careful account of public and private response. The elaboration of the author function then allows the communicative pattern of the theater to be incorporated into an even more comprehensive pattern of jurisprudence.

In Hobbes's *Leviathan*, the allocation of authority among actors and authors has become so well codified that it is used to formulate pivotal legal definitions of persons, actions, and the nature of direct and indirect responsibility. Hobbes begins from the etymological derivation of the term 'person' as a 'face' or integument.

> Persona in latine signifies the disguise, or outwarde appearance of a man, counterfeited on the Stage; and sometimes more particularly that part of it, which disguiseth the face, as a Mask or Visard: And from the Stage, hath been translated to any Representer of speech and action, as well in Tribunalls, as Theaters. So that a Person is the same that an actor is, both on the stage, and in common Conversation.[10]

A person exists at the surface, where identity is seen and known by others. A person's acts are conceived as possessions, but there are cases when a person represents 'the words or actions of an other', and in these it is necessary to distinguish between actor and author.

> Of Persons Artificiall, some have their words and actions Owned by those whom they represent. And then the Person is the Actor; and he that owneth his words and actions, is the Author: In which case the actor acteth by Authority. For that which in speaking of goods and possessions, is called an Owner, and in latine, Dominus . . . speaking of actions is called Author. And as the Right of possession, is called Dominion, so the Right of doing any Action, is called Authority.[11]

The convergence of authority with domination and with ownership transforms it into an object relationship; initiative and creative power become identified with a particular thing rather than with a diffuse energy or process. The diffusion of authority through free mimicry is impermissible, and in fact inconceivable, since an actor is no longer a 'player' possessed of improvisatory competence but merely a 'lieuten-ant, a Vicar, an Attorney, a Deputy, a Procurator'. Hobbes's analysis thus provides for a clear and orderly delegation of authority from a coherent center. And just as the sovereign impersonates the civil society and gathers together all its dispersed authority in his own person, so the author brings together a collectively dispersed creativity in his own *œuvre*. The singularity of the author is achieved through the separation of his own literary language from the undifferentiated and omnipresent flow of all other speech types both in the domain of words and in the broader domain of actions. The integration of literary and verbal creativity into more general forms of ownership and delegation of authority is the enabling act for the professionalization of creativity and its legitimation as a means of livelihood. This individualization of artistic production is the basis for the legitimation of the theater. The author is defined as the owner of his text and thus as an individual who might be punished or subjected to litigation. The audience is decomposed into private individuals who appreciate a text without interpreting it; the actor is an artificial person whose words originate from and are delegated by a well-defined center of authority. In this allocation of functions, there is no one left who can say forbidden things with impunity, and the dangers of an ambiguously allocated or dispersed authority are safely contained.

In his analysis of the author function, Michel Foucault points out that, although the paradigmatic conception of 'the man and his works' has become the decisive element in both the creation and the reception of literary texts, it is not the only possible form by which verbal art may be created. The author function is only one among several possible pro-cedures for the production of narrative material, and not necessarily the oldest or most natural one.

> There was a time when the texts that we today call 'literary' (narrative, stories, epics, tragedies, comedies) were accepted, put into circulation and valorized without any question about the identity of their author; their anonymity caused no difficulties since their ancientness, whether real or imagined, was regarded as a sufficient guarantee of their status.[12]

The author function has emerged more than once in the history of literature, but never to the complete exclusion of anonymous, dispersed creative processes. However, when the author function is in the ascendancy, it is difficult to recognize patterns other than those of individualized production, except by means of such marginalizing conceptions as 'folk narrative' or the 'oral tradition'. And this marginalization is compounded by developmentalist points of view that identify real literature with individualized, definitively attributed works of art and thus use the author function as an implicit teleology for the elucidation of alternative forms of cultural production.

The polemic against the stage and the subsequent deployment of the author function and its collateral structure of authority are systematic responses to an alternative form of cultural production that found an extremely favorable setting for energetic dissemination in the public playhouses. In this form of cultural production, publicly and collectively 'owned' narrative and aphoristic material exists 'objectively', prior to any singular act of creativity by any individual. That material is valorized by its antiquity and by its homely familiarity to a wide public; there is no distinction between the activities of 'original creation' and 'performance'. Particular concretizations are not 'memorable' or preserved in durable and definitive form, but collective memory nevertheless sustains the narrative resources to which there is unrestricted access. In this process the text does not stand out as a monumental presence but functions within a 'heteroglot' exchange of experience. [13]

The communicative exchange of experience in such anonymous forms as storytelling is, towards the end of the sixteenth century, displaced from the private spaces of the workshop into the politically open spaces of inns, taverns and eventually actual playhouses. This theater is, like storytelling, an artisan form deeply embedded in the experience of everyday social labor. The amateur theaters of homogeneous social groups confined this exchange of experience within a well-defined and authorized social milieu. The public playhouses, however, substantially altered the pattern of dissemination. To the already pervasive exchange of cultural experience in the free, public spaces of the street it added the anonymous, impertinent forms of the players, in the shape of familiar stock routines and innovative improvisatory competence. The playhouse is not simply a theater in which a literary heteroglossia is performed, but an actual heteroglot institution in which the exchange of experience crosses every social boundary, and the diversity of speech types traverses the genres of literature and of authoritative discourse.

This is cultural activity mandated by a 'dialogic imperative' rather than by any prior allocation and structuring of authority.[14] Poetic language, rhetorical ornament and classical learning are compelled to share communicative space with vernacular speech and with vernacular misinterpretations of high culture. This is a virtual and immediate form of heteroglossia, not simply a literary reproduction within a text, and it corresponds to Stubbes's conception of the 'scurrilitie' of playing. The theater is the site of experimental institution-making, purposefully antithetical to any aesthetic program that seeks to create a 'unified' and comprehensive language for the interpretation of social complexity.

In a theater dominated by such an ethos of creativity there is stubborn resistance, not only to the entrenchment of any unifying language or code of representation, but also to the monumentalization of any particular text. The existence of unforgettable works of art is incompatible with the strongest possible continuity of tradition, remembrance and recollection of lived experience as it is transmitted across social space and from one generation to another. Unforgettable works of art also weaken the tactical versatility of the collective and diminish its resourcefulness in responding to social change.

Literature enters into this pattern of cultural production as a relative latecomer, and for a considerable time it was forced to contend with an environment quite unfavorable for the reception of literary art. The subsequent success of the great Elizabethan playwrights and the prestige accorded to their work have made it difficult to appreciate the priority of a heteroglot theater, its capacity to arouse genuine political anxiety, and its impact on social discipline and the structure of authority. The theatrical performances that took place within this environment were created by means of a coalition strategy shared among writers and their texts, players and their repertoire of 'business', and integral groups of spectators and their proverbs, jokes, curses and improvised commentary. Social discontinuity is never hidden and certainly not by the compelling power of a disembodied art or a universally shared ideology. The strong forms that emerge from this *mise-en-scène* are likely to be disjunctive and highly ephemeral. They are also likely to be effective as a form of cultural or political work in which specific aspects of the social relations of production may be interrogated critically. But this 'heteroglot' condition of the theater as an institution cannot be fully analyzed by the investigation of specific 'works' or authors, though such specific textual analysis does help to make this form of cultural production more fully intelligible. Many of the important texts are, however, peculiarly unfinished, incompletely determined structures that presuppose a complex philosophy of *serio-ludere* embodied in a particular dialectic of laughter and in the theatrical conventions of clowning and devilment. The patterns of grotesque, popular laughter, and the mobilization of that laughter by the public figures of the clown and the devil, constitute a distinct structure of authority which is the precondition both for the writing and the reception of the dramatic text.

CHAPTER 8
THE DIALECTIC OF LAUGHTER

T HE MIXTURE of jest and earnest has been a well-understood norm of
literary practice since antiquity. E. R. Curtius has shown that the
seriocomic continued to be an important topos throughout the Middle
Ages, in preaching as well as in literature, where its main function was
ridendo dicere verum, to speak truth laughingly.[1] The mixture of mirth
and truth remains a conspicuous feature of 'high' and of 'popular'
literature throughout the Renaissance.

In his prefatory remarks to the encomium of the Red Herring, Thomas
Nashe supplies an exhaustive list of precedents for the mixing of jest and
earnest, enumerating works in praise of insects and other vermin,
household objects, diseases, parts of the body, and even a witty encomium dedicated to 'the reformation of close-stooles and houses of office'
(*Lenten Stuffe*, p. 177). The existence of a rich and venerable literary
tradition in which serious matter and irreverent expression are combined
does not, however, explain the peculiar cognitive strategies inherent
both in the forms themselves and in the pattern of responses to those
forms. Laughter appears to be fundamentally incompatible with philosophical statements, this incompatibility deriving from the connection
laughter has with what is socially and intellectually low and common-

place, and from the privileged status that jesting provides for logical contradiction and equivocation. Because of this, many theories of laughter stress its subordination to rational categories and its capacity to reinforce social and intellectual norms. According to V.A. Kolve in his discussion of 'religious laughter', this is the basis for the accommodation of laughter by the medieval church.[2] Laughter is accepted by religious authority when it points out the aberrations of individual sinners and the deformity of their sin. But laughter enjoyed for its own sake, taking delight in worldly experience, is unaesthetic and morally reprehensible.

The socially normative character of satirical laughter can be seen in the epilogue to *Summer's Last Will and Testament*. Here laughter attains legitimacy by its capacity to reinforce status, hierarchy and class difference.

> To make the gods merry, the coelestiall clown Vulcan tun'de his polt-foot to the measures of Apolloes Lute, and daunst a limping Gallyard in Ioue's starry hall. To make you merry, that are the Gods of Art and guides unto heaven, a number of rude Vulcans, unweldy speakers, Hammer-headed clowns (for so it pleaseth them in modestie to name themselves) have set their deformities to view, as it were in a daunce here before you.[3]

As Keith Thomas has pointed out, the mockery of deformity, deviance and inferior status was socially accepted in the culture of Tudor and Stuart England.[4] Ridicule is a recognized element in law enforcement, in the punishment of insubordination and in the everyday feeling of superiority enjoyed by nobles in respect of their servants. Laughter is also an important element in the strategies of social appeasement used by servants in respect of their masters. Self-abjection and self-ridicule are significant elements in an elaborate system of deferential gesture and compliment. 'Beare with their wants, lull melancholie asleepe with their absurdities, and expect hereafter better fruites of their industrie.'[5]

The strategy of self-ridicule reveals the social uneasiness expressed through laughter, even when that laughter is sanctioned by mutually acknowledged norms of social conduct. This view of laughter is theorized by Sir Philip Sidney, who criticizes the mixed decorum of early Elizabethan plays that 'be neither right Tragedies, nor right Comedies'.[6] Sidney's analysis of laughter begins with his conviction that the governing aim of poetic or theatrical representation is 'delightful teaching'.

The pleasure of representation lies in the careful discrimination of responses, so that there is no confused mixing of joy and sorrow, of 'hornepipes with funerall'. In addition, 'teaching delightfulness' arises from equally careful delineation of social and ethical types.

> A busy loving Courtier, a hartles threatening Thraso, a selfe-wise-seeming schoolemaster, a awry-transformed Traueller: These if we sawe walke in stage names, which wee play naturally, therein were delightfull laughter and teaching delightfulnes.[7]

Sidney differentiates between a precise, moderated and intellectual laughter, proper to literature and to literary drama, and the indiscriminate laughter he finds in the theatrical performances of his contemporaries. Pleasurable literary laughter requires more than outward conformity to a social system and profession of belief in its ideology. The members of society must live their hierarchically ordered relationships inwardly, with full emotional engagement.

Sidney's philosophy of laughter reveals a fundamental distrust of ludicrous situations and the complex attitudes of shared pleasure and derision experienced in viewing such situations. These disturbing feelings are particularly awkward and objectionable in public social settings such as the theater.

> But our Comedians thinke there is no delight without laughter; which is very wrong, for though laughter may come with delight, yet commeth it not of delight, as though delight should be the cause of laughter, but well may one thing breed both together: nay, rather in themselves they have, as it were, a kind of contrarietie: for delight we scarcely doe but in things that have a conveniencie to our selves or to the generall nature; laughter almost ever commeth of things most disproportioned to ourselves and nature. Delight hath a joy in it, either permanent or present. Laughter hath onely a scornfull tickling. For example, we are revished with delight to see a faire woman, and yet are far from being moued to laughter. We laugh at deformed creatures, wherein certainly we cannot delight.[8]

Laughter is a response to exceptional, inconvenient and deformed aberrations from the harmonious regularity of ordered social life. In this view, laughter, considered by itself, is mainly negative, and therefore useless, unless it is combined with instruction that promotes corrective action.

The theory of laughter adopted by Sidney was later articulated more bluntly by Hobbes, who explained laughter as a pleasurable response to the inferiority or degradation of another.

> Sudden glory, is the passion which maketh those Grimaces called Laughter; and is caused either by some sudden act of their own, that pleaseth them; or by the apprehension of some deformed thing in another, by comparison whereof they suddenly applaud themselves.[9]

Sudden glory, like 'scornful tickling', is derived from invidious comparison, self-congratulation and overt aggression. Hobbes stigmatizes the attitude as one that is incompatible with honor and magnanimity.

> . . . it is incident most to them, that are conscious of the fewest abilities in themselves; who are forced to keep themselves in their own favour, by observing the imperfections of other men. And therefore much Laughter at the defects of others, is a signe of Pusillanimity. For of great mind, one of the proper workes is, to help and free others from scorn; and compare themselves only with the most able.[10]

Laughter is linked to scorn; it is cowardly; it is, above all, consciousness of inferiority and superiority in the individual subject. The specific complex of attitudes and social reactions accounts for Sidney's desire to exclude laughter from theatrical performance, unless it arises as a secondary manifestation of the more positive complex of feelings he identifies as delight.

Sidney recoils from laughter and from the feelings of aggression connected with it partly out of a sense of courteous restraint. It is clear from his correspondence that he is very much preoccupied with courtesy, not only toward his peers, but also toward his servants, dependents and, indeed, every individual with whom he comes into contact. Social life, for Sidney, demands scrupulous attention to the appropriate courtly response to every situation, and most particularly to the observance of fine points of etiquette connected with the system of deference and *noblesse oblige*. However, exactly that same consciousness of differences in wealth, rank, status and authority can also give rise to scorn, and thus to laughter, which must therefore be proscribed because it reveals far too much about the nature of that social system. The laughter that Sidney rejects as unaesthetic is the undisguised expression of aristocratic arrogance. Laughter can, and often does, reveal the self-congratulatory belligerence of those in privileged situations in their relationship with those who serve them.

Despite its capacity for therapeutic social correction, laughter is too corrosive, even in its normative, satirical function. There is the further danger that the scornful and hostile laughter of social superiority will rebound upon those in positions of privilege. The amusing doltishness of servants may be something other than a strategy of deference and appeasement. The gestures of self-ridicule may represent a stubborn refusal to conform fully to the elaborate requirements of an hierarchical society. The 'mingling of Kings and Clownes', and the laughter such mingling evokes, constitute for Sidney a formal public display of attitudes that are better left unexpressed. His theory of laughter reveals a strong distrust of seriocomic discourse, a distrust derived from a sensitive and insightful sociology of laughter. Sidney sees very clearly that laughter is social, that it is a shared pleasure in which the participants experience strong feelings of intimacy or solidarity, together with equally strong feelings of exclusion and difference.

Sidney's position represents the gentle and courtly solution to the problem of laughter, and to the literary and theatrical mixture of jest and earnest. His view excludes most of the stronger forms of satirical denunciation and normative ridicule. Most seriocomic literature of the Renaissance fails to conform to Sidney's aesthetic preferences, even though his theory does give recognition to the cognitive and social ambivalence and complexity of the counter between jest and earnest. What Sidney recognizes in the *Apologie*, and what is overlooked or neglected by more conventional theorists and apologists for the corrective or pedagogical value of satire, is that laughter cannot easily be regulated. It is linked, not only to clearly recognizable aberration and deformity, but also to structural ambiguity in the social system and to discord experienced as a result of that ambiguity. Furthermore, laughter is not only a reaction to some particular discontinuity or rupture, to an erroneous 'philosophy', but is, in some texts at least, a substantive philosophy in its own right, and one that presents itself as a full and genuine alternative to all serious world views.

Laughter, rather than any formalized system of rational concepts, is the primary philosophy expressed throughout Erasmus's *Praise of Folly*.

> . . . mine is not the first of this kind, but the same thing that has been often practiced even by great authors: when Homer so many ages since, did the like with the battle of frogs and mice; Virgil, with the gnat and the puddings; Ovid with the nut; when Polycrates and his corrector Isocrates extolled tyranny; Glauce, injustice; Favorinus, deformity and the quartan ague; Synescius, baldness; Lucian the fly and flattery; when Seneca made such sport with Claudius' canonizations; Plutarch with his dialogue between Ulysses and Gryllus; Lucian and Apuleius with the ass.[11]

Erasmus's purpose is to recuperate laughter as philosophy. He plays with the name of his correspondent, More, whose name 'comes so near the word Moriae (folly) as you are far from the thing'. Thus the Latin title, *Encomium Moriae*, becomes a kind of global equivocation in which the praise of foolishness is at the same time the praise of a wise man. More himself is characterized as a laughing philosopher, like Democritus, 'neither unlearned . . . nor altogether insipid'. Laughter thus constitutes a way of knowing the truth about the world that is accessible neither to solemn academic discourse nor to the reduced genres of topical or personal satire.

Laughter is built into the fictional *mise-en-scène* of Folly's oration. As soon as she appears, she tells her audience:

> [You] cleared your brows, and with so frolic and hearty a laughter [gave] me your applause, that in truth as many of you as I behold on every side of me seem to me no less than Homers gods drunk with nectar and nepenthe; whereas before, you sat as lumpish and pensive as if you had come from consulting an oracle. And as it usually happens when the sun begins to show his beams, or when after a sharp winter the spring breathes afresh on the earth, all things immediately get a new face, new color, and as it were a certain kind of youth again; in like manner, by but beholding me you have in an instant gotten another kind of countenance.
>
> (*The Praise of Folly*, pp. 7–8)

As the embodiment of equivocation, fallacy and unreason, Folly insinu-
ates her authority throughout the social and intellectual domain, but the
universality of unreason and its preeminence in the sphere of wisdom
and learning are neither ominous nor threatening. On the contrary, the
celebration of unreason is a relief. The laughter evoked by Folly's
appearance at the lectern is scorn powerfully transformed to self-
derision and self-acceptance.

Erasmus theorizes laughter in Folly's parodic account of the ancient
pantheon, made tolerable mainly by the presence of Bacchus.

> Why is it that Bacchus is always a stripling, and bushy-haired? but
> because he is mad, and drunk, and spends his life in drinking,
> dancing, and May games, not having so much as the least society
> with Pallas . . . O foolish god, say they, and worthy to be born as
> you were of your father's thigh! And yet who had not rather be
> your fool and sot, always merry, ever young, and making sport for
> other people. (*The Praise of Folly*, p. 23)

The clownish Bacchanalian celebration is a version of the popular
utopian 'fools paradise'. Folly suggests that this is the wish horizon of
most men and women, and a counter-statement to the demands of
authority, wisdom and hard work, which are 'laughed away' by celebratory practice and irreverent spectacle. Laughter exposes the entire
Olympian hierarchy as a farcical imposture and at the same time reveals
the narrow limits within which ordered reason may function. With
reason carefully circumscribed, there is ample scope for living, for
surrender to pleasure and communality in the acceptance of weakness,
frailty and imperfection.

> . . . there was never any pleasant which folly gave not the relish to.
> Insomuch that if they find no occasion of laughter, they send for
> 'one that may make it', or hire some bufoon flatterer, whose
> ridiculous discourse may put by the gravity of the company. For to
> what purpose is it to clog our stomachs with dainties, junkets, and
> the like stuff, unless our eyes and ears, nay whole mind, were
> likewise entertained with jests, merriments, and laughter?
> (*The Praise of Folly*, p. 29)

This festive laughter is the social presence of Folly, who completes the satisfactions of the banquet by nourishing both the senses and the spirit.

Folly's rhetoric gradually changes, and, through much of the text of *Encomium Moriae*, she performs the role of a moralizing satirist. In these passages, describing worldly vanity and dissimulation, Folly denounces false priests and dishonest merchants whose actions are tolerated by the easy compromises of conventional social morality. From the standpoint of this detached moral wisdom, laughter is a healthy and cathartic defense against temptation, false reason and false consciousness. These satirical passages provide a reassuring sense that there are standards of rationality and that the grotesque energies of folly and unreason may somehow be contained.[12] The fiction of a public performance, however, provides a most uneasy foundation for the strategies of satire. The counsels of wisdom are offered by a character whose name and appearance make her auditors laugh, so that the entire argument stands on equivocation, logical contradiction, fallacy. In a world of unreason, what can it possibly mean to be reasonable? If the categories which organize practical knowledge of the world are so saturated with unreason, then any wisdom that offers to distinguish between 'benign' and 'malignant' forms of folly can only be approximately and relatively valid.

Erasmus's philosophy of jest and earnest, as well as his philosophy of social life, is not predicated on absolute standards of perfection or even perfectability. The relationships that link one person to another and sustain collective interaction rest on arbitrary roles, on a 'self-fashioning' of the social integument that bears an ominous relationship to theatrical masquerade and the will to deception.[13] These 'roles' that men and women play are 'foolish', but they receive collective valorization from the participants provided they are performed with appropriate conviction and cheerful disregard for the often threadbare and patched social surface.

The universality of folly as the fundamental 'truth about the world' is Erasmus's main 'argument'. Laughter is indiscriminate and tends towards dissolution of all forms of worldly and institutional knowledge. Even religion is a laughing matter.

> Christ himself, that he might better relieve this folly, being the wisdom of the Father, yet in some manner became a fool when taking upon him the nature of man . . . nor did he work this cure

any other way than by the foolishness of the cross and a company of fat apostles, not much better, to whom he also recommended folly but gave them a caution against wisdom and drew them together by the examples of little children, lilies, mustard seed, and sparrows, things senseless and inconsiderable. (*The Praise of Folly*, p. 141)

Laughter is a saving response because it places everything in a down-to-earth perspective. It offers a capacity to revitalize fundamental impulses of love and belief by dissolving the authoritative claims of temporal institutions such as church and state. It is, therefore, antithetical to conceptions of 'sudden glory' that arise from scorn, from social contempt and in general from any claim of hierarchical advantage. It is powerfully antithetical to the 'pusillanimity' of pretended superiority, whether that superiority derives from social privilege or from some kind of self-righteous position of moral dignity and worth, including the moral dignity of the satirist. Laughter is, additionally, an antidote to fear and intimidation. Even Holy Writ can be grasped as the narrative of a familiar and laughable world represented at a human scale. The figures of Christ and his 'fat apostles', even the cross itself, are seen as homely and ludicrous rather than as terrifying.

Erasmus's 'learned oration' is a 'Carnivalization' of literature that deploys the grotesque laughter of popular festive form.[14] Folly's stance of self-ridicule is itself a characteristic gesture of that form, and, in her extensive use of proverbial expressions and sayings, she reveals her familiar relationship with the language of plebeian culture. Two of these proverbs figure importantly in her concluding remarks. 'Sometimes a fool may speak a word in season' suggests the prevailing theme of seriocomic discourse, of *ridendo dicere verum*. The truth uttered in laughter is not, however, a formal concept or memorable doctrine. 'I hate one that remembers what's done over the cup': Folly opposes dogmatic recollection of particular words or ideas. The truth expressed in Carnival laughter acknowledges pleasure in the things of this world, and the pathos of their transience and fragility. Truth is grasped as a mingling of joy and grief.[15] It is in this linking of strong contrary feelings that Erasmus's 'theology' of laughter may be compared with the most 'scientific' of Renaissance theories of laughter, the *Traité du Ris* of Laurent Joubert.

The *Treatise on Laughter* was evidently first published in 1579, though it had been written, according to Joubert, much earlier. Its author was a physician, and his approach to laughter is based very extensively on his knowledge of physiology and on direct observation of the physical and material basis of laughter and the ludicrous. His prologue reveals a wide-ranging curiosity about the world and a desire to know and to understand diverse phenomena such as the reason why 'fruit puts our teeth on edge' or 'iron [is] drawn by a magnet'.[16] Among the unexplained curiosities mentioned, laughter deserves particular scrutiny and attention as 'one of the most astounding actions of man . . . which counteracts old age, is common to all, and proper to man' (*Treatise on Laughter*, p. 17). Joubert does not pose the problem of laughter in terms of an individualistic conception of a 'sense of humor'. Laughter is an aspect of the individual's relationship to other people: established collective life is the precondition for individual laughter and for distinctive variations in the capacity to create laughing matter.

Joubert begins his analysis with axiomatic propositions derived from common knowledge as to the nature of 'laughing matter'.

> The most known things (those which each man understands and accords) are accepted by the populace, and such that they can never be denied. What aids much in proving something is the putting forth of propositions so evident that they cannot be refuted, and from these to deduce as much as possible. So it is with what we are attempting: to show from general acceptance what is the matter of laughter.　　　　　　　　　　　　　　(*Treatise on Laughter*, p. 19)

Joubert thus concedes to common knowledge considerable intellectual authority. Common knowledge is characterized as 'general acceptance' – propositions that are 'already everywhere'. For Joubert, 'scientific axioms' are most reliable and persuasive when they correspond to common opinion. In this respect his philosophy of science resembles More's philosophy of religion. In both writers there is strong conviction that no fundamental discontinuity exists between things that common people understand and higher realms of complex, difficult, formal knowledge.

The 'matter of laughter' is a series of objective situations and states of affairs commonly acknowledged to provoke a laughing response. Laughter is stimulated by objects that are ugly, deformed and indecorous, provided that the pain or sorrow ordinarily occasioned by such objects is in some way modified. Things that are ugly but 'unworthy of pity or compassion' constitute the domain of the ludicrous. Certain parts of the body, when suddenly revealed in public, are recognized universally as laughing matter.

> . . . if perchance one uncovers the shameful parts which by nature or public decency we are accustomed to keeping hidden, since this is ugly yet unworthy of pity, it moves the onlookers to laughter. . . . It is equally unfitting to show one's arse, and when there is no harm forcing us to sympathize we are unable to contain our laughter. But if another suddenly puts a red-hot iron to him, laughter gives way to compassion unless the harm done seems light and small, for that reinforces the laughter. (*Treatise on Laughter*, p. 20)

These objects of laughter are not merely examples of the ludicrous. The human genitals and buttocks, what Bakhtin has called the 'lower bodily stratum', constitute the definitive category of laughing matter. The buttocks are 'out of place' in a social situation. Nevertheless, they are objects of desire and in any case their existence is 'common knowledge'. This form of 'laughing matter' has logical priority over all other forms because it has the widest applicability. Every other type of laughing matter refers to this one, as the origin and the meaning of the ludicrous.

The second class of laughing matter discussed by Joubert is 'seeing someone fall in the mire'. Downward movement, especially sudden, precipitous and inadvertent downward movement, is as universally laughable as the revelation of the lower body. Further, the greater the fall, the heartier and more powerful is the laughter.

> . . . children and drunkards fall often, and make us laugh: but we will laugh incomparably more if a great and important personage who walks affectedly with a grave and formal step, stumbling clumsily on a heavy stone, falls suddenly in a quagmire. . . . there is nothing so disgusting, and that causes less pity, than if this same personage is unworthy of the rank he holds and of the honor one gives him, if he is hated for his pride and excessive arrogance, resembling a monkey dressed in crimson, as the proverb has it. And who, seeing such a man stumble stupidly, would be able to keep from laughing. (*Treatise on Laughter*, p. 20)

This is the laughter that Bakhtin interprets as 'uncrowning'; it is also recognizable as the inversive form of Hobbes's concept of 'sudden glory', except that downward movement is seen from below and satisfaction derives from seeing 'superiority' brought low.

Following his discussion of these two categories of the 'lower bodily stratum' and 'downward movement', Joubert proceeds to a series of more abstract classes of laughing matter. Gregory de Rocher identifies two of these as 'error' and 'inconsequential loss', both of which may come about either by misadventure or as the result of a deliberate prank.[17] In each instance, however, it is possible to refer to the basic gestures that disclose the ambivalent reality of the human body (showing of the genitals and buttocks) and unmask pretension and social pride (falling in the mud). Many of Joubert's examples – 'if for example, when somebody is unaware, we undo his clothes, or if we throw water on somebody who was not expecting it' (*Treatise on Laughter*, p. 22) – reveal a predominant interest in the more boisterous and physical forms of the ludicrous. This fascination with physical humor and with the riskier forms of public humiliation corresponds to Joubert's central theoretical doctrine, in which laughter is described as an exterior, social manifestation of a physical and affective, rather than an intellectual, reaction.

In Joubert's theory, the precondition for laughter is an objective situation or state of affairs that incorporates either sudden disclosure of the lower body or downward movement. The physical concreteness of the ludicrous provocation corresponds to the primarily physiological character of the laughing response.

> Everybody sees clearly that in laughter the face is moving, the eyes sparkle and tear, the cheeks redden, the breast heaves, the voice becomes interrupted; and when it goes on for a long time the veins in the throat become enlarged, the arms shake, and the legs dance about, the belly pulls in and feels considerable pain; we cough, perspire, piss, and besmirch ourselves.
>
> (*Treatise on Laughter*, p. 28)

Unlike gaiety, or sadness, laughter is a mixed or impure emotion that expresses both joy and sorrow over laughing matter. The characteristic rapid, spasmodic sound of laughter is caused by the extreme expansion and contraction of the heart and diaphragm as the body moves between opposite poles of feeling.

This is how laughter is made up, of the contrariety or battle of two feelings, holding the middle ground between joy and sadness. . . . Laughter can therefore be called a false joy with a false displeasure, being a participant in both that retains the nature of neither.

(Treatise on Laughter, p. 44)

The ambivalent feeling experienced in laughter is composed of delight or pleasure in a 'lightness' of the laughing matter that makes awareness of the pathos of ugliness, pain or suffering bearable. Because it is an experience of the heart, laughter is composed of both voluntary and involuntary movements; as knowledge, laughter is not confined to discretionary judgment or conclusive interpretation. In laughter, the individual is in touch with his world, in particular the embodied social world of self and other, and knowledge of that world is achieved by mimetically reproduced 'feelings' – 'false joy' and 'false displeasure'.

Renaissance theories of laughter all posit a human collective as the precondition for laughter. The social environment in which laughter takes place is complex and highly differentiated; interaction between social groups provides the most usual occasion for creating or discovering laughing matter. This often takes the form of crude social give and take, as in the Carnival incident related in *The Courtier*. Bernardo, who loves to play tricks on friars, persuades one to mount up behind him and ride through the town square, where the friar is pelted with eggs. However, the 'friar' soon turns the tables:

without my knowing, the rascal got certain lackeys, who had been stationed there for the purpose, to pass him some eggs, and pretending to hold me tight so as not to fall, he crushed some of them on my chest, more on my head, and several on my face until I was streaming with them. At length, when everyone was tired of laughing and throwing eggs, he jumped down, threw back his scapular to show his long hair, and said: 'Bernardo, sir, I'm one of your grooms of San Pietro in Vincoli, the one who looks after your little mule.'[18]

Laughter interprets the complexity of social relations by drawing attention to a structure of differences, especially those 'vertically' distributed differences so important to a hierarchy of social positions. Both upward movement in the form of social pretension and downward movement in the form of 'uncrowning' produce abundant laughing matter. Laughter addresses every possible source of disjunction, including those that arise from transgression of norms and those that arise from structural ambiguity in the norms themselves. Even more fundamentally, however, laughter discloses the relative weakness of a social structure and the impunity with which its constraints may be violated.

The spontaneous, elusive and 'harmless' character of laughter makes it an extremely valuable resource and instrument for any social group that lacks power but seeks to retain a strong feeling of solidarity. For the plebeian culture of Renaissance England, laughter is a central element of an active critical consciousness.[19] That consciousness produces an ensemble of tactical responses to the enormously complicated power structure and to its pervasive demands on time, energy and attention. The maneuvers of self-abjection and self-ridicule so frequently encountered in popular festive form do not always reinforce the constraints of the social system, and may in fact be most useful to plebeian culture as a prophylaxis against violent coercion, strict and severe administration of law, and other forms of expropriation. In any case, these familiar patterns of deference and social appeasement are defensive aspects of plebeian culture that enhance the relative security of the subordinated group. From this position, plebeian culture may deploy laughing matter in more aggressive ways. In the laughter of popular festive form, the community gets away with a refusal to conform to the social system or to accept its ideological and cosmological claims. Thus popular 'folk' laughter may not only take particularly appreciative note of inadvertent 'downward movement' but may also take the initiative to actually bring it about, either symbolically or, at times, through grossly irreverent practical jokes and limited, tactical social violence.

These tactics of delay and petty harassment, and the gradual accumulation of small victories, are predicated on a specific vision of history and historical change. The survival of any collectivity requires perpetual struggle within an historical world conceived and represented tragically rather than idyllically. Plebeian culture acknowledges the pathos of desire, the brevity of individual life and the vulnerability of the body. It also takes particular note of the arbitrary, ramshackle structure of authority and political power, and of the relative incapacity of that power substantively to alter the objective and material conditions of life. The grotesque physically oriented laughter of common people objectifies a pre-ideological, implicit political doctrine. As Bakhtin describes it, that doctrine is 'the defeat of power, of earthly kings, of the earthly upper classes, of all that oppresses and restricts'.[20] This is very similar to the conclusion reached by Freud in his analysis of the structure of jokes.

> What these Jokes whisper, may be said aloud: that the wishes and desires of man have a right to make themselves acceptable alongside of our exacting and ruthless morality. . . . it has been said in forceful and stirring sentences that this morality is only a selfish regulation laid down by the few rich and mighty who can satisfy their wishes at any time without any postponement . . . so long as social arrangements do no more to make it more enjoyable, so long will it be impossible to stifle the voice within us that rebels against the demands of morality.[21]

CHAPTER 9
CLOWNING AND DEVILMENT

Discovery and disclosure of laughing matter is a special and privileged function of clowns, whose presence turns even the most serious drama into 'mungrell tragi-comedy'. Sidney's objection to the 'mingling of kings and clowns' speaks of a relationship more complex than the mixing of literary genres. A clown is a mock-king who mimics royal gesture.[1] He may even switch places with a prince, as Ralph Simnel does in *Friar Bacon and Friar Bungay*. The exchange of identity is easy for the clown, because he refuses to take seriously any discriminations of rank, status or individuality. He calls everyone Ned, including Prince Edward, and is on terms of candid familiarity with every other character. The clown in a versatile substitute whose resourcefulness is derived from his inability or refusal to understand differences. But the clown who mingles with the *dramatis personae* of a dramatic text is not simply a character in a play. He traverses the boundary between a represented world and the here-and-now world he shares with the audience.

A clown is a real public figure, who may 'wander into' a narrative, as Feste does in *Twelfth Night*, reappearing in Illyria after an unexplained absence. But though as a character he is a servant to Olivia, as a clown his relationship to the other characters is that of a self-conscious professional in a world full of amateurs. Though the fool nominally understands less than other men and women, Feste, like all fools, is in a situation of enhanced understanding because he has experience of the 'other side'. In addition to his role within the narrative, he is also a chorus who stands outside it and draws attention to what the other characters do not 'know' – that they have only a limited, purely nominal existence. This extra-literary status confers a distinct cognitive advantage upon the clown.

CLOWN. . . . To see this age! A sentence is but a cheveril glove to a good wit. How quickly the wrong side may be turned outward!
VIOLA. Nay, that's certain. They that dally nicely with words may quickly make them wanton.
CLOWN. I would therefore my sister had no name, sir.
VIOLA. Why, Man?
CLOWN. Why sir, her name's a word, and to dally with that word might make my sister wanton. But indeed words are very rascals since bonds disgraced them.

(*Twelfth Night*, III. i. 11–12)

An equivocator and a 'corrupter of words', Feste understands the wrong side as well as the right side of language. The careful separation of names from things is necessary to sustain the identities and differences that keep things in their place. But the 'wrong' or wanton side of language permits things to be treated as if they were only names, and vice versa. The equivocal character of words is transferred to the domain of actual things, and socially inscribed rationality is transformed into 'laughing matter'.[2]

The power of the clown over other *dramatis personae* corresponds to the power of an objective social domain over the nominal individuality of a particular character or person. But this power does not depend on the clown's 'good wit'. He is just as effective as a buffoon, half-wit or ignoramus. In *Mucedorus*, the clown, Mouse, is a rustic character who is 'captured' by the pastoral adventure-narrative and forced to act as a servant to the hero's chief rival. Mouse avoids harm to himself and to Mucedorus by the tactics of 'not understanding'. He is prolifically inventive in the elaboration of this device, manifested as partial deafness, inattention, ignorance of the correct meaning of words, mispronunciation and severely diminished intelligence. But the results of his 'not understanding' are just as successful as they would be if he possessed unusual perspicacity. The rustic character is, moreover, a partial and temporary identity of convenience to be used in deference to the requirements of a narrative action. When he is alone on stage, however, Mouse is fully cognizant of his audience and of the here-and-now reality he shares with them.

The independent, public relationship between the clown and his audience disregards the conventional boundary between a dramatic performance and the social occasion that provides its surrounding environment. In addition, the clown may leave the confines of the theater altogether in order to create a more diffuse public spectacle in the streets. Will Kemp's legendary performance of the Morris Dance from London to Norwich, the 'nine days wonder', is the best-known example of such an event, though it was not an isolated incident. The feat was performed during Lent. On each of the nine days, Kemp rose early in the morning, and, accompanied by a servant, a drummer, and an 'overseer' or official witness, he would dance part of the distance between London and Norwich. The nine days were not danced consecutively: in the intervals between dancing days, Kemp rested at various inns and private houses, where he was entertained by townspeople. The largest crowds were gathered at those points where he passed through the city gates, either coming in or going out.

> My setting forward was somewhat before seauen in the morning, my Taberer stroke up merrily, and as fast as kinde peoples thronging together would giue mee leauue, thorow London I leapt: By the way many good olde people, and diuers others of younger yeeres, of meere kindnes, gaue me bowd sixpences and grotes, blessing me with their harty prayers and God-speedes. . . . many a thousand brought me to Bow, where I rested a while from dancing, but had small rest with those that would haue urg'd me to drinking.[3]

His performance does not have sharp, well-defined boundaries between actors and an audience but is rather a form of participatory scenario that combines dance, comic improvisation and athletic endurance with an atmosphere of festive spontaneity and informal hospitality.

Kemp describes many incidents, including several in which spectators join in his dancing, and others in which he has to improvise in order to contend with some obstruction or unanticipated intervention. Among these incidents is a brief social drama that arises from the capture of two thieves among the crowd.

> In this town [Burntwood] two Cut-purses were taken, that with other two of their companions followed mee from London (as many better disposed persons did:) but these two dy-doppers gaue out when they were apprehended, that they had laid wagers and betted about my iourney. Whereupon the Officers bringing them to my Inne, I iustly denied their acquaintance, sauing that I remembered one of them to be a noted Cut-purse, such a one as we tie to a poast on our stage, for all people to wonder at, when at a play they are taken pilfering.[4]

Kemp is familiar with the close and immediate relationship between a planned performance and an unplanned social drama. Such conjunctions occur within the playhouse just as they do in the streets, and they are mediated by resourceful cooperative 'scripts' shared by performers and their audience.

Because he is a public figure, the clown's intrusion into a dramatic narrative does more than provide a farcical commentary on the 'main action'. In fact, clowning cannot be understood 'in context' as a literary device, because it belongs to the bigger, extra-literary context of everyday life. In an anonymous popular play such as *Locrine*, the effectiveness and the cogency of the clown's crude interpretation of epically distanced, heroic ideology is comprehensively worked out as he mingles with the early kings of Britain and is eventually 'recruited' into a narrative of obsessive desire, political intrigue and violence. Like many other texts of similarly uncertain and ambiguous authorship, *Locrine* represents the structural ambiguity and persistent discontinuity of social life by the convergence of erotic and political themes. It is a version of the epic 'matter of Britain', the story of the Trojan 'king Brutus' and the troubled founding of the first royal dynasty. The first scene represents the death of Brutus and his disposition of the succession. As in *King Lear*, there is a division of the inheritance; but this is evidently achieved without political strife, because Brutus' brothers, as well as his sons, all agree to acknowledge Locrine as king and supreme ruler over all Britain. This scene proceeds through several ritual events: the testamentary allocation of the kingdom to the sons, the betrothal of Locrine to Guendoline, the coronation of Locrine, and, finally, the formal leave-taking and death of King Brutus. The events unfold against the epic background of prolonged suffering and eventual victory of the Trojans, who come to occupy Britain after their conquest of the Gauls and, later, of the giants who were its primordial inhabitants.

> Arriued on the coasts of Aquitaine,
> Where with an armie of his barbarous Gaules
> Goffarius and his brother Gathelus
> Encountering with our hoast, sustained the foile.
> And for your sake my Turnus there I lost,
> Turnus that slew six hundred men at arms
> All in an houre, with his sharpe battle-axe.
> From thence upon the strond of Albion
> To Corus hauen happily we came,
> And queld the giants, comme of Albions race,
> With Gogmagog sonne to Samotheus,
> The cursed Captaine of that damned crew.
> And in that Ile at length I placed you.[5]

The heroic figures exist as part of an epic discourse; they belong to a distant and completed past articulated in 'ennobled language'. The task now set for Locrine is to consolidate the political harmony achieved by Brutus through his own dedication to the responsibilities of the role of warrior-king. This problem is objectified in the coincidence in the action of two decisive rites of passage: the betrothal of Locrine to Guendoline and the funeral obsequies for Brutus. The conjunction of marriage and funeral is the crucial link between the accumulated experience of the past and the possibility of its continuation into the future. As the rest of the play reveals, however, this is a perilous conjunction.

The heroic capabilities of Locrine and his brothers are at first used in the service of Britain's defense against the maniacally cruel and vindictive Huns, or Scythians, led by Humber and his son Hubba. The fortunes of the two sides ebb and flow, though in the end the Scythians are defeated. The world of epic deeds and misdeeds is entirely filled with strife and with physical violence that seems to serve no other purpose than to provide an occasion for the satisfaction of private feelings of spite, revenge and desire for personal glory.

Eventually the cause of sustaining the harmony of the state is set aside by Locrine as the result of his erotic preoccupation with the captured wife of the defeated Scythian king. This private sexual obsession becomes for Locrine a crucial challenge to his own political will and royal authority. In order to satisfy his intermingled erotic and political desire, he banishes his wife, who flees to her brother's protection. Bloody civil war ensues, leading to the defeat of Locrine's forces and to the double suicide of the king and his mistress. The play concludes with the following moralizing epilogue.

> Lo here the end of lawless trecherie
> Of usurpation and ambitious pride;
> And they that for their private amours dare
> Turmoile our land, and set their broiles abroach,
> Let them be warned by these premisses.
> And as a woman was the onely cause
> That civil discord was then stirred up,
> So let us pray for that renowned mayd,
> That eight and thirtie yeares the scepter swayd.
> In quiet peace and sweet felicitie;
> And every wight that seeks her graces smart,
> Wold that this sword wer pierced in his hart!
>
> (*Locrine*, v. iv. 1261–72)

The epic 'matter of Britain' concludes with a powerful disclosure of the essential political nihilism inherent in the ethos of military conquest and its justificatory ideology of 'defense of the state'. That ideology is recuperated, however, in the brief but obviously compelling reference to Queen Elizabeth, who 'makes good' on the archaic futility of the legendary dynastic founders, their fatal confusion of the private and the public, and their grotesque inability to actualize the human community known as Britain. Nevertheless, even this recuperation rests somewhat ambiguously on the partnership between the power of prayer and the power of the sword. The sword is displayed by the character of Ate, who has retrieved it from the on-stage carnage, where it was used as the instrument of social control and stability, and equally as the instrument of private lust and bloody discord.

The heroic characters of the epic narrative are stiff and hieratic images of archaic violence. The nihilistic and self-destructive ethos of this archaic past is epically distanced from the audience by the formality of its language and by its drift towards the most turgid and exaggerated rhetorical stylization. This obvious woodenness of the heroic characters reveals the extent to which epic forms have lost their authenticity and their power adequately to represent 'man' and his social life.

> The epic world knows only a single and unified world view, obligatory and indubitably true for heroes as well as for authors and audiences. . . . The destruction of epic distance and the transferral of the image of an individual from the distanced plane to the zone of contact with the inconclusive events of the present result in a radical re-structuring of the individual. . . . Its first and essential step was the comic familiarization of the image of man. Laughter destroyed epic distance.[6]

In *Locrine*, this destruction of epic distance through laughter is accomplished by Strumbo the clown. The play's first scene consists of a series of elaborate formalities conducted by legendary figures of the epic past. It is followed by the entrance of Strumbo, who belongs to the very same contingent, inconclusive space and time occupied by the audience as they view his performance. His first speeches are a straightforward acknowledgment of that shared contemporaneity.

> STRUMBO. . . . trust me, gentlemen and my verie goode friendes, and so foorth, the little god, nay the desperate god Cuprit, with one of his vengible birdbolts, hath shot me unto the heele: so not onlie, but also, oh fine phrase, I burne, I burne, and I burne a, in loue, in loue, and in loue, a. (*Locrine*, I. ii. 16–20)

The forms of direct address redefine the theatrical space as a familiar and contemporary communicative environment in which direct social contact is permitted. The speech reveals not only the linguistic incompetence and ignorance of the clown in his mispronunciation of the names of classical figures, but also his facility in precise mimicking of fine phrases in the language of scholarship and poetry.

The clown displays this complex blending of learning with gross ignorance as he pens a letter to 'mistresse Dorothy', and the scene concludes with a brief and successful wooing.

> DOR. Truly, Maister Strumbo, you speake too learnedly for mee to understand the drift of your mind, and therefore tell your tale in plaine termes, and leaue off your darke ridles.

STRUM. Alasse, mistresse Dorothie, this is my lucke, that when I
most would, I cannot be understood; so that my great learning
is an inconvenience unto me. But to speake in plaine termes, I
loue you, mistress Dorothie, if you like to accept me into your
familiarite.

DOR. If this be all I am content.

STRUM. Saist thou so, sweet wench; let me lick thy toes. Farewell,
mistress.

[Turning to the people.]

If any of you be in loue, prouide ye a capcase full of new coined
wordes, and then shall you soone haue the *succado de labres*, and
something else.

(*Locrine*, II. ii. 91–109)

This scene establishes two kinds of 'crude contact' with the formalities of
literary speech and official ideology. Strumbo is in the most immediate
sense conducting a burlesque of the social conventions of aristocratic
courtship and of the literary objectification of those sentiments. A
'capcase of new words' might be effective, but if 'great learning is an
inconvenience . . . speak in plain terms'.

Crude contact is intensified and made more explicit in a later scene,
where Albanact and Thrasimachus come to Strumbo's cobbler's shop to
impress him for an army needed in the war against the Huns. The scene
begins with Strumbo, Dorothy and Trompart, the clown's servant,
'cobling shoes and singing'. The song 'We coblers lead a merry life' is a
rhythmic celebration of a way of life in which there is a most satisfying
combination of 'work and ease', where labor is in a harmonious relationship with bodily satisfaction and where the cobblers 'worke for
companie'. This plebeian social environment is not, however, secure
from intrusion by the insistent demands of another ethos, for the
'epically distanced' figures are somehow able to enter the contemporary
space and time of Strumbo's cobbler's shop and carry him off to their
war. He attempts to resist the impressment.

STRUM. King Nactaball. I crie God mercy! what haue we to doo with
him, or he with us? But you, sir master capontaile, draw your
pastebourd, or else I promise you, Ile giue you a canuasado with a
bastinodo over your shoulders.   (*Locrine*, II. ii. 59–66)

This cogent objection to the captain's demands is futile, as is Strumbo's attempted physical resistance. In his farewell to Dorothy acknowledges his own tactical error, but it is clear that the strategic objective of survival is not relinquished.

Even after his house is burned by the Huns, and his loving wife Dorothy roasted in the flames, his crude strategic misinterpretation of the war and of the king's policies defines a persistent, comical resistance to the heroic ethos.

> ALBANACT. We must remedie these outrages,
> And throw revenge upon their hatefull heads,
> And you, good fellowes, for your houses burnt,
> We will remunerate you store of gold,
> And build your houses by our pallace gate.
> STRUM. Gate? O pettie treason to my person!
> Nowhere else but by your backside?
> Gate! O how I am vexed in my coller!
> Gate! I crie God mercie! Doo you hear, master king?
> If you mean to gratifie poore men as we bee,
> you must build our houses by the Tauerne.
>
> (*Locrine*, II. iv. 77–88)

Despite 'Wild fire and pitch', the loss of his home and workshop, and the death of his wife, Strumbo survives, and he persists in his crude and clownish response to events and to the way those events are explained and justified by his superiors. Open defiance of authority is not an effective tactic, and so his survival is predicated on the resources of strategic misinterpretation and versatile improvisatory competence. He understands as little as possible, avoids risks and, in the end, evades the demands of authority, finds a new wife and settles down again in clownish content.

During the course of the play, Strumbo appears as a poet-courtier, a cobbler, a soldier and, in his final scene, as a farmer with 'a pitchefork and a scotchcap'. He has lost his first wife, the docile and affectionate Dorothy, and has married again, this time to the aggressive and shrewish Margery. His difficulties with her are finally resolved by sexual means.

> STRUM. How do you, maisters, how do you? how haue you scaped
> hanging this long time? Yfaith, I haue scapt many a scouring this

yeare, but I thanke God I haue past them all with a good couragio, couragio, and my wife and I are in the great loue and charite now, I thank my manhood and my strength.   (*Locrine*, IV. ii. 21–6)

Despite his engagement in the heroic narrative for a brief interval, Strumbo remains very much in the sphere of direct and familiar social contact with the audience and he shares with that audience his own comical, vulgar experience with violence and sexual desire that has created such personal and social havoc within the epic and heroic sphere. Strumbo's marital harmony is achieved when he comes home drunk one night to find his wife waiting for him, with her baby in her arms. The wife takes up a 'fagot stick' to beat him and begins to scold and threaten.

> STRUM. Now, althogh I trembled, fearing she would set her ten commandements in my face, I ran within her, and taking her lustily by the midle, I carried her valiantly to the bed, and flinging her upon it, flung my selfe upon her; and there I delighted her so with the sport I made, that euer after she wold call me sweet husband, and so banisht brawling for euer. And to see the good will of the wench! she bought with her portion a yard of land, and by that I am now one of the richest men in our parish.   (*Locrine*, IV. ii. 33–43)

Sexual thrashing and sexual gratification are ways to achieve domestic peace and to consolidate social wealth. Strumbo's story of sexual and social success is a crude and visceral paraphrase of the epically distanced 'matter of Britain'. The clown, who has a fluid social identity, speaks for the perdurable vitality of plebeian culture and its ability to survive the persistent assaults of the heroic ethos. The majestic figures of the epic 'matter of Britain' are constrained to reappear in this zone of crude contact where the obsessive narrowness of their interests is made evident. Despite their exaggerated idealization, the interests of the epically distanced characters—dynastic marriage and war—can generate nothing other than betrayal, revenge and despair. The clown survives all of this by 'refusing to understand' the cultural fantasy he is called on to participate in, choosing instead to remain at home in the vernacular discourse of everyday productive life and domestic interaction.

The clown's refusal to understand, his 'scurrilitie' and his easy complicity with the crowd bring heroic ideology into a 'zone of crude contact', forcing that ideology and its claims into the situation of self-travesty. Clowning thus creates openings both in the literary text and in the social structure that a text purports to reflect. The extra-literary and even anti-literary interventions of clowns and their devilish accomplices reduce texts to schematic structures, partial scenarios that coexist somewhat uncomfortably with the crude improvisations of public entertainers who abuse the integrity of literary form.

Clowning and devilment are actually the predominant element in Marlowe's *Doctor Faustus*, though this is not an anonymous, popular playscript, but a serious literary work with a definite author. The play has a heterogeneous structure, consisting of a serious theological frame, concentrated in the opening and closing scenes, combined with a kind of anthology of popular material in which Faustus's diabolical powers are an excuse for slapstick, practical jokes and irreverent disregard of theological matters. It is a 'mungrell tragi-comedy', despite its ostensibly theological and religious themes, consisting almost entirely of clownish interruptions and farcical variations on the story of Faustus's contract with the devil.

> WAG. Sirra boy, come hither.
> CLO. How, boy? swowns boy, I hope you haue seen many boyes with such pickadevaunts as I haue. Boy quotha?
> WAG. Tel me sirra, hast thou any commings in?
> CLO. I, and goings out too, you may see else.
> WAG. Alas poor slaue, see how pouerty iesteth in his nakedness, the vilaine is bare, and out of seruice, and so hungry, that I know he would giue his soule to the Diuel for a shoulder of mutton, though it were blood rawe.
> CLO. How, my soule to the Diuel for a shoulder of mutton though twere blood rawe? not so good friend, burladie. I had neede haue it wel roasted, and good sawce to it, if I pay so deere.[7]

This exchange mimics the more elaborate and ominous transaction between Faustus and Mephistophilis. In this scene, the conception of selling a soul to the devil is parodically reinserted into vernacular and idiomatic speech. The language of Wagner and the clown is conditioned by the experience of poverty, hunger and candid appreciation of the needs of the body. Even a poor vagabond has some self-respect; if poverty requires the clown to sell his soul in exchange for something to eat, he insists that his mutton be well cooked and well sauced. Theology is dissolved into the speech type of everyday vernacular expression in which 'the Diuell' is nothing more than a figure of speech used to emphasize feeling and appetite. The transformation of the theological vocabulary is part of a more general shifting of context.

This scene – 'Wagner attempts to hire the clown as his servant' – is a standard clownish routine or skit that belongs to a preexisting vocabulary of popular entertainment. As in *Mucedorus*, the clown uses the device of apparent partial deafness as an abusive form of jesting response.

> WAG. Sirra, wil thou be my man and waite on me? and I will make thee go, like Qui mihi discipulus.
> CLO. How, in verse?
> WAG. No sirra, in beaten silke and staues acre.
> CLO. How, how, knaues acre? I, I thought that was al the land his father left him: Doe yee heare, I would be sorie to robbe you of your living.
> WAG. Sirra, I say in staues acre.
> CLO. Oho, oho staues acre, why then belike, if I were your man, I should be ful of vermine.
> WAG. So thou shalt, whether thou beest with me, or no. But sirra, leave your iesting, and your self presently unto me for seaven yeeres, or Ile turne all the lice about thee into familiars, and they shal teare thee in peeces.
> CLO. Doe you heare sir? you may saue that labour, they are too familiar with me already, swowns they are as bolde with my flesh, as if they had payd for my meate and drinks.
>
> (*Doctor Faustus*, A. 374–91)

As in the discussion of selling souls in exchange for raw mutton, the clown insists on a crude physical meaning for words like 'familiar'. The torments of hell hold no terrors for a man already infested with fleas and lice.

Even after he has been pursued and thrashed by the two devils summoned up by Wagner, the clown continues to view his own experience in bodily terms and to apply that view to both the natural and the supernatural world.

CLO. . . . there was a hee diuell and a shee diuell, Ile tell you how you
shall know them, all hee diuels has hornes, and all shee diuels has
clifts and clouen feet.   (*Doctor Faustus*, A. 415–17)

This clownish refusal to understand devils as anything more than a
momentarily uncomfortable practical joke invites the spectators to view
supernatural reality as a laughing matter. The cheerful resiliency of the
clown's response to 'devilish torment' reveals an important part of the
truth about the supernatural reality experienced by Faustus. Hell is only
'a cautionary fable', the devil is a bogeyman contrived to compel
obedience and subordination; devilish manifestations are mainly noise,
firecrackers and scary masks. The safety of the clown's soul, of course,
depends on the absolutely pristine foolishness of his refusal to understand, his complete lack of interest in acquiring any serious knowledge
of religious and spiritual matters. More urgently, the safety of the
clown's body depends on his ability to make a realistic estimate of
relative coercive power. Because Wagner has demonstrable ability to in-
flict pain by means of diabolical agency, the clown agrees to become
his servant. This strategic self-abjection is derived from the clear sense
that it is wise to submit to superior force and to relatively mild
thrashing in order to avoid more painful and permanently damaging
violence.

Just as in *Locrine*, an epically distanced admonitory drama – here the
story of Faustus's fatal and apocalyptic contract with Lucifer – is brought
into crude contact with the contemporaneity of clownish pranks and
impertinence. These two incommensurable discursive and communicative domains intersect at several points. Faustus's compulsive resistance
to God's authority, his vague but passionate desire to fashion a self of
immense power, is only fitfully and intermittently sustained.[8] Mephistophilis is obliged periodically to devise entertainments in order to
reinforce Faustus's denial of faith and repentance. One of these entertainments is a pageant of the Seven Deadly Sins. The sins are homely
variations on the conventional allegorical representation, except for
Gluttony, who presents himself in terms of popular festive imagery of
material abundance.

GLUT. I am Gluttony, my parents are al dead, and the diuel a peny
they haue left me, but a bare pention, and that is 30 meales a day,
and tenne Beauers, a small trifle to suffice nature. O, I come of a

royall parentage, my grand father was a gammon of bacon, my grand mother a hogs head of Claret-wine; My godfathers were these, Peter Pickle-herring and Martin Martlemas-biefe, O but my godmother, she was iolly gentlewoman, and welbeloued in euery good towne and Citie, her name was mistresse Margery March-beere: now Faustus, thou hast heard all my Progeny, wilt thou bid me to supper?

FAU. No, Ile see thee hanged, thou wilt eate up all my victualls.

GLUT. Then the diuell choake thee.

(*Doctor Faustus*, A. 770–83)

Though gluttony considered as excessive private and individual visceral gratification is manifestly a sin just like other sins, this particular representation of it is an image of universal abundance – food and wine, herring and beef. Faustus refuses to invite Gluttony to supper, fearing he will eat up all the food; Gluttony naturally enough curses this churlish refusal of hospitality.

Faustus's magical powers, for which he has exchanged his immortal soul, are objectified in an evidently trivial capacity to carry out elaborate practical jokes. Faustus uses his devilish power in several different social settings, including the pope's palace in Rome, where he steals food, overturns wine and finally gives His Holiness a sound box on the ear. The scene ends with an elaborate exorcism ritual, interrupted with a climactic piece of explosive slapstick comedy.

Cursed be hee that stole away his holiness meate from the table.
    maledicat dominus.
Cursed be hee that strooke his holiness a blowe on the face.
    maledicat dominus.
Cursed be he that tooke Frier Sandelo a blow on the pate.
    male, etc.
Cursed be he that disturbeth our holy Dirge.
    male, etc.
Cursed be he that tooke his holiness wine.
    maledicat dominus.
Et omnes sancti Amen.
Beate the friers, and fling fier-workes among them
    and so Exeunt.   (*Doctor Faustus*, A. 1115–25)

'Diabolical power' is primarily a crude form of abusive counter-festivity that turns serious ceremonial form into hilarious burlesque. In the scenes involving the horning of the emperor's knight and the swindling of the horse courser, the same abusive counter-festive impulse is acted out. In all these farcical episodes, including the scenes with Dick and Robin, laughing matter is created out of very crude physical circumstance. Even though the pranks are committed by 'devils' and by 'damned souls', the audience is likely to share a feeling of complicity with the pranksters. Certainly there is no likelihood of any sympathy for the victims. The triviality of Faustus's powers, the identification of devilish power with crude practical jokes, might be interpreted as indicating the radical spiritual folly of Faustus, who has exchanged an eternity of spiritual peace for the dubious pleasure of setting off firecrackers at a banquet. But this vocabulary of devilment – firecrackers, thrashing, horns, animal masks, drenchings – is a collectively sanctioned practice of physically abusive mummery useful for settling old scores and for punishing unamiable or arrogant individuals. In these scenes where Faustus enjoys his devilish power most fully, he is no longer a character in a theological *mise-en-scène*, but the ringleader of a Carnivalesque disturbance. Faustus the damned magician has become Faustus the low-life, hanging about in taverns and living by his wits. In this world of ordinary vulgar entertainment the only devils are manmade, funny monsters, animated spooks used to frighten the credulous.

It is possible to devise interpretive strategies that absorb the burlesque, popular-festive forms of this play into a comprehensive, doctrinally consistent reading. Judith Weil, for example, argues that Faustus's radical foolishness is ironically recapitulated in the simpler foolishness of the clowns and servants. The viewers' horrified appreciation of Faustus's impending spiritual destruction is reinforced by the very much more limited worldly folly of the clowns.

> Differences within a general resemblance between Faustus and the clowns retain importance. While the clowns mimic the shallow art of magic, they neither invert heavenly wisdom nor presume upon deity. Their magic is a worldly means without damnable ends, zany, relatively harmless, and not very exciting.[9]

If the play is viewed as a unified expression of a systematic eschatology, then Faustus's spiritual folly can be contrasted ironically with the relatively harmless devilment of the clowns. Such a view, however, depends on a prior choice. The pattern of a theologically controlled irony that unifies the diverse elements of the text is a preconceived interpretive artifact that is bound to reveal the unity it seeks, a unity predicated on the assumption of a finished work of literary art, and on the hierarchical subordination of other forms of cultural production to that work. But clowning and devilment are theatrical practices in their own right, and they exist precisely in order to evade and willfully to misinterpret prior authority. Devils and clowns double as characters and as critical interpreters of a play's crude and immediate continguity with the wider world of public and collective life. Their presence within the theater, and their intrusion or capture by a dramatic narrative, are an active discouragement to projects of unity and of closure.

PART IV
CARNIVALIZED LITERATURE

I N A SUBJECTIVE and highly idiosyncratic essay entitled. 'The Influence of the Audience on Shakespeare's Drama', Robert Bridges concludes with some severe strictures on the relationship between the dramatist and his public.

> . . . the foolish things in his plays were written to please the foolish, the filthy for the filthy, and the brutal for the brutal, and . . . if out of veneration for his genius we are led to admire . . . such things, we may be thereby not conforming ourselves to him, but only degrading him to the level of his audience, and learning contamination from those wretched beings who can never be forgiven their share in preventing the greatest poet and dramatist of the world from being the best artist.[1]

This is now a thoroughly discredited opinion. Modern humanistic scholarship has responded to the critical challenge suggested in these remarks by discovering and elaborating much less narrow canons of literary form, together with a more comprehensive sociology of reception. This more congenial and broad-minded view undertakes to explain away every possible difference between genuine art and foolish, filthy, brutal trash. But one consequence of the broader view is its tendency retrospectively to deny the possibility of any objection to, or even a second opinion about, the value of art and the patterns of cultural and political domination to which it corresponds. The virtue of Bridges's position is his refusal of any presumption of innocence either on the part of writers or of their audiences. This facilitates the project of questioning the integrity of the *œuvre* and of raising the issues of contamination and complicity.

The canon of Shakespeare's work is well established and the attribution of that canon not open to serious question. Nevertheless, the Shakespearean *œuvre* remains highly resistant to exact and definitive resolution. There is a general, theoretical problem in specifying the unity of any author's work.[2] There is also the specific historical problem of the Shakespearean text. Shakespeare is the creator of a body of texts that contains a large number of anomalies, exceptional cases and untypical examples – 'early plays', 'problem plays' and possible collaborations. Furthermore, many texts are problematic, deriving from a haphazard collection of 'good quartos' and 'bad quartos' with differing relationships to what is assumed to be the author's own original composition. Despite the very considerable efforts of many editors to resolve these disparate problems, the outcome of the project as a whole remains in doubt. Editors proceed from aesthetic and ideological convictions.[3] The most fundamental of all these convictions has been belief in an individual work of art created by an author, and in the possibility of access to that singular work. But in the case of some authors, Shakespeare, for example, and Marlowe, evidence suggests that there is no reason to assume that any single, finished original ever existed. The texts, with their conflicting variant forms, are exactly what they appear to be – that is, schematic, incompletely determined and highly variable, resourceful structures that function best in a *mise-en-scène* where they are traversed, or 'contaminated', by other 'texts' inscribed in the social life of the audience. These are often texts of popular festive form, the concerns they objectify subverting or rupturing the integrity of literary structures in favor of a more immediate, and of course more ephemeral, interrogation of elementary political relationships. The contamination – or to reverse ethical signs, the Carnivalization – of literature forces a dramatic text to 'speak up for the interests of its own times'. For Shakespeare and for many of his contemporaries this is accomplished through such distinct Carnival structures as charivari, 'mirth in funerals', and the festive agon or Battle of Carnival and Lent. In the discussions that follow, each of these narrative forms will be analyzed as it traverses and is disseminated by works of the literary canon.

CHAPTER 10
WEDDING FEAST AND CHARIVARI

IN MANY cultural settings, courtship, betrothal and marriage make up a complex and perilous *rite de passage* in which the health and prosperity of the community are inextricably bound up with the harmony and satisfaction achieved by the bride and groom. Marriage, in the context of Elizabethan society, is a largely public matter in which personal desire and preference are always open to external scrutiny. The allocation and selection of marriage partners are never carried out exclusively within the private and domestic sphere. Since traditions of collective life are sustained through the productive and reproductive capacity of marriage, the community retains a vital stake, not only in the matching of suitable partners, but also in the way married life is actually lived.[1] Marriage is therefore a complex institution with an elaborate system of prohibitions and injunctions both in respect of the choice of partners and of the requirements for suitable marital conduct. But the success of marriage may depend not so much on the willingness of the partners to conform to all the rules as on their ingenuity in transgressing some constraints and on their ability to overlook the transgressions of others.

Good God! What divorces, or what not worse than that, would daily happen were not the converse between a man and his wife supported and cherished by flattery, apishness, gentleness, ignorance, dissembling . . . how few marriages should we have, if the husband should but thoroughly examine how many tricks his pretty little mop of modesty has played before she was married.

(*The Praise of Folly*, p. 32)

Although essential to harmonious collective life, marriage is in fact a fragile and tenuous social artifact that does not bear much looking into.

In the sixteenth and early seventeenth centuries, marriage is characterized by a high degree of structural ambiguity that affects the procedures of courtship and the selection of partners, as well as the relative ability of bride and groom to sustain a relationship that conforms reasonably well to the standards of the community. It is precisely those communal standards that give rise to the most intensely complicated situations, because the prospective couple is likely to be confronted with several different systems of conflicting imperatives. First, the choice itself and the initiative for that choice are governed by parental authority and filial obedience. However, there is also strong sentiment for the conflicting 'rule' of mutual desire and preference, and although these two imperatives are not antagonistic in principle, the possibility for conflict is present in virtually every partnership.

Conflict between parents and children is likely to be compounded and intensified by efforts to conform to various socially inscribed rules and prohibitions that affect the suitability of a particular match. Although man and wife should be well matched in respect of wealth, social status and traditional kinship alliances, partners cannot always be found that suit all the various criteria equally well. Furthermore, although marriage is an institution that is supposed to function in support of a particular social hierarchy, it is in fact often used to facilitate social mobility. The conflict between parent and child over choice of marriage partners is not, therefore, a simple division between expediency and sentiments, or between family interests and romantic love. Conflict is likely to arise over the hierarchy of imperatives – a parent favours a match that upholds family honor well, but the child seeks a match that offers greater economic security – so that a general willingness to conform to the rules of society does not in itself assure a harmonious outcome.

In addition to potential conflict between generations and to further conflict between conflicting social imperatives, there is, finally, a chronic antagonism that arises from sexual difference itself, and from contradictions in the logic of male solidarity and gender hierarchy.[2] Although men and women are equally marked by differences in social status, the hierarchy of class does not correspond to the traditional hierarchy of male dominance. Although every individual husband has a compelling interest in his wife's sexual fidelity and in satisfying erotic and affective reciprocity, men collectively desire the subordination and the sexual availability of all women. From this perspective the selection of a partner is a distinctly secondary consideration. The much more arduous and difficult choice is that between marriage on any terms at all, and the freedoms and privileges of the unattached male. Marriage requires at least partial exclusion from the solidarity of the male community, together with the perpetual insinuation of cuckoldry. For women the hierarchy of male dominance makes marriage an even more perilous situation. In addition to partial exclusion from the compensatory solidarity of women and from the protection of family and friends, a prospective bride faces the potential hazards of sexuality itself, which is physically as well as socially risky.

Considerable social and individual resourcefulness is required for anyone successfully to negotiate such a complicated pattern of transition to full participation in erotic and communal life. And because marriage is a substantively political institution that constitutes the texture of social relations and facilitates the redistribution of wealth and authority, it cannot be sustained only by the sentimental idealization of romantic love and sexual desire.

The complexity of marriage as an institution was objectified and worked through in a variety of representational forms. The community could express itself through a variety of social dramas, gossip, public quarrels and the more organized public forms of the archdeacon's court. The organization of marriage, its structural rules and characteristic transgressions, could also be represented in a complex of festive forms, which included both the ceremonial formalities of the wedding and the informal and irregular counter-festivities of charivari or 'rough music'.[3] This complex of festive customs provides the necessary procedures for a transition that has significance both for the bride and groom and for the community to which they belong. The formalities solemnize the bond between the parents and constitute an image of personal and social harmony. The counter-festivities have a variety of functions. Because the community reserves to itself certain rights of surveillance and regulation of sexual conduct, the charivari may be used for admonitory purposes; related to this admonitory function, the charivari is also used to redress grievance or chastise impropriety. However, as Natalie Davis has clearly shown, the charivari has particular importance to 'young men' – that is, to the unmarried males in a community, who exploit the counter-festivity, not only to correct the waywardness of individuals, but also as a general protest against the exclusions and prohibitions of marriage as an institution.[4]

The social complexity of courtship and marriage is evident even in the simplest representational forms, such as the jig. In *The Black Man*, the pattern of courtship begins with the reciprocal and consensual choice of two partners, Thumpkin and Susan.

> THUMP. Sweet Susan remember the words I have said.
> SUS. I'le rest on my Thumpkin, I'le do as I may.
> THUMP. Then soon in the night I will come to thy Bed, And spend the whole time in sweet pleasure and play. I'le chace thee.
> SUS. I'le embrace thee, my Love and delight.
> THUMP. And spend the whole time in sweet sports of the night.
> SUS. But what if you afterwards should me mislike; And not be contented to make me your Wife.
> THUMP. Ne're fear, I will stand to it if I do strike, Although Sue, it cost poor Thumpkin his Life.[5]

This procedure clearly violates the socially sanctioned norms of sexual conduct, which require that the partners observe all the formalities of marriage, that they be made one flesh in the eyes of God and man before they experience sexual intercourse. The exchange between Susan and Thumpkin certainly articulates the risk of sexual betrayal and rejection in premarital sex, as well as the antithetical risk of permanent marital dissatisfaction inherent in marriage vows made prior to any sexual experience. Elopement or clandestine sexual contact may represent the optimum strategy for accommodating the desires of the partners with the socially constituted patterns of marital obligation, even though that strategy is necessarily both transgressive and highly risky. Thumpkin and Susan mutually agree to this strategy; opposition to their choice comes, not from representatives of lawful sociosexual conduct, but from crude sexual rivalry. Two gentlemen appear, and notice that Thumpkin has a 'pretty companion beside' whom they decide to abduct. Thumpkin resists the intrusion until the gentlemen threaten violence and he exits. The gentlemen endeavor to make Susan 'look chearily' but she objects that she cannot, 'Since my true love is not hear'.

> 1ST GENT. Hold thee contented, thou shalt have thy liking
> We but for kindness put in for a share:
> Thou shalt get no harm by our striking,
> We'l play fair, and stake fair, and play ware for ware.[6]

The abduction of Susan objectifies the claim of unattached males on every available sexual partner, and the consequent hostility of men collectively to the exclusions that result from marriage. In addition, the situation expresses a fundamental sexual anxiety and hostility between disparate social classes. The abduction of Susan acts out a cultural fantasy in which men of one social class are seen as threatening rape and sexual expropriation of the women of another.[7]

These conflicts are worked through in *The Black Man* through a sequence of disguisings, pranks and public humiliations, culminating finally in a redressive action that restores Susan to Thumpkin and routs the gentlemen-rivals. Thumpkin wins back Susan by disguising himself as an old man and stealing her away while the two gentlemen fight between themselves. They soon abduct her a second time, and Thumpkin is compelled to wrap himself up in a sheet and 'cry mum' to everyone who passes by. This 'terrifying apparition' or spook eventually frightens the Black Man, who is passing by selling his wares – blacking for boots and shoes. Thumpkin and the Black Man change places, and, changing their cry from 'Mum' to 'Ho, ho, ho', they finally frighten away the rival suitors, who believe they are pursued by devils 'come to plague us for our evil'.

In representing courtship and marriage, the roles of bride and groom may be assumed by a young man and a young woman. However, these roles may also be misrepresented by a clown and a transvestite or boy-woman. Examples of this situation are numerous in the dramatic literature: Strumbo and Dorothy in *Locrine*, Touchstone and Audrey in *As You Like It*, Bottom/Pyramus and Flute/Thisby in *A Midsummer*

Night's Dream. This mummery hides the actual identity of the participants and draws attention to the artificiality of gender as a socially
encoded 'fact'. The clown and transvestite express sexual and biological
'facts of life' with impunity and also reveal the ludicrous contradictoriness of marriage as a sexual and social arrangement. Marriage is
accomplished against multiple resistance, both from the duly constituted
social order that seeks to regulate the sexual pleasure of the bride and
groom, and from the 'outlaw' community of bachelors whose access to
sexual partners is constrained by marriage as an institutionalization of
sexual exclusivity. The bride and groom, therefore, must participate in a
series of games and mummings, in order successfully to negotiate these
transitions.

No matter what forms resistance to marriage may take, the final
resolution of the procedure and the determination of the identity of the
partners are achieved by the active intervention of a third party, who
often assumes the guise of a 'black man'. This devil disguise is one
element in the ensemble of festive personae through which the complexity of courtship and marriage procedure is objectified. This group
includes the bride/transvestite, the groom/clown and the 'suit of black'
which may be used as a spook to frighten away rival suitors, as the
punisher of sexual or conjugal transgression, or as the scourge and
nemesis of marriage itself. In this latter capacity the black man may
persecute one or both partners in an unsuitable match (like Iago) or he
may indiscriminately harass perfectly suitable matches out of a general
hostility to domestic sexual arrangements (Don John). The complex as a
whole – clown, transvestite and 'suit of black' – constitutes a counter-
festive vocabulary through which marriage as a social and political as
well as a sexual form is subjected to critical scrutiny and possible
revision.

The politics of marriage are represented with exemplary clarity in a
very popular anonymous play, *The Merry Devil of Edmonton.* In this
text, the prospective bride and groom, Millicent Clare and Raymond
Mounchesney, are well matched in age and social position and have been
betrothed by the mutual agreement of their respective families. In
addition, they share a warm, even passionate sexual and emotional
attachment to each other. Despite these very favorable circumstances,
there is powerful resistance to the proposed marriage, Millicent's
father determining to obstruct the match on the grounds that the
Mounchesney estate has decayed.

CLARE. For looke you, wife, the rioutous old knight
　　Hath o'erun his annual reuenue
　　In keeping iolly Christmas all the yeere:
　　The nostrilles of his chimny are still stuft
　　With smoake, more chargeable than Cane-tobacco;
　　His hawkes deuoure his fattest dogs, whilst simple,
　　His leanest curres eate him hounds carrion.
　　Beside, I heard of late, his yonger brother,
　　A Turky merchant, hath sure suck'de the knight
　　By meanes of some great losses on the sea,
　　That, you conceive mee, before God all is naught,
　　His seate is weake: thus each thing rightly scand,
　　You'le see a flight, wife, shortly of his land.[8]

This 'fatherly concern' is based on the narrowest economic and practical considerations. Clare is willing to go back on his word in violation both of family honor and the happiness of his own child for 'foggy gaine'. Mounchesney has fallen on hard times because he has upheld traditional and customary values of hospitality ('keeping iolly Christmas all the yeere') and filial or kinship loyalty (aiding his younger brother), but Clare sees only the immediate economic consequences of all this and determines to prevent his daughter's marriage through a complex strategy of evasion. His daughter is to be placed in 'Cheston Nunry', but this is only a temporary evasion, after which she will be married to 'the lusty heire of Sir Raph Ierningham', whose prospects are decidedly better than Raymond Mounchesney's.

The actions contemplated by Sir Arthur Clare link the widely sanctioned norm of patriarchal authority over children with the much more dubious value of 'primitive accumulation'. This strategy is in its turn aligned with an image of archaic repression and false consciousness – the nunnery at Cheston – as a complex metaphor of individual bad faith and malignant social practice. The counter-plot that is to bring about a more satisfactory state of affairs is initiated by Raymond Mounchesney, Millicent's brother Henry Clare, and the putative rival, Frank Ierningham. The solidarity of the young men is dedicated to bringing the lovers together in order to preserve family honor, and to promote and foster the sentimental and sexual satisfactions of the bride and groom as the central purpose of courtship and marriage. This project is carried out with the assistance of Fabel, the merry devil of Edmonton himself, who is a scholar and a magician like Faustus or Friar Bacon, but one who has 'beaten the devil' and evaded the terms of his contract. This counter-plot works as an ingenious extension of the original deception practiced by Sir Arthur Clare. Since the promise originally made to Raymond has been broken by making Millicent assume the guise of a nun, the counter-plot works by disguising Fabel and Raymond as, respectively, the abbot of a neighboring monastery and the young confessor sent by him to shrive the nuns. The two lovers then appear in the guise of religious celibates and declare their mutual passion.

> MILL. O my deere life! I was a dream't to night
>   That, as I was a praying in mine Psalter,
>   There came a spirit unto me as I kneeld,
>   And by his strong perswasions tempted me
>   To leave this Nunry: and me thought
>   He came in the most glorious Angell shape,
>   That mortall eye did euer looke upon.
>   Ha, thou art sure that spirit, for theres no forme
>   Is in mine eye so glorious as thine owne.
> MOUNCH. O thou Idolatresse, that dost this worship
>   To him whose likenes is but praise of thee!
>   Thou bright unsetting star, which through this vaile,
>   For very envy, mak'st the Sun looke pale. . . .
>   Nor will I absolve thee of that sweete sin, though it be venial
>   Yet have the pennance of a thousand kisses.
>   (*The Merry Devil of Edmonton*, III. ii. 90–102)

During this exchange Raymond reveals to Millicent the plans for an elopement to a lodge in Enfield Chase, where they will be able to elude the pursuit organized by Sir Arthur Clare. Millicent agrees to share the dangers of this plan, as she has shared with Raymond this spiritualized and sentimentalized expression of love. As soon as she has left the stage, Raymond reports his success to his companions in a noticeably different idiom. 'She may be poore in spirit, but for the flesh,/'Tis fat and plumpe, boyes' (*The Merry Devil of Edmonton*, III. ii. 124–5). Both romantic and ethereal love poetry and the coarse language of masculine solidarity are uttered by a character wearing the garments of a priest, so that there is an intensified and exaggerated transgressive sense to the entire scene. These transgressions, including the elopement itself and the defiance of patriarchal authority, are sanctioned by adherence to other social imperatives – particularly to 'traditional values' of family honor, friendship and hospitality.

There is a second plot in *The Merry Devil of Edmonton*, which features Blague, the innkeeper, and his plebeian companions, Banks the Miller, Smug the Smith and Sir John the Priest. Their project is to 'wend . . . merrily to the forrest, to steale some of the kings Deere' (*The Merry Devil of Edmonton*, II. ii. 64–6). The poaching of the deer proceeds simultaneously with the elopement of Millicent and Raymond, and both sets of 'outlaws' – the poachers and the young lovers – must find a way to come to terms with Brian, the gamekeeper and local representative of the king's authority. Blague, the host, reassures his fellow poachers at the very beginning of their escapade that they are not to unduly concern themselves over this potential obstacle.

> HOST. Tush, the knaue keepers are my bosonians, and my pensioners. Nine a clacke! be valiant, my little Gogmagogs; Ile fence with all the Iustices in Hartford shire. Ile haue a Bucke til I die: Ile slay a Doe while I liue. Hold your bow straight and steady.
> (*The Merry Devil of Edmonton*, II. ii. 74–80)

The climax of the play is a series of farcical chase sequences in which Millicent is 'severed' from her companions and subsequently rescued by Brian. At the same time the poachers succeed in killing a great buck and carrying it off, though only after a series of painful misadventures. The old knight, Sir Arthur Clare, is mistaken for the poachers by Brian, who threatens to shoot them for their misdeed. In the confusion, both the lovers and the poachers escape.

> BRIAN. Ile complaine unto the King you spoile his game:
> 'Tis strange that men of your account and calling
> Will offer it. . . .
> I charge you both ye get out of my ground!
> Is this a time for such as you,
> Men of your place and of your gravity.
> To be abroad a theeuing? tis a shame;
> And, afore God, if I had shot at you,
> I had serude you well enough.
> (*The Merry Devil of Edmonton*, IV. i. 186–97)

The king's authority is the immediate instrument that secures the happy ending, though the king himself acts indirectly and at a distance through Brian the gamekeeper, who achieves the good results 'by mistake'. If happy endings and happy marriages are good, then disobedience to parents and even poaching the king's deer are also good, since all these actions and states of affairs are accomplished with the implicit and inadvertent approval of the king.

Raymond and Millicent are married by Sir John and spend their wedding night in Blague's inn, The George. Sir Arthur Clare and Old Ierningham are prevented from catching them there by Fabel, who switches the signs on the inns so that Clare and Ierningham spend the night in the wrong beds and discover the extent of the deceptions only after it is too late to do anything about it. The successful defiance of patriarchal authority and the concomitant overthrow of socially repressive institutions, both old (the enforced chastity of the nunnery) and new (the dishonorable rapacity of accumulation), are orchestrated by the 'devilish' Fabel, who excuses himself on the grounds that his actions are motivated by love.

> FABEL. These for his loue, who once was my deere puple,
>   Haue I effected. Now, mee thinks, tis strange
>   That you, being old in wisedome, should thus knit
>   Your foreheade on this match, since reason failes;
>   No law can curbe the louers rash attempt;
>   Yeares, in resisting this, are sadly spent.
>   Smile, then, upon your daughter and kind sonne,
>   And let our toyle to future ages proue,
>   The deiull of Edmonton did good in love.
>   (*The Merry Devil of Edmonton*, v. ii. 145–52)

For the devil to do good, he must outwit the 'bad fathers' and their avaricious disregard for the multiple bonds of love between bride and groom, between friends of the same gender, and between various members of the community, to whom a particular deference is owed in respect of the dignity of their calling as well as their place in the social structure. The 'overthrow' of 'bad' patriarchal authority requires the multiple chastisement of Old Clare and Old Ierningham, who are not only defeated by the counter-intrigue of the younger generation, but also admonished and scolded for their presumptive arrogance by their 'lower-class' neighbors, Brian the gamekeeper and Blague the host.

The thrashing of aristocratic and patriarchal authority that exceeds socially tolerable limits is depicted directly and physically in *The Merry Devil of Edmonton*, as Old Clare and Old Ierningham, having awakened in the wrong beds, appear in the final scene stiff and aching from their futile exertions in the forest. In *A Midsummer Night's Dream* a similar heuristic is represented, using a similar vocabulary of festive and counter-festive personae and conventional actions. In this play, however, there is no physical abuse or thrashing: the admonitory purposes of plebeian culture in respect of socially constituted authority are achieved through 'obscene' and 'tragically mirthful' spectacle.

The wedding feast of Theseus and Hippolyta provides a narrative framework for the action of *A Midsummer Night's Dream*. Theseus invites all of Athens to join in a period of festivity celebrating his marriage; his eloquence expresses the poise and authority appropriate to his privileged, aristocratic status. The names and parts of the story identify the couple as characters from classical mythology, but their language is a poetic representation of the speech of a lord and lady contemporary with Shakespeare's audience.[9] By conflating the image of a gentle lord and lady with an epically distanced one of figures from classical mythology, the dramatist reproduces the ceremonial form of aristocratic spectacle.[10] The noble couple assume the identity of figures from an idealized past because in their individuality they embody ideal, timeless categories. Theseus intends to confirm a harmony between the natural and the social order. Within this frame, however, the play represents several stories of resistance and discord, counter-models of the reconciliation and accommodation Theseus proposes. Among these counter-models is a burlesque parody of high literature, 'Pyramus and Thisby', an 'interlude' to be offered to the Duke and his lady by Bottom and his associates.

The wedding celebration of Duke Theseus is to be a time of social liberty, in which mirth will reign, melancholy will be banished and conflict will resolve into harmony. The pageantry and feasting are to show the social and moral significance of his marriage, and its importance as a symbol of the structure of social relations. The marriage is a change in status for both Theseus and Hippolyta, a change that results from mutual consent to a pattern of hierarchy and subordination. That pattern is represented by images of conquest and abduction.

THE. Hippolyta, I woo'd thee with my sword,
    And won thy love doing thee injuries;
    But I will wed thee in another key,
    With pomp, with triumph, and with revelling.
                        (*A Midsummer Night's Dream*, I. i. 16–19)

The lord and lady whose marriage is celebrated are clothed in identities derived from classical literature. Following the practice of their real-life Renaissance contemporaries, they create a mythologically distant and idealized space and time for themselves to occupy. As images of antiquity, their meaning is already established and iconographically codified. From within this perfected space and time, the characters of Theseus and Hippolyta create an authoritative discourse that matches the language of constituted authority in the dramatist's own society. This authoritative discourse divides and distinguishes; it schedules the flow of emotions and names the roles and social positions each individual must occupy.[11] Social and individual well-being depends above all on obedience to that discourse.

THE. Be advis'd, fair maid.
    To you your father should be as a god
    One that compos'd your beauties, yea, and one
    To whom you are but as a form in wax
    By him imprinted, and within his power
    To leave the figure, or disfigure it.
                        (*A Midsummer Night's Dream*, I. i. 46–51)

Identity assigned by authority is fixed and unchanging. Change in status – marriage, for example – is a change from one categorically distinct social position to another within a fixed structure. The rites and processes of this kind of change occur under the careful surveillance of constituted authority. Theatrical symbols and the narrative interanimation of those symbols are allegorical, and meanings are generated by natural resemblances between objects and signs, among social roles, the individuals who occupy them and the insignia of rank they bear. Theseus' nuptial revels are a festive enactment of his authoritative discourse. It is in this sense that he 'stands in' for the noble couple whose marriage the play commemorates, using celebratory mirth and feasting to control the changes ordained by his wedding and to insure stable continuity in the social fabric.

Bottom's company of clowns, sometimes referred to as the 'mechanicals', are, in contrast to the antique images of Theseus and his retinue, solidly contemporary. They represent specific plebeian crafts, all of which were important in the economic life of Shakespeare's England.[12] The image of a company of gentlefolk, distanced by projection into the mythological past, is disrupted by the intrusion of the practical world of the present. The language of Bottom and his friends is strongly contrasted to the ennobled language of the court, not only in its sound and diction, but also in its orientation to the space and time of the audience. The mundane practicality of everyday, collective decision-making is undertaken here by a group of blundering clowns and represents a parodic image of everyday social life.

Bottom, like Theseus, has a 'theory' of representation to guide him in his function as organizer of a public spectacle. Theseus' semiotics of resemblance sees the sign imprinted on the thing in permanent, authoritative form. Bottom, on the other hand, sees external signs as freely interchangeable and is therefore ready to play any part in the interlude, in any color beard, regardless of sex or even of species. He presents himself as vain, overenthusiastic and obviously foolish, but his ambition to play all the parts should not be interpreted as a manifestation of his folly as an individual. Bottom is not an individual subject or character at all, but a temporary name assumed by a public figure whose willingness to play all parts is a comic uncrowning of limited identity and social discrimination. In playing the scene, Bottom mimics tyrant and lover, man and woman, lion and nightingale. His confused misuse and abuse of language is a property of the clown's mask, with its inherent capacity of strategic misinterpretation.

In the rehearsal scene, Bottom applies his theory of representation to specific problems of theatrical form and its social implications. In this scene the *ad hoc*, improvisatory nature of group decision-making leads to a ludicrous patchwork of compromises and cobbled-up solutions to technical problems. The working process of theatrical production is swamped by the sheer mechanical perversity of telling a story to a socially privileged audience without offending anyone. To dispel the ladies' fear of lions, for example, Bottom recommends that 'you must name his name, and half his face must be seen through the lion's neck; and he himself must speak through . . . and tell them plainly he is Snug the joiner' (*A Midsummer Night's Dream*, III. i. 36–45). 'Baring the device' – 'speaking through' the costume, drawing attention to artifice while at the same time using artifice to represent a second reality – is a basic resource of Elizabethan drama. The 'transparency' of the character of Lion, the disclosure of the actor's artifice, does not work for other devices in the interlude, where things are not represented at all but appear as themselves, like the dog and thornbush that 'represent' a dog and thornbush. This convention of disclosure of artifice does not permit 'suspension of disbelief'; as Barber suggests, it draws attention to 'the continual failure to translate actor into character'.[13] But this artistic 'failure to translate', inherent in Carnivalized forms, is a purposeful critique of fixed, private self-identification.

The pattern of versatile improvisatory competence is most forcefully objectified in Bottom's translation, in which the head of an ass is superimposed on the already asinine mask of the clown. Bottom is courageous in responding to his transformation. His ability to accept the gross violation of normal expectations and categories of the everyday comes from his status as a clown or comic mask, not from any clearly bounded individual subjectivity. Bottom can even bring the extraordinary or supernatural world of fairies into a familiar relationship to his own mundane contemporaneity.

> BOT. I shall desire you of more acquaintance, good Master Cobweb: if I cut my finger, I shall make bold with you. Your name, honest gentleman?
>
> PEAS. Peaseblossom
>
> BOT. I pray you, commend me to Mistress Squash, your mother, and to Master Peascod, your father. Good Master Peaseblossom, I shall desire of more acquaintance too. Your name, I beseech you sir?
>
> MUS. Mustardseed.
>
> BOT. Good Master Mustardseed, I know your patience well. That same cowardly giant-like ox-beef hath devoured many a gentleman of your house: I promise you your kindred hath made my eyes water ere now. I desire you of more acquaintance, good Master Mustardseed.
>
> (*A Midsummer Night's Dream*, III. i. 175–90)

What Bottom sees in the fairy world is the natural process of growth and productivity which, through human labor, leads to ease and abundance.

His next scene is a brief comic Utopia, a Lubberland or Cockaigne in which fairy attendants cater to all his wishes. Bottom's choice of pleasures is mundane, but his language has become a frenchified parody of the ennobled language of his social superiors, just as his action here is a parody of gracious *noblesse oblige*.

> BOT. Mounsieur Cobweb, good monsieur, get you your weapons in your hand, and kill me a red-hipped humble-bee on the top of a thistle; and good mounsieur, bring me the honey-bag. Do not fret yourself too much in the action, mounsieur; and good mounsieur, have a care the honey-bag break not. I would be loath to have you overflown with a honey-bag, signior.
>
> (*A Midsummer Night's Dream*, IV. i. 10–16)

Bottom, waited upon by the fairy attendants, is the parodic double of a nobleman waited upon by his servants. His travesty of the gentle manners of a lord may not resemble the actual behavior of any gentleman who ever lived, but it does portray the image of the privileged as they are perceived by their social inferiors. This rude and irreverent mimicry of what purports to be elegant, gentle manners is conducted with impunity, by virtue of the clown's resourcefulness in 'not understanding'.

Before they are interrupted by the metamorphosis of Bottom, the plebeian characters are occupied with the project of presenting an interlude for the wedding feast of Theseus and Hippolyta. They see this enterprise as a vehicle for their own personal aspirations to wealth and status, their desire to move up the social ladder. The poverty of their artistic means makes the production of 'Pyramus and Thisby' into a self-parodying, botched achievement, but 'Pyramus and Thisby' is more than a witty put-down of folk drama, or a distant allusion to *Romeo and Juliet*. It is also 'rough music', a noisy, burlesque counter-festivity that is an admonitory gloss on the ceremonial formality of a wedding.[14] Pyramus and Thisby are, like Hermia and Lysander, young lovers blocked in their desires by arbitrary and oppressive parental restrictions. In the main comic action of *A Midsummer Night's Dream*, the young lovers successfully negotiate the intricacies of courtship not so much by outwitting parental opposition as through the activity of Oberon, the King of Shadows, and his representative, Puck, the hobgoblin. As in *The Merry Devil of Edmonton*, good results are accomplished by devilish means, and the ominous and violent potentiality of the Black Man is favorably deployed to bring about a sexual and social happy ending. The violent and tragic 'other side' of marriage is actualized in 'Pyramus and Thisby', which represents the complex risks and hazards of sentimental and idealized love. Bottom (as Pyramus) and Flute (dressed as a woman – Thisby) mime the attitudes of romantic love and restate its idealizations in coarse bodily language.

> PYR. O kiss me through the hole of this vile wall.
> THIS. I kiss the wall's hole, not your lips at all.
>
> (*A Midsummer Night's Dream*, v. i. 198–9)

The sexual side of romantic love has been talked about euphemistically and indirectly by the lovers. The physical desire that animates them is crudely paraphrased by the bawdy innuendo of the language and by the Carnivalized theatricality of the interlude as a whole. Men in animal costumes, men dressed as women, ludicrous misrepresentations of classical literature and popular legend, are all common Carnival devices. The interlude is, moreover, an example of 'Mungrell tragi-comedy'. According to the rational decorum of the court audience on the stage such a concept is absurdly self-contradictory, but tragical mirth is a dominant characteristic of Carnivalesque mimesis. The cheerful death and immediate resurrection of the comic lovers in the interlude reformulate the passionate sentiments of infatuated youth as seen from the bottom of the social order. Bottom's comedy is an 'obscene' parody of that infatuation. His benign ignorance, an ignorance that is often witty and appropriate, is an attitude in itself – one of strategic misinterpretation, not merely the absence of someone else's supposedly correct way of construing things.

The burlesque of the conventions of romantic love, like a charivari or a jig, makes a mockery, not only of the harmony of the wedding feast, but more generally of the contradictions of aristocratic marriage, where the pattern of conflicting imperatives is as likely to result in violence as in harmony. The deaths of Pyramus and Thisby are the antithesis of joyous reconciliation: they suggest the other side of marriage – disappointment, separation and death. In a way, 'Pyramus and Thisby' is a kind of cautionary tale, although it has an ambivalent moral. It seems to warn equally against the dangers of filial disobedience and of arbitrary parental rigidity. Its tragedy negates the reconciliation of the lovers; its mirth negates the solemnity of their festive celebration.

Bottom and his friends do not set out to change or even to criticize the established order of social relations. However, the presence of 'hard-handed men' – weavers, carpenters, joiners – within an epically distanced mythological realm brings that realm into crude contact with the contemporaneous world of productive life and the familiar language of the street, the workshop and the marketplace. The mechanicals use the power of disguise and their own transgressive theory about performing theatrical roles to reveal the insubstantiality of social identity. In their 'offering' they ridicule the desires, as well as the behavior, of their upper-class audience. This negative critical activity exposes the ideology of dominance behind the sentimental justification of hierarchized erotic love. The social and artistic creativity of the mechanicals enjoys only mixed success within the play. Their undertaking falls short of its hoped-for goals: Bottom is not awarded a pension and might be lucky to escape hanging. The enterprise of drama does, however, bring authoritative discourse into a close, proximate relationship with the experience of everyday productive life so that it can be viewed experimentally, and irreverently.

'Pyramus and Thisby' is social critique by inadvertency. Its cogency does not depend in any way on the conviction that Bottom and company are knowingly engaged in the production of a purposeful or tendentious art. The refusal to understand is also a refusal to concur fully and wholeheartedly with structures of feeling regarded as natural and necessary by Theseus and the powerful social groups of which he is a symbol. The 'bloody farce' of 'Pyramus and Thisby' is a substantive admonition as to the dangers concealed by the injunctions surrounding marriage, and most particularly in the effort to reconcile the economic and social purposes of dynastic marriage with the sexual and personal satisfactions of the bride and groom. This is finally dependent, not only on the goodwill of the partners, but also on the willingness of the community impersonated by the 'suit of black' to refrain from malicious persecution of the bride and groom. But the 'suit of black' reserves the right to intervene, to alter and readjust the organization of sexuality, because domestic erotic life is an elementary political form, the primary allocation of pleasure, of wealth and of power.

CHAPTER 11
TREATING DEATH AS A LAUGHING MATTER

DEATH is treated as a laughing matter in many of Shakespeare's tragedies, as it is in the tragic drama of his predecessors and his contemporaries. The juxtaposition of low comedy with death scenes and funerals, and the resulting confusion of generic distinction, was one of the specific objections to the theater raised by Sidney.

> . . . neither the admiration and commiseration, nor the right sportfulnes, is by their mungrell Tragy-comedie obtained. . . . So falleth it out that, hauing indeed no right Comedie, in that comicall part of our Tragedy we haue nothing but scurrility, unwoorthy of any chast eares, or so extreame shew of doltishness, indeed fit to lift up a loude laughter, and nothing else.[1]

The laughter evoked by an 'extreme show of doltishness' at a deathbed or the gallows or the graveyard is certainly not edifying, at least not in Sidney's sense. For Shakespeare and for many of his contemporaries, however, death is a particularly favorable subject for laughter, and funerals are often the occasion for clowning, burlesque and irreverent language. Tragical mirth is by no means confined to comedy. Extended bouts of clowning occur in relation to death scenes of a fundamentally serious kind, as in the Porter scene in *Macbeth* and the Gravedigger scene in *Hamlet*. The low comedy of these disrupts the solemnity and fear connected with death by drawing attention to the experience of the body and to the continuity of collective life. According to Robert Weimann, they also express ideological values of English and German peasant-revolutionary movements.[2] Laughing in the presence of death is an aspect of a comprehensive political heuristic common to all of plebeian culture and objectified in popular festive form. Both 'extreme doltishness' and the grotesque laughter it evokes represent a collective and communal rejoinder to the ideology of established political power.

Laughing at death may come about in a variety of ways. Death itself may be farcical, as in the drowning of the drunken Clarence in a 'butt of Malmsey' or in the catalogue of horrors recited by Barabas to Ithamore in *The Jew of Malta*. Gallows humor and jesting dialogues between prisoners and their jailers is another frequently encountered pattern. There are also burlesque resurrections, as in 'Pyramus and Thisby', *Locrine*, *The Jew of Malta* and *1 Henry IV*. Finally, and perhaps most puzzling, there are instances of crude, abusive laughter, often with sexual overtones, connected with the death of innocent or 'martyred' characters. Laughter is a central, privileged response to the death even of an exemplary image of kingship such as Duncan in *Macbeth*.

Like marriage, death is an existential transition for the individual who experiences it and a political transition for the social milieu in which the event occurs. As a social transformation it is, again like marriage, characterized by complex structural ambiguity. Every death is consequential; each time someone dies there is a reallocation of authority and a redistribution of wealth. One way to grasp and to objectify the complexity of this situation is by treating death as a joke. This is especially pertinent when the individual death has a wide public impact, and when the issue of succession is consequential for a relatively wide community. An individual dies, but social life is sustained despite this local discontinuity.

Burlesque resurrection, as it is represented in plays such as *Locrine* or *1 Henry IV*, is a crude schematization of continuity achieved by the temporary evasion of death. This tactic of sham-death in favor of preserving one's life is, at least in the examples cited, juxtaposed to an image of honorable death and self-sacrifice. Strumbo, the clown of *Locrine*, has been conscripted by the officers of Albanact to fight in the wars against the Huns. He participates in the battle scene in which the defenders of Britain are routed by their enemies. Albanact, the leader of the British army and brother to Locrine, sees that the British cause in this battle is hopeless and kills himself rather than suffer the dishonor of flight or capture. Strumbo has in the meantime already 'fallen' in the battle. In the midst of the turmoil he makes the following observation:

> STRUM. Lord have mercy upon us, masters, I think this is a holie day; euerie man lies sleeping in the fields, but, God knowes, full sore against their wills.
>
> (*Locrine*, II. v. 70–3)

Strumbo states openly what some members of his audience might feel, that is that no one willingly dies an honorable death. Furthermore, by his cowardly evasion of actual combat, Strumbo objectifies the conviction that a dishonorable life is preferable to a noble death. Strumbo, counterfeiting death, and Albanact, who is 'actually dead', lie side by side upon the stage; Strumbo's servant Trompart enters, and the two deaths are observed and respected by an 'extreame show of doltishness'.

> TR. Looke where my maister lies. Master, Master.
> STRUM. Let me alone, I tell thee, for I am dead.
> TRUM. Yet one word, good master.
> STRUM. I will not speake, for I am dead, I tell thee.
> TRUM. And is my master dead?
> O sticks and stones, brickbats and bones,
> and is my master dead?
> O you cockatrices and you bablatrices,
> that in the woods dwell:
> You briers and brambles, you cookes shoppes and
> shambles, come howle and yell.
> With howling and skreeking, with wailing and weeping,
> come you to lament,
> O Colliers of Croyden, and rusticks of Royden, and
> fishers of Kent;
> For Strumbo the colber, the fine mery cobler
> of Cathnes towne:
> At this same stoure, at this very houre,
> lies dead on the ground.

O maister, theeues, theeues, theeues.

STRUM. Where be they? cox me tunny, bobekin! let me be rising. Be
gone; we shall be robde by and by.

(*Locrine*, II. v. 93–116)

Strumbo 'falls in battle' to save his skin and 'rises from the dead' to save
his purse. The lament over his death, with its 'howling and skreeking', is
a ludicrous acknowledgment of the public significance of this clownish
death, a death that is to be observed throughout the productive sphere –
'cookes shoppes' and shambles – and indeed throughout the wider public
sphere: Croyden, Royden and Kent. The laughter evoked by this
temporary triumph over death is diffuse and may spill over into
unsympathetic mirth at the representation of the 'actual death' of
Albanact, whose body must be removed from the stage because, unlike
Strumbo, he cannot leave the scene of the battle under his own power.

The much better-known example of the death and resurrection of
Falstaff in *1 Henry IV* objectifies a very similar interpretation of social
life and the claims of 'honorable death'. The gloss on the ideology of
noble sacrifice is provided by Falstaff himself, who first observes Blunt,
wearing the arms of the king, dead on the field.

FAL. Though I could 'scape shot free at London, I fear the shot here.
Here's no scoring but upon the pate. Soft! Who are you? Sir Walter
Blunt. There's honour for you! Here's no vanity! I am as hot as
molten lead, and as heavy too. God keep lead out of me.

(*1 Henry IV*, v. iii. 29–40)

Like Strumbo, Falstaff wishes to go on living, and, from the perspective
of the crude thinking that such a wish mobilizes, he sees the actuality of
honor as 'a mere scutcheon' and as the grinning face of a corpse. This is
not the admirable view of honor bodied forth in the character of Blunt
or of Harry Monmouth in his identity as Prince of Wales. Falstaff,
however, draws attention to the pertinence and the cogency of the
'unbalanced' view that rejects the justificatory ideology of honorable
death.

FAL. . . . 'Sblood, 'twas time to counterfeit, or that hot termagant
Scot had paid me scot and lot too. Counterfeit? To die is to be a
counterfeit, for he is but the counterfeit of a man who hath not the

life of a man. But to counterfeit dying when a man thereby liveth is to be no counterfeit, but the true and perfect image of life indeed.

(1 Henry IV, v. iv. 110–20)

Falstaff engages the persistent suspicion that it might really be better to be a live coward than a dead hero, especially since the duty to die an heroic death may depend more on the credulity of the fallen hero than on any demonstrable and concrete social benefit gained through sacrifice. He has already seen his ragamuffins 'peppered' and the survivors reduced to eventual beggary. By treating honorable death as a joke, Falstaff speaks to a plebeian consciousness that maintains itself despite sacrifices demanded in the name of the nation-state.

The roguish and cowardly clowns who are 'miraculously' resurrected on the battlefield walk away under their power; their noble counterpart must be somehow carried offstage. Strumbo and Falstaff are both clownish paraphrases of the political doctrine of *dignitas non moritur*: the king's mystical identity or dignity never dies.[3] Both king and clown are 'twin-born' or two-bodied, existing both as individuals and as the temporary embodiment of a social and corporate persona. The pathos of the twin-born king whose natural body dies but whose corporate and mystical body is immortal has been analyzed by Ernst Kantorowicz in his reading of Shakespeare's *Richard II*:

> kingship itself comes to mean Death, and nothing but Death. . . . The king that 'never dies' here has been replaced by the king that always dies and suffers death more cruelly than other mortals. Gone is the oneness of the body natural with the immortal body politic. . . . all that remains is the feeble human nature of a king.[4]

Richard is himself aware of his affinity with the abject and ludicrous figure of the fool, and he sees the bitter humor in his situation along with the grim sadness that situation evokes. He is not, however, in a position to see just how funny that situation might be when interpreted by a clown who is also a diabolical rogue. The clown, who insists on surviving and who therefore arranges for his own resurrection, explicates the suffering and death of kings according to a simple philosophy. You can't fall off the floor. The 'kynges games . . . playde upon scafoldes' may be less significant and less consequential than they appear.

The clown dies and is reborn 'in jest'; the king dies 'in earnest'. This pattern applies even to an exemplary image of kingship like Duncan in *Macbeth*, whose death is interpreted as a laughing matter in the Porter scene that immediately follows his murder. The sound of knocking and the figure of the porter himself are images of the underworld, but this is not a terrifying and intimidating picture of hell. The underworld appears here as a familiar and funny monstrosity.

> PORTER. If a man were porter of hell-gate, he should have old turning the key. Knock, knock, knock! Who's there, i' th' name of Beelzebub? Here's a farmer, that hanged himself on th' expectation of plenty: Come in, time-server; have napkins enow about you, here you'll sweat for't.
>
> (*Macbeth*, II. iii. 1–6)

As the porter plays at being the gatekeeper of the inferno, we laugh at a variety of images of uncrowning: at the farmer who expected plenty, at the arrogance of those knocking to be admitted, even at the uncrowning of hell, turned into a homely place where a tailor might 'roast a goose'. The porter's hell is simultaneously hot and cold, ominous and funny, a place of feasting as well as a place of punishment: in other words it is equivocal. The porter himself is greatly preoccupied with equivocation, which has several different meanings in the scene. The porter himself links equivocation with treason and with drink. Equivocation is fallacy, a willful abuse of language, the use of different senses of a word in an argument to dissimulate or to confuse. Equivocation also has a physical meaning in terms of the ambivalent sexuality of the drunken man.

> PORTER. . . . much drink may be said to be an equivocator with lechery: it makes him, and it mars him; it sets him on, and it takes him off; it persuades him, and disheartens him; makes him stand to, and not stand to: in conclusion, equivocates him in a sleep, and giving him the lie, leaves him.
>
> (*Macbeth*, II. iii. 30–5)

The scene juxtaposes solemn horror at the murder of a noble king with a series of jokes about eating (roast goose), excrement (urine) and sexuality (lechery). In other words, the context shifts from the king to a lower-class character and, at the same time, from the 'ideal' to crudely material, bodily reality. Abuse of language, the processes of the visceral, lower body and the image of the underworld are deployed so as to interpret the murder of a king. In the symbolism of Carnival, these are the elements of festive uncrowning, debasement and renewal; they represent the essentially funny truth about death and its relation to worldly privilege. In this tradition, the death of the old is a constantly recurring event, linked always to images of the fecundating processes of eating and sexuality that bring forth new life.

This is not to suggest that the laughter in some way 'undercuts' our sense that Duncan is a good king. On the contrary, there is no doubt that Duncan is a benevolent ruler, or that Macbeth's betrayal is an evil deed that leads only to a succession of horrors and ever-increasing slaughter. Not until the murder is reenacted and Macbeth is himself physically 'uncrowned' will anything truly new and more hopeful emerge. But the laughter that comes just as Duncan is dying does show that the death of an individual is a laughing matter when that death is viewed from the standpoint of the social and biological process as a whole and not from a single, limited interpretation of that process. 'Duncan' is a political abstraction, the image of a king composed exclusively of good qualities. Nevertheless, the destruction of his natural body is accomplished with relative ease and facility by Macbeth and Lady Macbeth, and the identity of the king's natural body with the body politic is disrupted. Ironically, that 'oneness' is represented as both true and untrue in the action of Macbeth. The virtues embodied in Duncan are not permanently incorporated into the body politic; the oneness of the king with his kingdom is a doctrine refuted both by the murder itself and by the ensuing civil butchery. On the other hand, the political 'imbecility' of Macbeth as the usurping 'natural body' who makes himself the king is reproduced as a corresponding 'imbecility' in the body politic. The 'imbecility' of the high political action is already recognized in the Porter scene, but it is not expressed in the impressive rhetoric that Macbeth will use when he describes life as 'a tale told by an idiot'. In the porter's interpretation of political reality, the difference between a good king and a bad king is relatively slight and inconsequential. The slaughter that goes on as each succession is disputed is understood to be business as usual.

The patterns of crowning and uncrowning, of laughing at death, are perhaps more fully elaborated in *Hamlet* than in any other play. From the beginning, the action combines 'mirth in funeral and dirge in marriage'. Hamlet's 'suit of black' represents, not only his protracted grief over the death of his father, but also the disapproval he feels over the remarriage of his mother. Natalie Davis has suggested that *Hamlet* may be seen as 'a charivari of the young against a grotesque and unseemly remarriage, a charivari where the effigy of the dead spouse returns, the vicious action is replayed'.[5] There is not much doubt that much of what Hamlet does is a kind of 'rough music', an abusive counter-festivity that seeks not only to express disapproval of Claudius' remarriage, but to actually bring about its dissolution. Hamlet characterizes the wedding feast of Claudius and Gertrude as an occasion marked by unseemly haste. He jests bitterly with Horatio about the indecorousness of the situation.

> HAM. Thrift, thrift, Horatio. The funeral baked meats
> Did coldly furnish forth the marriage tables.
>
> (*Hamlet*, I. ii. 180–1)

Funeral baked meat represents a disturbing and disagreeable mingling of presumably disparate attitudes. As Claudius points out, the funeral banquet that is also a wedding feast objectifies a significant pattern of social continuity and suggests that Hamlet's excessive mourning for his dead father is a form of spiritual rebellion and impiety.[6]

> CLAUDIUS. 'Tis sweet and commendable in your nature,
> Hamlet,
> To give these mourning duties to your father,
> But you must know your father lost a father,
> That father lost, lost his, and the survivor bound
> In filial obligation for some term
> To do obsequious sorrow. But to persever
> In obstinate condolement is a course
> Of impious stuborness. 'Tis unmanly grief.
>
> (*Hamlet*, I. ii. 87–94)

The mournful prince with his stubborn impiety refuses to acknowledge the justice of this observation for the very good reason that the usurping uncle has stolen the place of both father and son. As a strategic response to a dangerous situation, the prince adopts the role of intriguer on his own behalf. The 'suit of woe' (the sign of mourning) now becomes more simply a 'suit of black' (the sign of 'persecution of marriage'). Hamlet takes on the persona of a devil-buffoon who interprets political reality by attempting to plot and to arrange political results. In his guise of an 'antic disposition', Hamlet finds it quite easy to treat death as a laughing matter. He kills Polonius by mistake, but he observes that this is at least a way to get the old man to shut up: 'this counselor / Is now most still, most secret, and most grave / Who was in life a foolish prating knave' (*Hamlet*, III. iv. 213–15).

The irreverence and disrespect expressed by Hamlet as he drags the corpse of Polonius offstage articulate an emerging solution to problems created by an individual's social integument with its enormous capacity both for rhetorical camouflage and for hypocrisy, dissimulation and the masking of vicious intrigue. The murder of Polonius comes about as a case of mistaken identity, but once he is dead there is no chance that his identity will ever be mistaken again. The murder reveals that violence does possess certain possibilities for clarification, because violence addresses the individual's physical reality and breaks through willful misrepresentation. A dead body is an instructive object that draws attention to processes of change and transformation that take place outside the scope of political intrigue.

> KING. Now Hamlet, where's Polonius?
> HAMLET. At supper.
> KING. At supper? where?
> HAMLET. Not where he eats, but where 'a is eaten. A certain convocation of politic worms are e'en at him. Your worm is your only emperor for diet. We fat all creatures else to fat us, and we fat ourselves for maggots. Your fat king and your lean beggar is but variable service – two dishes, but to one table. That's the end.
>
> (*Hamlet*, IV. iii. 16–25)

Hamlet's 'extreame show of doltishness' reinterprets the basic distinctions of social life: between food and corrupt, decaying flesh, between human and animal, between king and beggar. Temporal authority and indeed all political structures of difference are turned inside out.

> HAMLET. A man may fish with the worm that hath eat the king, and eat of the fish that hat fed of that worm.
> KING. What dost thou mean by this?
> HAMLET. Nothing but to show you how a king may go a progress through the guts of a beggar.
>
> (*Hamlet*, IV. iii. 27–31)

Hamlet assumes responsibility for a task that has meaning only in a world of coherent differences between father and uncle, king and usurper, Hyperion and satyr. But murder 'Carnivalizes' social difference and turns a person into 'laughing matter'. The logic of grotesque Carnival equivocation implies equivalence between Old Hamlet and Claudius. The royal 'progress', which affirms hierarchy, social superiority and political power, is internalized physiologically transformed by the lower functions of the body. By murdering Polonius, Hamlet has become a creator of laughing matter. He adopts the speech of grotesque equivocation so as to reinterpret and clarify the misleading representation of courtly intrigue and to simplify the vicious complications in the struggle to allocate political power.

Neither Hamlet – nor Claudius, another murderous equivocator and creator of laughing matter – are able to provide a full elaboration of this grotesque and irreverent language of death and dying. Authority for the comprehensive disclosure of death as a laughing matter resides with the two clowns, who enter this play to assume the roles of two gravediggers. The significance of their political philosophy is inversely proportional to their apparent insignificance as 'minor characters'. But their low and common speech, and their lack of interest in the events for which their participation is required, objectify their engagement with a plenitude of socially diverse speech types that exist vis-à-vis the text of *Hamlet*.

The clown's function is as a popular chorus, to reveal the nihilistic incoherence of privilege and its tendency fatally to confuse individual desire with political will.

> OTHER. Will you ha' the truth on't? If this had not been a gentlewoman, she should have been buried out o' Christian burial.
> CLOWN. Why, there thou say'st. And the more pity that great folk should have count'nance in this world to drown or hang themselves more than their even-Christen.
>
> (*Hamlet*, v. i. 24–30)

Christian burial is ostensibly given in accordance with the spiritual and moral condition of the deceased. The clowns perceive very clearly, however, how contingent, secular differences take precedence over religious distinctions supposedly blind to social advantage. The suicide of great folk is the occasion of admonitory humor. The clowns express resentment over privilege of any kind, resentment grounded in a principle of 'even Christen', the doctrine that all souls are equal in God's sight. At the same time the gravedigger expressed a certain grim satisfaction with the particular privilege claimed here, a privilege that the clown is willing to see granted. This *Schadenfreude* is derived not from a nebulous, comical refusal to understand social hierarchy but from a cogent and explicit critique of the basis for hierarchy in gentility and the privilege of 'bearing arms'.[7]

> CLOWN. There is no ancient gentlemen but gard'ners, ditchers, and
> gravemakers. They hold up Adam's profession.
> OTHER. Was he a gentleman?
> CLOWN. 'A was the first that ever bore arms.
> OTHER. Why he had none.
> CLOWN. What, are thou a heathen? How dost thou understand the
> scripture says Adam digged. Could he dig without arms?
>
> (*Hamlet*, v. i. 30–8)

The clown's reference to Adam digging restores a lost or subordinated meaning for 'arms' as something that all men – and women – share, along with the capacity to work so as to create subsistence.

> When adam delved
> And Eve Span
> Who was then
> The Gentleman.

The gravedigger's language reestablishes the connection between the circumscribed usage of a well-defined social class and the heteroglot vocabularies of productive life. Poetry, riddles, crude literalism and witty equivocation are all deployed by the clown in his presentation of a comprehensive doctrine of political economy and the distribution of temporal power.

> CLOWN. What is he that builds stronger than either the mason, the
> shipwright, or the carpenter?
> OTHER. The gallowsmaker, for that frame outlives a thousand
> tenants.
> CLOWN. I like thy wit well, in good faith. The gallows does well. But

how does it well? It does well to those that do ill. Now thou dost ill to say the gallows is built stronger than the church. Argal, the gallows may do well to thee.

(*Hamlet*, v. i. 41–50)

The authority of ordinary productive life is dominated by 'the gallows', the instrument of the state's coercive justice. The secular authority of civil institutions is subordinated to a higher authority embodied by the church. But neither church nor state answers the riddle: there is a secular authority even more durable than either of these forms.

> CLOWN. . . . . when you are asked this question next, say, 'a grave maker'. The houses he makes last till doomsday. Go, get thee in, and fetch me a stroup of liquor.
>
> (*Hamlet*, v. i. 58–61)

Against the perspective of death and burial all human effort is diminished, all the 'serious' claims of economic, political or moral systems become the objects of laughter. The doomsday image of the grave is from this viewpoint not something grim and gloomy, but, on the contrary, the occasion for 'drink' and merriment. The riddle is solved by a grotesque acknowledgment of concrete social antagonisms. The clown's riddle celebrates his direct, practical knowledge of a common fate to be shared by gentlefolk and common people.

Hamlet's response to the gravedigger recapitulates his reaction to the wedding feast of Claudius; again the prince reflects on the decorum of mingling contradictory emotions.

> HAMLET. Hath this fellow no feeling of his business? 'A sings in grave-making?
>
> (*Hamlet*, v. i. 66–7)

The association of death with laughter still puzzles him, but the gravedigger now provides him with skulls as exemplary objects of meditation. Hamlet and Horatio are at stage level and the clown is down below in the earth. Hamlet is up, the clown is down, both spatially and socially; the positioning defines the encounter between two speech types and two contrasting views of matters of life and death.

HAMLET. Whose grave is this, sirrah?
CLOWN. Mine, sir.
[*Sings*]   *O, a pit of clay for to be made*
          For such a guest is meet.
HAMLET. I think it be thine indeed, for thou liest in't.
CLOWN. You lie on't, sir, and therefore, 'tis not yours. For my part, I
   do not lie in't, yet it is mine.

>   (*Hamlet*, v. i. 121–6)

The clown and Hamlet talk at cross-purposes because the clown does not
make the same assumptions about authority and ownership that Hamlet
does.

HAMLET. What man dost thou dig it for?
CLOWN. For no man sir.
HAMLET. What woman then?
CLOWN. For none neither.
HAMLET. Who is to be buried in't?
CLOWN. One that was a woman, sir; but, rest her soul, she's dead.

>   (*Hamlet*, v. i. 132–8)

Hamlet is told that a thing is what it is, that there is to be no
circumlocution or substitution of terms, that 'we must speak by the
card or equivocation will undo us'. He also is shown the differences in
the way language is used by different social classes. The clown's
refusal to understand Hamlet's question is in fact an act of political
defiance.

HAMLET. By the Lord, Horatio, this three years I have took note of it,
   the age is grown so picked that the toe of the peasant comes so near
   the heel of the courtier he galls his kibe.

>   (*Hamlet*, v. i. 129–33)

The clown/gravedigger insists on choosing his own terms for things, the
materiality of his language expressing his perception of a world defined
by concrete experience. The absoluteness of his categories tends to
dissolve any special claims to pertinence implied by the use of formal
learning, which in this scene is just another speech type and not a
particularly powerful one. The gravedigger can answer questions about

such matters as madness and sanity (it all depends on the environment's standards of rationality) and the durability of bodies (it all depends on how and by what means a man lives). There *are* more things on heaven and earth than are dreamed of in your philosophy, and the gravedigger at this point provides the prince with a particularly rich and instructive illustration of this.

> CLOWN. Here's a skull that hath lien you i'th' earth three and twenty
> years. . . . A pestilence on him for a mad rogue! 'A poured a flagon
> of Rhenish on my head once. This same skull, sir, was, sir, Yorick's
> skull, the King's jester.
>
> (*Hamlet*, v. i. 174–82)

There is no reason to doubt the gravedigger's assertion as to the skull's identity – but there is nothing to confirm it either. A skull presents no identifying features, no countenance, that allows us to recognize individuality. As far as the audience can tell, Yorick's skull looks just like the other skulls tossed about on stage. But this absence of recognizable individual features is what makes the gravedigger's identification 'indisputable'. Identity is a mere surface artifact. The skull 'is' Yorick, although any skull would do equally well as his temporary embodiment.

Hamlet sees in Yorick's skull the pathos of change.

> HAMLET. Alas, poor Yorick! I knew him, Horatio, a fellow of infinite
> jest, of most excellent fancy. He hath borne me on his back a
> thousand times. And now how abhorred in my imagination it is!
> My gorge rises at it. Here hung those lips that I have kissed I know
> not how oft. Where be your gibes now? Your gambols, your
> songs, your flashes of merriment that were wont to set the table on
> a roar?
>
> (*Hamlet*, v. i. 185–93)

The happy festive community to which the prince belonged as a child is dead and buried, an object of nostalgia but not a motive for action.

The old jester is dead, but laughing matter is indestructible; the 'dead' mock the 'living', by revealing the transience of distinct identity. The contemplation of mortality becomes funny.

HAMLET. Imperious Caesar, dead and turned to clay,
Might stop a hole to keep the wind away.
O, that that earth which kept the world in awe
Should patch a wall t'expel the winter's flaw.

(*Hamlet*, v. i. 215–19)

The scene dramatizes the dissolution of individuality, by showing how all categories of social existence, gender, rank, *métier* and so forth, are merely contingent and impermanent. The image of imperial glory is uncrowned, but Caesar's death is not a total loss, for his earthly remains have a more durable utility as cheap building material.

The 'knowledge' Hamlet contemplates in Caesar's return to dust is not definitive. When the funeral procession for Ophelia comes on stage, concern for an individual person is reaffirmed. Imperious Caesar, whose function now is to stop a bunghole, is a suitable object for gaiety and derision, but the pathos of Ophelia's death is not diminished by treating it as a laughing matter. The ceremonies at the grave link death and marriage again, but in a more disturbing way than before. Death proscribes marriage and forestalls the possibility of emergent life. The past, objectified in Yorick's skull, has been 'resurrected' to mock the present. The future, or at least one possible future for Hamlet, has been buried. Death terminates every claim to individuality, destroying the essentially theatrical resources by which individuality is actualized. Despite this, however, Hamlet responds to Ophelia's death not by quietly accepting it but by 'making a scene'.

Although the gravediggers teach indifference to all contingent manifestations of social individuality, Hamlet's will to histrionic self-presentation is forcefully sustained until those histrionics are terminated in the usual way. In a sense, even Hamlet's death is a laughing matter, the result of miscalculation and farcical bungling that leave the succession to Fortinbras and his 'rights of memory'. The transfer of authority is solemnized by Hamlet's ceremonial removal. Like all other similar removals, this one has a funny side disclosed by grotesque laughter which refuses to understand the unfathomable contradictions of political succession.

In Dekker's *The Wonderful Year*, the complexity of succession and the allocation of political power are represented by the dialectic of mirth in funeral and dirge in marriage. The death of Queen Elizabeth is described as a terrifying catastrophe.

Never did the English nation behold so much black worn as there was at her funeral. . . . Oh, what an earthquake is the alteration of a state! Look from the chamber of presence to the farmer's cottage and you shall find nothing but distraction. The whole Kingdom seems a wilderness. . . .[8]

This sudden event plunges the entire nation into grief and, at the same time, inspires the brightest hope.

Oh, it were able to fill a hundred pair of writing tables with notes but to see the parts played in the compass of one hour of this new-found world! Upon Thursday it was treason to cry "God save King James, King of England!" and upon Friday high treason not to cry so. In the morning no voice heard but murmurs and lamentation; at noon nothing but shouts of gladness and triumph . . . as though Providence had enacted that one day those two nations should marry one another, and King James his Coronation is the solemn wedding day.

(*The Wonderful Year*, 39)

The convergence of wedding and funeral, and the 'mixed emotions' inspired by this sequence of events, are essential for an adequate setting forth of succession and its consequent reallocation of political loyalties. The political ambiguity is objectified and explicated jokingly by Dekker.

The Queen's removed in solemn sort,
Yet this was strange and seldom seen:
The Queen used to remove the Court
But now the court removed the Queen.

(*The Wonderful Year*, 37).

The Queen's physical remains are now 'laughing matter', her corpse is an inconvenient object that must be 'removed'. Words and categories of social activity reveal their equivocal, semantically elusive character. The punning language draws attention to the mundane, physical limitations of earthly majesty.

Dekker's narrative account of the death of Elizabeth and the accession of James are followed by the description of an outbreak of plague in London. This 'report' moralizes the succession and sets it in a very much larger context. Against the background of plague and sudden death, the authority of kings and queens is seen in diminishing perspective. Death has a different kind of authority in the affairs of men and women, and that authority often refutes the hopes and expectations of power and privilege. Dekker depicts a wealthy man who flees to his country estate, with his gold loaded on asses and mules, intent on protecting his only son and heir from the pestilence.

> Now is thy soul jocund and thy senses merry. But open thine eyes, thou fool, and behold that darling of thine eye, thy son, turned suddenly into a lump of clay. The hand of pestilence hath smoth him. . . . A tomb must now defend him from tempests. And for that purpose the sweaty hind that digs the rent he pays thee out of the entrails of the earth, he is sent for to convey forth that burden of thy sorrow. But note how thy pride is disdained. That weather-beaten sunburnt drudge that not a month since fawned upon thy worship like a spaniel, and like a bondslave would have stooped lower than thy feet, does now stop his nose at thy presence.
>
> (*The Wonderful Year*, 45)

This is graveyard humor in its strongest admonitory form; pride, arrogance and authority are all overthrown by death. The deferential and obedient 'drudge' is in a position openly to defy his master, because death has turned the social world upside-down. 'All thy gold and silver cannot hire one of those whom before thous didst scorn, to carry the dead body to his last home' (*The Wonderful Year*, 45).

The plague becomes a kind of grim and terrifying Carnival, a serio-comic transformation of the hierarchies of everyday existence.

> The plague is muster-master and marshal of the field; burning fevers, boils, blains and carbuncles the leaders, lieutenants, sergeants and corporals; the main army consisting like Dunkirk's of a mingle-mangle, viz. dumpish mourners, merry sextons, hungry coffin-sellers, scrubbing bearers and nasty grave-makers.
>
> (*The Wonderful Year*, 46)

The plague is, in these terms, a festive occasion and a source of merriment in which 'the three bald sextons of St. Giles, St. Sepulchre's and St. Olave's ruled the roast' (*The Wonderful Year*, 47–8). Grief over

Elizabeth's death coincides paradoxically with rejoicing over James's accession. A similar dialectic operates within the pestilence, which reallocates wealth and is therefore as much an occasion for mirth as it is for mourning. Among Dekker's 'merry tales' is the story of a tinker who 'valiantly' agrees to remove the body of a dead Londoner from a tavern and take it away for burial.

> . . . the tinker, knowing that worms needed no apparel saving only sheets, stripped him stark naked; but first dived nimbly into his pockets to see what linings they had, assuring himself that a Londoner would not wander so far without silver. His hopes were of the right stamp, for from one of his pockets he drew a leathern bag with £7 in it. This music made the tinker's heart dance. He quickly tumbled the man into the grave . . . [and] back again comes he through the town, crying aloud "Have ye anymore Londoners to bury? Hey down a down derry!" Have ye any more Londoners to bury?   (*The Wonderful Year*, 63)

The grotesque laughter of Dekker's pamphlet, and of the Porter and Gravedigger scenes, is an expression of a grim, barely suppressed *Schadenfreude* in which death is seen as an irresistible force that will 'expropriate the expropriators'. Awareness of death and of the precariousness of day-to-day existence is pervasive in every cultural setting in Elizabethan society. In plebeian culture this awareness can give rise to a vindictive sense of pleasure and satisfaction, especially in relation to the funerals of the great and powerful. More importantly, however, death is funny because death is fundamentally ambiguous. In the context of plebeian culture, with its constant awareness and rearticulation of 'the limits of the possible', death is never seen or represented as an isolated, individual event. Death is, on the contrary, continually reabsorbed and recycled into the rhythm of everyday life.

CHAPTER 12
THE FESTIVE AGON:
THE POLITICS OF CARNIVAL

R EPRESENTATION of larger forms of political life conforms to the same popular festive heuristic that interprets all local and circumscribed political form, and social process. This 'pathos of radical change and renewal' is given narrative form in dramatic actions organized around royal or political succession, and the successful or unsuccessful transfer of authority. Every transfer or reallocation of authority is accomplished by means of more or less stylized violence.[1] In a number of important plays, both chronicle histories and tragedies, a 'foolish' king is thrashed, uncrowned, and finally victimized and murdered by an energetic rival. The foolishness may appear gradually, as in *Richard II*, where Richard's arrogant disregard for public responsibility and his general unfitness to rule lead to humiliation, abjection and death. On the other hand, the foolish king may be a kind of devil-buffoon from the start, as in the case of *Richard III*. In either case, the persecution and eventual death of the foolish king has a sacred character, as well as a purely historical and contingent meaning.[2] These images of royal abjection and victimization do not have the purely redressive and exemplary features of an actual ritual. The violent uncrowning of the royal martyr or royal villain is invariably accompanied by a more generalized, pervasive social violence or civil war, 'the intestine shock / And furious close of civil butchery'. The relationship between victimized king and victimized kingdom is complex and elusive, as is the relationship among war, civil butchery and the state of affairs known as peace.

Although images of violent discontinuity and disruption saturate political drama beginning with *Gorboduc* and throughout the canon of well-known texts, analysis of these forms has in general proceeded from a hierarchized opposition between order and disorder, where order is the normative term.[3] It has frequently been implied, or suggested, that individual plays, and in the case of Shakespeare's 'tetralogies' whole cycles of plays, are organized in accordance with strategies similar to those of official pageantry. They consist of extended political anti-masques eventually routed by the appearance of a legitimate king. In such a project, disorder or misrule is a politically marginal impulse or tendency, a temporary and merely contingent rift or hiatus in the plenitude of social and cosmic harmony. C.L. Barber, in discussing this problem as it applies to the two parts of *Henry IV*, argues that 'the dynamic relation of comedy and serious action is saturnalian rather than satiric. . . . the misrule works, through the whole dramatic rhythm, to consolidate rule.'[4] This view of conflict recuperates the marginal experience of misrule by making it the instrument whereby rule, order or domination might be better defended and secured. This humanistic account of the history plays is part of a much wider cultural and political theodicy, variously articulated in respect to Shakespeare as 'the universe's hospitality to life' (Barber); a 'background of order' that gives meaning to 'pictures of civil war and disorder' (Tillyard); 'the unresolvable complexity of life [present to] the fullest human consciousness' (Rabkin).

Analysis of Shakespeare's plays that proceeds in accordance with one of these strategies will certainly appreciate structural complexity and will even take note of the failure of certain represented actions to conform with the norms of an ordered universe and a correspondingly ordered civil society. Nevertheless, conflict and misrule are interpreted as relatively small and localized turbulence that in the end cannot be permitted to expand beyond certain limits. This interpretive strategy is predicated on a commitment to order and to authority, as the necessary conditions for individual and collective well-being.

The hierarchical opposition order/disorder or rule/misrule coincides with certain explicitly political assumptions. Most prominent among these is the critical presupposition that the nation-state is the natural and necessary political form emerging from some kind of archaic disorder and consolidating itself against marginal forms of residual feudal anarchy or popular resistance. The English nation and the consolidation of its state apparatus were certainly substantially accomplished and very much part of the objective conditions of social life at the time Shakespeare's plays were written. In general, critics have argued from the implicit premise that it is definitely better for the state to exist than for it not to exist, even though the state is not the only form that civil society can take. Given this presupposition, that orderly collective life is only possible within the nation-state, interpretation of the plays may proceed to such secondary but consequential problems as 'the specialty of rule', the precarious historical transitions from ceremonially based kingship to practical and administratively based kingship, and the compelling urgency of Lear's division of the kingdom. Each of these questions is a way of thematizing the conviction that the state is a plenitude and, in fact, the only plenitude that could ever exist in the sphere of political life. A united kingdom is implicitly – and sometimes explicitly – asserted to be the exclusive guarantor of safety and of peace. The only legitimate purpose of any political activity, including kingship, therefore, is to sustain that united kingdom against all local and marginal initiatives and resistances.

Rule against misrule, the state against civil war, correspond to two additional hierarchized oppositions – everyday life/holiday and serious speech/jesting speech. Both of these distinctions correspond to governing categories of a real, substantive order, objectified in the state, and marginal disorder, objectified in disparate and disunited fragmentary social practices. The reintegration of the marginal term through such conceptions as 'saturnalian clarification', 'complementary perspective', 'burlesque or jesting counterpoint to a serious discourse', nevertheless insists on a subordinate and purely instrumental role for the marginal term. Thus to speak of 'clownish inversions' clearly implies that the unclownish version is right side up. And even the argument that folk festivals and popular theater are 'skeptical and anti-authoritarian' concedes that such activities are already peripheral to authority and to real political life.[5]

The characteristic dramatic images of political life iterated throughout chronicle history plays and tragedies include scenes of exaggerated, grotesque and often farcical violence; the suffering and abjection of a royal victim; treachery, usurpation and assassination, together with civil butchery, as the preferred means and as the inevitable consequence of every succession. As texts, many of these plays seem inversive in respect to the relationship between rule and misrule. Misrule and disorder are the pervasive, objective conditions of political life that correspond to the disunited fullness of the production, distribution and exchange of social wealth. Misrule and localized conflict on a small scale may be perfectly compatible with a general condition of relative social well-being; and the overthrow and abjection of the royal victim an acceptable and sometimes enjoyable element of business as usual.

The critical recognition of misrule and Carnival provides an alternative to a political theodicy of the nation-state. Misrule is not a merely negative idea, however, as in Jan Kott's conception of an absurd 'Grand Mechanism'.[6] The rhythmic succession of Carnivalesque uncrowning and renewal, the 'pathos of radical change', is the 'second life' of the people, a form of real politics, an ethos, a 'mode of production' existentially prior to the state and its administrative apparatus. This second life is lived in the public squares and also in the theater as a public space; it is mimetically represented in the forms of political drama. Bakhtin elaborates this 'second life' in his account of 'the folkloric bases of the Rabelaisian Chronotope', describing it as an alternative experience of time.

> This time is collective, that is, it is differentiated and measured only by the events of *collective* life; everything that exists in this time exists solely for the collective. The progression of events in an individual life has not yet been isolated (the interior time of an individual life does not yet exist, the individuum lives completely on the surface, within a collective whole). Both labor and the consuming of things are collective.
>
> This is the time of labor. Everyday life and consumption are not isolated from the labor and production process. Time is measured by labor events. . . . This sense of time works itself out in a collective battle of labor against nature. . . .
>
> This is the time of productive growth. It is a time of growth, blossoming, fruit-bearing, ripening, fruitful increase, issue. The passage of time does not destroy or diminish but rather multiplies and increases the quantity of valuable things. . . . [The] single items that perish are neither individualized nor isolated; they are

lost in the whole growing and multiplying mass of new lives. . . .
This time is profoundly spatial and concrete. It is not separated from the earth or from nature. It, as well as the entire life of the human being, is all on the surface.[7]

The culture of common people or plebeians in its political, social, philosophical and artistic manifestations is already everywhere; government and the nation-state as institutional forms are latecomers. Holiday, or holy-day, Carnival and misrule are not isolated episodes in a uniform continuum of regularly scheduled real-life: the experience of holiday pervades the year and defines its rhythm.[8]

The theater in its 'mature' or 'developed form' is an institution 'invented' by Jonson and by many others to oppose and displace a theater already practiced and appreciated throughout plebeian culture. Jonson, as the exemplary 'institution maker' proceeds by making a series of exclusions, redefining activities characteristic of traditional theatricality as aberrant and marginal. This project is carried out against the background of a very much larger and even more protracted struggle, in which the centralized authority of the state comes into being against social and political life already lived, and by means of traditionally dispersed, collective authority. One of the many engagements in that struggle concerns the local tradition of midsummer watches in London.

> This midsummer watch was thus accustomed yearly, time out of mind, until the year 1539, the 31st of Henry VIII, in which year, on the 8th of May, a great muster was made by the citizens of the Mile's End, all in bright harness, with coats of white silk, or cloth and chains of gold, in three great battles, to the number of fifteen thousand. . . . King Henry, then considering the great charges of the citizens for the furniture of this unusual muster, forbade the marching watch provided for at Midsummer for that year, which being once laid down was not raised again till the year 1548.[9]

The midsummer watch was, among other things, a procession of armed citizenry organized at the initiative of the common people. It was suppressed once in 1539, and again after the term of office as Lord Mayor of Sir John Gresham, during the reign of Edward VI. The initiative for this practice did not die out entirely, however, and, according to Stow, attempts were made to revive it during Elizabeth's reign. The antiquity and the scope of participation of such a manifestly powerful and independent urban politics could not in the end be compatible with the coalition of interests that support the centralized state, whose representatives find reasons quietly to discourage such activities. But the political life of plebeian culture is not effaced by these tactics; it persists in other popular festive events, in processional life, and in the theatrical performance of dramatic texts where elements of a 'second life' in the pattern of misrule provide the organizing scheme for exemplary, mimetic actions. A central instance of this Carnival or popular festive structuration of politically significant narrative is the use of characteristic festive personae and the festive agon or Battle of Carnival and Lent as a narrative scheme governing both comic and serious actions. The festive agon reinterprets political succession, and other transitional procedures, as the double and reciprocal thrashing and expulsion of the Carnivalesque and Lenten tendencies.

The festive agon is fully played out in *Twelfth Night*, as Carnival misrule in the persons of Toby and his companions – the gull, the clown and the mischievous servant – contends with Lent in the person of Malvolio. This is often referred to as the 'comic sub-plot' – a series of episodes that constitute a marginal, non-serious commentary on the main action. The position taken here, however, is that the festive agon *is* the 'main action,' continuous with the wider world indicated in the clown's 'return from the outside' and in Malvolio's Parthian shot – 'I'll be revenged on the whole pack of you'. The confrontation between the Carnivalesque and the Lenten principles is represented in the long drinking scene, where Toby, Andrew, Feste and Maria gather to enjoy hospitality with drink, laughter and singing. The scene begins by transgressive rescheduling of the normal order of day and night typical of Carnival and other forms of misrule.

> SIR TO. Approach, Sir Andrew. Not to be abed after midnight is to be up betimes; and 'diluculo surgere', thou knowst——
>
> SIR AND. Nay by my troth, I know not. But I know to be up late is to be up late.
>
> SIR TO. A false conclusion. I hate it as an unfilled can. To be up after midnight, and to go to bed then, is early, so that to go to bed after midnight is to go to bed betimes. Does not our life consist of four elements?

SIR AND. Faith, so they say, but I think it rather consists of eating and
drinking.

SIR TO. Thou'rt a scholar. Let us therefore eat and drink.

(*Twelfth Night*, II. iii. 1–14)

This symposium combines bodily satisfaction with philosophical debate
and dialogue. The Carnivalesque principle of knowledge operates here,
as both crudely material, literal description and ingeniously transgressive redescriptions are equally necessary to an adequate account of 'our
life'. The simple-minded, tautological view that 'late is late' is a 'false
conclusion' that is none the less compatible with the abusive casuistry
that maintains that 'late is early'. The hateful 'unfilled' tautology of the
simple-minded Andrew that seems to require habits more abstemious
than Toby likes is 'filled up' by the same simple-minded character's view
that man's life is 'eating and drinking', rather than the four elements.
Harmonizable disagreement and the 'abundance of the material principle' are celebrated in jokes and song until the intervention of
Malvolio, whose Lenten severity is mandated by his perfectly cogent
understanding of precedence and due order.

MAL. My masters, are you mad? Or what are you? Have you no wit,
manners, nor honesty, but to gabble like tinkers at this time of
night? Do ye make an alehouse of my lady's house that ye squeak
out your coziers catches without any mitigation or remorse of
voice. Is there no respect of place, persons, nor time in you?

(*Twelfth Night*, II. iii. 92–9)

Irrespective of person, place or time, the rejoinder offered by Carnival is,
as always, a celebration of food and drink.

SIR TO. . . . Art any more than a steward? Dost thou think because
thou art virtuous, there shall be no more cakes and ale?

(*Twelfth Night*, II. iii. 122–5)

As the festive agon unfolds, this acrimonious feeling gives rise to the
active persecution, humiliation and confinement of Malvolio. But the
pattern of festive agon is not compatible with asymmetrical, one-sided
and conclusive outcomes. The combatants, Carnival and Lent, each have
certain obligations, in particular the obligation to be thrashed. Toby

organizes the persecution of Malvolio and then in a more improvisatory entertainment orchestrates the farcical duel between Andrew and Viola, the boy-woman. The compensatory thrashing of Toby is given by Sebastian near the end of the play. Toby, escorted by the clown, appears briefly to display his bloody coxcomb and is then escorted to his bed. This brief appearance is important, as it visibly and materially confirms the fact of Toby's thrashing and also the importance of that wider world offstage where significant events that have the potential to upset the plots and the intentions enacted on the stage continually occur. Malvolio also has some scores to settle which he will attend to offstage. 'And thus the whirligig of time brings in his revenges.' The battle of angry Carnival and sullen, vindictive Lent is not concluded in the represented world of Illyria, nor is it ever concluded in the world offstage.

The Battle of Carnival and Lent is an explicit structuring device in the two parts of *Henry IV*. These plays are seriocomic, anachronistic recreations of epically distanced chronicle history within the familiar *mise-en-scène* of the streets and taverns of contemporary London. Falstaff's girth, his perpetual drinking and eating, his disrespect of time, place and person are typical features of Carnival as a festive persona. His companion and Lenten antagonist, a character known variously as Hal, Harry Monmouth and the Prince of Wales, is a 'stockfish' who continually chastises Falstaff and admonishes him in respect of a less abundant future. Falstaff, like Carnival, is an ambivalent and grotesque figure. Hal, miming his own father, characterizes Falstaff as a vicious and decaying fat old man.

> PRINCE. There is a devil haunts thee in the likeness of an old fat man, a
> tun of man is thy companion. Why dost thou converse with that
> trunk of humors, that bolting hutch of beastliness, that swollen
> parcel of dropsies, that huge bombard of sack, that stuffed cloak bag
> of guts, that roasted Manningtree ox with the pudding in his belly.
>
> (*1 Henry IV*, II. iv. 493–8)

This denunciatory language, in which Falstaff is mainly described as a series of large vessels or containers filled with vile, excremental matter, is suddenly interrupted with an image of savory, festive abundance. This is the language Bakhtin identifies as belonging to 'lower bodily stratum', in which degraded excremental images coexist with images of the digestive organs that consume food – dead meat – and turn it into 'beastliness' which is both living flesh and bodily waste.[10]

Falstaff is socially as well as ethically ambivalent. He is Sir John, but prefers to name himself Jack, the most versatile and familiar name for every nameless hero of plebeian culture, including, paradoxically, Jack-a-Lent.

> Of Jack-an-apes I list not to indite
> Nor of Jack Daw my goose's quill shall write;
> Of Jack of Newbury I will not repeat,
> Nor Jack of both sides, nor of Skip-Jack neat.
> To praise the turnspit Jack my Muse is mum,
> Nor of the entertainment of Jack Drum
> I'll not rehearse: nor of Jack Dog, Jack Date,
> Jack fool, or Jack-a-Dandy, I relate:
> Nor of black Jacks at gentle buttery bars,
> Whose liquor oftentimes breeds household wars:
> Nor Jack of Dover that grand jury Jack,
> Nor Jack Sauce (the worst knave amongst the pack).
>
> (*Iacke-a-Lente*, 3)

As Falstaff's apology for himself suggests, his iniquitous conduct is typical of a wider world where 'every man jack' has to make his way in the best way he can manage.

> FAL. . . . If to be old and merry be a sin, then many an old host that I know is damned. If to be fat be to be hated, then Pharaoh's lean kine are to be loved. No, my good lord. Banish Peto, banish Bardolph, banish Poins. But for sweet Jack Falstaff, kind Jack Falstaff, true Jack Falstaff, valiant Jack Falstaff, and therefore more valiant, being as he is, old Jack Falstaff, banish not him thy Harry's company, banish not him thy Harry's company. Banish plump jack, and banish all the world.
>
> (*1 Henry IV*, II. iv. 517–26)

Falstaff multiplies and refracts his identity to blend with 'every man jack'; his plea is also an admonition. To proscribe Carnival is the undoubtedly fatal project of 'banishing all the world', a consolidation of rule by the ruthless and permanent suppression of misrule. As Falstaff hints, however, misrule is the amoral and ungovernable pattern of social life itself.

Falstaff's companionable antagonist and eventual 'successor' as Carnival king is Hal, the exemplary embodiment of Lenten civil policy. Both Carnival and Lent are grotesque, double-valued personae who enjoy temporary and limited sovereignty and who submit to thrashing and to abjection. Hal's project, however, is eventually to break the rhythmic alternation between the abundance of the material principle embodied in Carnival and the abstemious social discipline embodied in Lent by establishing a permanent sovereignty of Lenten civil policy. This project is very much out in the open, publicly acknowledged in respect of the contemporaneous space-time of the performance, as Hal informs the audience of his overall intentions.

> PRINCE. I know you all, and will a while uphold
> The unyoked humor of your idleness. . . .
> If all the year were playing holidays,
> To sport would be as tedious as to work.
> But when they seldom come, they wished-for come,
> And nothing pleaseth but rare accidents.
>
> *(1 Henry IV*, I. iii. 218–30)

Under the supervision of a comprehensive social discipline, a holiday will be an isolated episode, a limited release that is all the more appreciated for its rarity. This is the social discipline that Hal undertakes to establish. His project is, in respect of the represented, epically distanced narrative action, covert and unacknowledged. To secure the conditions of Lenten civil policy, Hal plays out his role of Jack-a-Lent, the festive, transgressive and feasting side of the Lenten reality. He wins support from 'all the lads in east cheap', a constituency that certainly includes a number of butcher's apprentices. In the politics of authoritarian populism, 'Lenten butchery' emerges as a sanctioned response to a putative need for social order. The 'Lenten butcher with a license to kill' emerges from an ambiguous and obscure status to become the necessary instrument of prudential political foresight. The civil state arrogates to itself the authority both to proscribe 'Lenten butchery' and to sanction it for the sake of larger social purposes. In order to accomplish this comprehensive administrative project, it is not sufficient merely to thrash Carnival and misrule. All competing local authority or suspensions of authority must be either permanently abolished or incorporated into the machinery of civil policy and the administration of social discipline. Hal's success in accomplishing this project – revealing himself to be the true prince – is ominous in the context of a wider world. He has evaded his obligation to submit to compensatory thrashing and abjection. The rhythm that requires Lenten civil policy to be ceremonially expelled in the mock-trial of Jack-a-Lent is a piece of unfinished cultural and political business in the celebratory imagery of the final scenes of each of the *Henry IV* plays.

The political action of *Hamlet* unfolds against a wider horizon of geopolitical struggle characterized by military thrust and counter-thrust, diplomatic missions, and intellectual and cultural exchange. From the represented center in the court of Denmark the characters move to a wider world offstage, into particular locales known as Norway, France, Germany, England and Poland. This geography is recognizable as the *mise-en-scène* of the northern Renaissance, and equally as the 'theater' in which the war for religious and political hegemony in the region of the Baltic and the North Sea will be waged.[11] In *Hamlet* the demographic and political pressures of this wider world are depicted as acting at a distance upon the intrigues of the Danish court. Within that more narrowly constituted setting, a struggle for the Danish succession is enacted as a seriocomic variant of the festive agon, with Claudius adopting the identity, the gestures, the pattern of feeling typical of Carnival misrule, and Hamlet adopting the identity, first of a sober, Lenten civil policy, and second of an antic Jack-a-Lent. The characters adopt these personae, not because either one of them as a character enjoys any motivated relationship with authentic popular energies, but because these personae are the resources that theater makes available for constituting the image of political and dynastic struggle.

Claudius, in the usurped finery of royal majesty, is a Carnivalesque Lord of Misrule, a sovereign figure of authority who is also pleased to indulge in drinking bouts and indiscreet public fondlings. Claudius makes a mockery of kingship by appearing in public in the robes of the 'real' king, but this mockery is complex and ambivalent. As a Lord of Misrule he is both the object of derision by virtue of the falseness of his claims and the agent of derision directed against the office he holds and its previous incumbent. He has killed and buried his predecessor, and replaced him in the queen's bed. His coronation and marriage are an occasion of Carnival mirth – an affirmation of the abundance of the material principle in both its sexual and its gustatory aspects. In his first

scene Claudius proclaims a period of festivity and celebration, a protracted interlude characterized by the mixed emotions that accompany
the wedding feast/funeral obsequy contiguous in every political
succession.

> CLAUDIUS. Though yet of Hamlet our dear brother's death
> The memory be green, and that it is befitted
> To bear our hearts in grief, and our whole kingdom
> To be contracted in one brow of woe,
> Yet so far hath discretion fought with nature
> That we with wisest sorrow think on him
> Together with remembrance of ourselves.
> Therefore our sometime sister, now our Queen,
> Th' imperial jointress to this warlike state,
> Have we, as 'twere with a defeated joy,
> With mirth in funeral, and with dirge in marriage,
> With an auspicious and a dropping eye,
> In equal scale weighing delight and dole,
> Taken to wife.
>
> (*Hamlet*, I. ii. 1–14)

In this speech Claudius articulates the political scope of the festive agon
as a practice in which the violent and precarious procedures of succession
may be securely negotiated. Claudius compares the mortality of the king
with the continuity of his office and affirms that the continuing vitality
of society is independent of the transitoriness of individuals. The death
of the old gives scope to the new and emergent. By marrying Gertrude,
Claudius objectifies this principle of succession and renewal at a sexual
and bodily level. The disturbing and offensive candor of that sexuality
'brings down' the projects and ambitions of kingship to the material and
earthly level of appetite and human desire.

Festive mixed emotions, the linking of death and marriage, and the
reinterpretation of succession in terms of domestic sexuality are Carnivalesque patterns that Claudius appropriates in order to reinforce and
legitimate his own ambiguously sanctioned authority. Claudius does not
directly acknowledge himself as a Lord of Misrule; his language is a
philosophical 'transformation upward' of Carnival. Claudius is a peculiar
embodiment of Carnival: he presides over the indecorous celebration
that links the living and the dead, but he has no connection with the

whole life of the people. His Carnival is a private feast – it does not embrace any wider social world.

Hamlet's project as the embodiment of Lenten civil policy is to pursue, to thrash and finally to uncrown Carnival. As Hamlet quickly realizes, misrule is pervasive, and the project is daunting in its scope and its resistance to the intervention of any organized political planning. He makes the pursuit of sexuality, the domestic legitimation of carnal appetite, the particular focus of his persecutory, Lenten function. The task requires him to kill, and indeed, indirectly or directly, he is responsible for a number of violent deaths. However, though he is a sanctioned Lenten butcher, with the particular duty of executing the murderer of his own father, it is not clear that this act of violent uncrowning is to be a restitution of orderly and stable social rule. As the play unfolds, there are numerous suggestions that the action of revenge against the murderer of a father is not so much a redressive action as it is a purely iterative and compulsive reoccurrence of the festive agon, refracted through endless historical time and space. Hamlet is then just a local and transitory incarnation of the dark persecutory figure already anticipated by ancient literature and shared as a textual memory by both Hamlet and the Player King.

> HAMLET. The rugged Pyrrhus, he whose sable arms,
>   Black as his purpose, did the night resemble
>   When he lay couched in the ominous horse,
>   Hath now this dread and black complexion smeared
>   With heraldry more dismal. Head to foot
>   Now is he total gules, horridly tricked
>   With blood of fathers, mothers, daughters, sons.
> (Hamlet, II. ii. 474–80)

The struggle in the Danish court between Claudius as Carnival misrule and Hamlet as Lenten civil policy is very greatly diminished against the horizon of the wider world. In the perpetual battle of Carnival and Lent this is an insignificant episode, an event of purely ephemeral interest. From the standpoint of plebeian culture, every succession has just such an ephemeral and iterative character. The forms of the festive agon offer the possibility for the containment within tolerable bounds of the social violence that characterizes all procedures of political transition.

In *King Lear*, the Battle of Carnival and Lent is acted out in an extremely painful variant. The central scenes showing the 'liminary outcasts' on the heath are a procession of defeated and expelled Carnival, pursued by the temporarily victorious energies of Lenten civil policy.[12] It is easy to recognize Lear as a figure of Carnival misrule. From the very beginning of the narrative action he has renounced all the serious worldly duties of kingship in order to embrace only the outward manifestation and amenities of his position. This withdrawal from the arduous political efforts of kingship into the celebration of festive hospitality is objectified in Lear's determination to retain his company of one hundred knights. This is, in effect, to 'keep Christmas' or to celebrate hospitality all the year long, and the daughters who must bear the expense of such an elaborate practice of social generosity object most forcefully. In reply to these considerations of economic necessity, Lear replies: 'Oh reason not the need. Our basest beggars / Are in the poorest thing superfluous.' This is Lear's own refusal to understand the virtues of fiscal prudence and, equally, his unyielding commitment to the traditional values that demand the personal loyalty of his retainers and his reciprocal material obligations to them. The painful domestic quarrel with the two elder daughters over the scope of hospitality to be offered to the knights eventually leads to the expulsion, abjection and victimization of the king. That process of abjection begins with the initial processes of uncrowning at the beginning of the action.

The fool draws attention to Lear's transformation into a mock-king when he suggests 'sirrah, you were best take my coxcomb', and then elaborates on his gesture.

> That Lord that counseled thee
> To give away thy land
> Come place him here by me
> Do thou for him stand
> The sweet and bitter fool
> Will presently appear
> The one is motley here
> The other found out there.
>
> (*King Lear*, I. iv. 154–61)

Even as a Carnival, King Lear's sovereignty is brief and painful. He has only limited scope for the celebration of hospitality before he and his motley retinue are stripped, humiliated and driven out into the countryside. His train is gradually diminished as the recipients of festive abundance decrease in number from 100 to 50 and then to 25, to 10, and to nothing. The capacity of Carnival to sustain hospitality, to perpetuate the abundance of the material principle, is subjected to the radical necessity of unimproved nature, where the body is maximally exposed and where conditions are maximally privative. The liminary outcasts – the mock-king, fool, madman and the Carnival bully (Kent or 'Caius') – nevertheless recreate a form of social reality even under conditions of extreme physical duress.

> LEAR. Come on, my boy. How dost, my boy? Art cold?
> I am cold myself. Where is this straw, my fellow?
> The art of our necessities is strange,
> That can make vile things precious. Come, your hovel.
> Poor fool and knave, I have one part in my heart
> That's sorry yet for thee.
> (King Lear, III. ii. 69–73)

In this radically diminished social and economic *mise-en-scène*, the obligations of hospitality as a sharing of resources is still a capable and in fact a favored response.

Lear has been driven out on to the heath by the voices of Lenten severity, social discipline and civil policy. His daughter Goneril accuses him of wanton riot and misrule.

> GONERIL. Not only, sir, this your all-licensed fool,
> But other of your insolent retinue
> Do hourly carp and quarrel, breaking forth
> In rank and not to be endured riots . . .
> Here do you keep a hundred knights and squires,
> Men so disordered, so deboshed and bold,
> That this our court, infected with their manners,
> Shows like a riotous in. Epicurism and lust
> Make it more like a tavern or a brothel
> Than a graced palace.
> (King Lear, I. iv. 220–3, 262–7)

Once Lear as Carnival king has been driven away, however, Lenten severity is unmasked; the misrule created by Lear is not succeeded by peace and harmonious order. There is, on the contrary, a continuation and intensification of violence.

The Battle of Carnival and Lent is elaborated as each of the warring principles is subjected to trial by proxy by its antagonist. Each of the trial scenes is a ludicrous travesty of the other, and both are travesties of the dignity of justice as conventionally represented. In the first of these mock-trial scenes, Lear's guilty daughters are tried *in absentia* for filial treachery by judges impersonated by a fool and a madman. At the same time the victims sit in judgment on their persecutors. In the second trial, Gloucester, who is guilty of lechery, is tried for treason; the guilty sit in judgment upon the wrongfully accused though not entirely innocent party. Both the trial scenes are painful *and* funny; both represent the code-switching and uncrowning of 'serious' and 'responsible' ideology by the topsy-turvy discourse of Carnival. From this standpoint, neither the noble purposes nor the ignoble ambitions of kingship are taken very seriously. Lear is constrained and suffered to understand the world in these terms by virtue of his own abjection, and to accept himself as an ephemeral and transitory image of authority answerable finally to the cry 'poor Tom's a-cold'.

The multiple deaths at the end of the play do not create a reconciliatory image of 'saturnalian' clarification. The representation of dead bodies is not, on the other hand, a nihilistic image of an absurd and meaningless universe. The patterns of social violence have been completed; the succession and transfer of authority have been achieved. Secular authority, in both its majestic, charismatic and its practical, administrative manifestations, has been changed into a festive effigy and symbolically destroyed. The most powerful images of 'good' and 'evil' have been thrashed and murdered – all except Edgar, the most versatile and most enigmatic figure in this violent Carnival mummery. Edgar is a master of disguise and an accomplished mimic of many diverse speech types. He is able to play all parts, from wretched naked victim to chivalric hero. The dispossessed brother is mysterious because, unlike the usurping 'natural' brother, he has no fixed and final individuality. He is the *refus d'identité*. After the festive agon is concluded, the energy of a resourceful improvisatory competence is the only authority that remains. This same resourceful repertoire of strategic responses to struggle and change is the characteristic energy both of theater and of popular festive form.

Carnival is not anti-authoritarian. But Carnival is a general refusal to understand any fixed and final allocation of authority. It is – equally – a refusal to understand any fixed and final allocation of social wealth or to concede that any expropriation of production proceeds in accordance with an uncontested and uncontestable natural order. This refusal arises, not from ignorance, but from knowledge. The monopoly of knowledge retrospectively claimed for education and 'the educated' is itself a willful suppression of the disparate forms in which knowledge can be objectified and disseminated. The vocabulary of Carnival and the Carnivalesque is the 'other' form of knowledge, a comprehensive 'art and science' of social and collective life. Clowning, devilment, abusive and summary popular justice, hospitality and entertainment, and the deployment of Carnival artifacts such as masks and giants, are the tactical instruments of a resourceful collectivity with an active and independent will to sustain itself. Carnival is put into operation as resistance to any tendency to absolutize authority, and to the disruptive radicalizations of social life proposed and implemented by powerful ruling elites. This resistance is purposeful, and proceeds in accordance with the ethical imperatives of plebeian culture. According to these imperatives, differential and hierarchical allocations of wealth and power are not indiscriminately resisted out of a vague and inarticulate principle of equality. But such allocations must answer the purposes of collective life embodied in the philosophical doctrine of 'every horse his loaf', an expression of the deeply entrenched expectation that society will sustain each of its members. For plebeian culture, theater is valued mainly as a social institution where this ethos of collective life may be sustained and experimentally renewed.

Notes

ABBREVIATIONS

EETS   Early English Text Society
ELH   *ELH: A Journal of English Literary History*
ELR   *English Literary Renaissance*
NLB   New Left Books
NLH   *New Literary History*
RES   *The Review of English Studies*
SP   *Studies in Philology*
SQ   *Shakespeare Quarterly*
TLS   *The Times Literary Supplement*

PART 1   THEORETICAL PERSPECTIVES

1 Muriel Bradbrook, *The Rise of the Common Player* (Cambridge, Mass.: Harvard University Press, 1964); Robert Weimann, *Shakespeare and the Popular Tradition in the Theater* (Baltimore: Johns Hopkins University Press, 1978); Victor Turner, 'Variations on a Theme of Liminality', in *Secular Ritual*, ed. Sally F. Moore and Barbara G. Myerhoff (Amsterdam: Van Gorcum, 1977), 35–57; Louis A. Montrose, 'The Purpose of

Playing: Reflections on a Shakespearean Anthropology', *Helios*, NS 8 (1980), 51–74.
2 John Stow, *A Survey of London*, ed. H. Morley (London: G. Routledge & Sons, 1890), 370.
3 Stow, *A Survey of London*, 119.
4 Walter Benjamin, 'Theses on the Philosophy of History', in *Illuminations*, ed. Hannah Arendt (New York: Schocken Books, 1969), 256.

CHAPTER 1   PLAYING THE OLD WORKS HISTORICALLY

1 Bertolt Brecht, *The Messingkauf Dialogues*, trans. John Willnet (London: Eyre Methuen, 1965), 63.
2 Brecht, *Messingkauf Dialogues*, 101.
3 Brecht, *Messingkauf Dialogues*, 63
4 E.M.W. Tillyard, *The Elizabethan World Picture* (New York: Vintage Books, 1948), vii.
5 E.M.W. Tillyard, *Shakespeare's History Plays* (London: Chatto & Windus, 1961), 21.
6 Tillyard, *Elizabethan World Picture*, 13. Emphasis added.
7 Norman Rabkin, *Shakespeare and the Common Understanding* (New York: Free Press, 1967), 12.
8 Rabkin, *Common Understanding*, 12
9 Rabkin, *Common Understanding*, 27. Emphasis added.
10 Norman Rabkin, 'Rabbits, Ducks, and *Henry V*', *SQ* 28 (1977), 279–97.
11 Stephen Greenblatt, *Renaissance Self-Fashioning: From More to Shakespeare* (Chicago: University of Chicago Press, 1980), 113.
12 Greenblatt, *Renaissance Self-Fashioning*, 120.
13 Jonathan Dollimore, *Radical Tragedy: Religion, Ideology and Power in the Drama of Shakespeare and his Contemporaries* (Brighton, Sussex: Harvester Press, 1984), 4.
14 Dollimore, *Radical Tragedy*, 267.
15 D.W. Robertson, 'Some Observations on Method in Literary Studies', *NLH* 1 (1969), 21–33.
16 D.W. Robertson, 'A Medievalist Looks at Hamlet', in *Essays in Medieval Culture* (Princeton: Princeton University Press, 1980), 312–31.
17 Dollimore, *Radical Tragedy*, 29.
18 Michael Holquist, 'Answering as Authoring: Mikhail Bakhtin's Trans-Linguistics', *Critical Inquiry* 10 (1983), 307–20; Edward W. Said, *Beginnings: Intention and Method* (New York: Basic Books, 1975), 133.
19 P.N. Medvedev and M.M. Bakhtin, *The Formal Method in Literary Scholarship: A Critical Introduction to Sociological Poetics*, trans. Albert J. Wehrle (Baltimore: Johns Hopkins University Press, 1978), 18.
20 Medvedev and Bakhtin, *Sociological Poetics*, 19.
21 Holquist, 'Answering as Authoring'.
22 Medvedev and Bakhtin, *Sociological Poetics*, 7.

23 Mikhail Bakhtin, *The Dialogic Imagination*, trans. Michael Holquist and Caryl Emerson (Austin: University of Texas Press, 1981), 263.
24 Bakhtin, *The Dialogic Imagination*, Glossary, 426.
25 Bakhtin, *The Dialogic Imagination*, 7.
26 Mikhail Bakhtin, *Rabelais and His World*, trans. Hélène Iswolsky (Cambridge, Mass.: MIT Press, 1968), 301.
27 Bakhtin, *The Dialogic Imagination*, 132.
28 Bakhtin, *Rabelais and His World*, 275.

CHAPTER 2   THE SOCIAL FUNCTION OF FESTIVITY

1 Jean-Pierre Dupuy, 'Randonnées carnavalesques', in *Ordres et désordres: Enquête sur un nouveau paradigme* (Paris: Éditions du Seuil, 1982), 187 ff.
2 Johan Huizinga, *Homo Ludens: A Study of the Play Elements in Culture* (New York: Harper & Row, 1970); Roger Caillois, *Man, Play, and Games*, trans. Meyer Barash (New York: Free Press, 1961); Edmund Leach, *Rethinking Anthropology* (London: Athlone Press, 1961).
3 E.K. Chambers, *The English Folk Play* (Oxford: Clarendon Press, 1933), 221.
4 Emile Durkheim, *The Elementary Forms of the Religious Life*, trans. J. Swain (London: George Allen & Unwin, 1915), 348.
5 Durkheim, *Elementary Forms*, 347.
6 Durkheim, *Elementary Forms*, 349.
7 Arnold Van Gennep, *The Rites of Passage*, trans. Monika Vizedom and Gebrielle Caffee (Chicago: University of Chicago Press, 1960), 10–11.
8 Van Gennep, *Rites of Passage*, 179.
9 C.L. Barber, *Shakespeare's Festive Comedy: A Study of Dramatic Form and Its Relation to Social Custom* (New York: Meridian Books, 1963), 3–16.
10 Barber, *Festive Comedy*, 7.
11 Barber, *Festive Comedy*, 8.
12 René Girard, *Violence and the Sacred*, trans. Patrick Gregory (Baltimore: Johns Hopkins University Press, 1977), 306–7.
13 Roger Caillois, *Man and the Sacred*, trans. Meyer Barash (Glencoe, Ill.: Free Press, 1959), 125–6.
14 Caillois, *Man and the Sacred*, 123.
15 Victor Turner, *Dramas, Fields, and Metaphors: Symbolic Action in Human Society* (Ithaca: Cornell University Press, 1974); *The Ritual Process: Structure and Anti-Structure* (Ithaca: Cornell University Press, 1977).
16 Turner, 'Variations on a Theme of Liminality', 43.
17 Turner, 'Variations on a Theme of Liminality', 46.
18 Victor Turner, 'Social Dramas and Stories About Them', *Critical Inquiry* 7 (1981), 141–68; Richard Schechner, 'Selective Inattention', in *Essays in Performance Theory, 1970–1976* (New York: Drama Book Specialists, 1977), 140–57.

CHAPTER 3 CARNIVAL AND PLEBEIAN CULTURE

1 Peter Burke, *Popular Culture in Early Modern Europe* (New York: New York University Press, 1978).

2 Claude Gaignebet, 'Le cycle annuel des fêtes à Rouen au milieu du XVIᵉ siècle', in *Les Fêtes de la Renaissance*, III (Paris: Editions du Centre National de la Recherche Scientifique, 1975), 569–78.

3 Thomas Dekker, *The Shoemakers Holiday*, in *The Dramatic Works of Thomas Dekker*, ed. Fredson Bowers, 4 vols (Cambridge: Cambridge University Press, 1953), I, 80.

4 Perry Anderson, *Lineages of the Absolutist State* (London: NLB, 1974), 113–42; P. Clark and P. Slack, *Crisis and Order in English Towns, 1500–1700* (London: Routledge & Kegan Paul, 1972); Agnes Heller, *Renaissance Man*, trans. Richard Allen (New York: Schocken Books, 1981); Christopher Hill, *Reformation to Industrial Revolution* (London: Weidenfeld & Nicolson, 1967); and *The World Turned Upside Down: Radical Ideas during the English Revolution* (London: Temple Smith, 1972); B.A. Holderness, *Pre-Industrial England: Economy and Society from 1500–1750* (London: J.M. Dent, 1976); Barrington Moore, *Social Origins of Dictatorship and Democracy* (Boston: Beacon Press, 1967); Lawrence Stone, *The Causes of the English Revolution 1529–1642* (New York: Harper & Row, 1972).

5 In addition to Hill, Holderness and Moore, see Brian Manning, *The English People and the English Revolution* (London: Heinemann, 1976); P. Laslett, et al., *Household and Family in Past Time* (Cambridge: Cambridge University Press, 1972); J.F.C. Harrison, *The Common People* (London: Fontana Paperbacks, 1984).

6 J.H. Hexter, 'Property, Monopoly, and Shakespeare's *Richard II*', in *Culture and Politics from Puritanism to the Enlightenment*, ed. P. Zagorin (Berkeley: University of California Press, 1980), 1–24.

7 E.P. Thompson, 'Patrician Society, Plebeian Culture', *Journal of Social History* 7 (1974), 382–405.

8 Karl Marx, *Grundrisse: Foundations of the Critique of Political Economy*, trans. Martin Nicolaus (New York: Random House, 1973), 541–2, et passim.

9 Natalie Z. Davis, 'The Reasons of Misrule: Youth Groups and Charivaris in Sixteenth Century France', *Past and Present* 50 (1971), 49–75; Bernard Capp, 'English Youth Groups and *The Pinder of Wakefield*', *Past and Present* 76 (1977), 127–33.

10 Emmanuel Le Roy Ladurie, *Carnival in Romans*, trans. Mary Feeney (New York: G. Braziller, 1979).

11 Burke, *Popular Culture in Early Modern Europe*; Carlos Ginzburg, *The Cheese and the Worms*, trans. John and Anne Tedeschi (Baltimore: Johns Hopkins University Press, 1980).

12 Michel Foucault, *Madness and Civilization: A History of Insanity in the*

Age of Reason, trans. Richard Howard (New York: Vintage Books, 1973); Ginzburg, *The Cheese and the Worms*, Introduction.

13 Weimann, *Shakespeare and the Popular Tradition.*

14 Peter Burke, ed. *Economy and Society in Early Modern Europe* (London: Routledge & Kegan Paul, 1972); P. Laslett *The World We Have Lost* (New York: Scribner, 1965); Lawrence Stone, *The Crisis of the Aristocracy: 1558–1641* (Oxford: The Clarendon Press, 1965); Paul M. Sweezy, ed., *The Transition from Feudalism to Capitalism* (London: NLB, 1976); R.H. Tawney, *The Agrarian Problem in the Sixteenth Century* (New York: Harper & Row, 1967); Immanuel Wallerstein, *The Modern World System: Capitalist Agriculture and the Origins of the European World Economy in the Sixteenth Century* (New York: Academic Press, 1974).

15 Fernand Braudel, *Civilization and Capitalism: 15th–18th Century*, trans. Siân Reynolds, 3 vols (New York: Harper & Row, 1984); Emmanuel Le Roy Ladurie, 'History that Stands Still', in *The Mind and Method of the Historian*, trans. Siân Reynolds (Chicago: University of Chicago Press, 1981), 1–28; Gregor McLennan, 'Braudel and the Annales Paradigm', in *Marxism and the Methodologies of History* (London: Verso Editions and NLB, 1981), 129–53; Immanuel Wallerstein, *Historical Capitalism* (London: Verso Editions, 1983).

16 Fernand Braudel, *Afterthoughts on Material Civilization and Capitalism*, trans. Patricia Ranum (Baltimore: Johns Hopkins University Press, 1977), 5–6.

17 Le Roy Ladurie, *Carnival in Romans*, 292.

18 Allon White, 'Pigs and Pierrots: The Politics of Transgression in Modern Fiction', *Raritan Review* 2 (1982), 35–51.

19 Le Roy Ladurie, *Carnival in Romans*, 279.

20 Natalie Z. Davis, 'The Rites of Violence: Religious Riot in Sixteenth Century France', *Past and Present* 59 (1973), 51–91.

PART 2   THE TEXTS OF CARNIVAL

CHAPTER 4   TRAVESTY AND SOCIAL ORDER

1 Sydney Anglo, *Spectacle, Pageantry, and Early Tudor Policy* (Oxford: Clarendon Press, 1969); David Bergeron, *English Civic Pageantry: 1558–1642* (Columbia, SC: University of South Carolina Press, 1971); Stephen Orgel, *The Illusion of Power: Political Theater in the Renaissance* (Berkeley: University of California Press, 1975).

2 John Nichols, *The Progresses and Public Processions of Queen Elizabeth*, 3 vols (London: John Nichols & Son, 1823), II, 46.

3 Nichols, *Progresses*, III, 220.

4 Stephen Orgel, 'The Poetics of Spectacle', *New Literary History* 2 (1971), 367.

5 Rosemond Tuve, *Allegorical Imagery*, ed. Thomas P. Roche (Princeton: Princeton University Press, 1966), 57–143 et passim.

6 Walter Benjamin, *The Origins of German Tragic Drama*, trans. John Osborne (London: NLB, 1977), 175.

7 Harry L. Berger, *The Allegorical Temper* (New Haven: Yale University Press, 1957), 211–41.

8 Michel Foucault, 'The Prose of the World', in *The Order of Things* (New York: Vintage Books, 1973), 17–45.

9 Ulrich von Hutten, *Letters of Obscure Men*, trans. F.G. Stokes (New York: Harper Torchbooks, 1964), 8–9.

10 *Rabelais and His World*, 7; Julia Kristeva, *Le Texte du roman: approche sémiologique d'une structure discursive et transformationnelle* (Paris and The Hague: Mouton, 1970), 162–77.

11 Bakhtin, *The Dialogic Imagination*, 159.

12 George Puttenham, *The Arte of English Poesie*, in *Elizabethan Critical Essays*, ed. Gregory Smith, 2 vols (Oxford: Oxford University Press, 1959), II, 159.

13 John Taylor, *Iacke a Lent: His Beginning and Entertainment: With the Mad Prankes of his Gentleman Usher Shroue Tuesday . . .* , in *Works of John Taylor the Water Poet*, ed. Charles Hindley (London and Westminster: Reeves & Turner, 1872), 7. Subsequent references to this work are given in the text.

14 White, 'Politics of Transgression'.

15 Desiderius Erasmus, *The Praise of Folly*, trans. John Wilson (Ann Arbor: University of Michigan Press, 1958), 44.

16 Sir Thomas More, *The History of King Richard III*, ed. Richard Sylvester, *The Yale Edition of the Complete Works of St Thomas More*, II (New Haven: Yale University Press, 1963), 81.

CHAPTER 5   BUTCHERS AND FISHMONGERS

1 E.P. Thompson, 'Patrician Society, Plebeian Culture', *Journal of Social History* 7 (1974), 382–405.

2 R. Chris Hassel, Jr, *Renaissance Drama and the English Church Year* (Lincoln: University of Nebraska Press, 1979), 6–17.

3 Hassel, *Drama and the Church Year*, 68.

4 Thomas Nashe, *Pierce Penniless his Supplication to the Devil*, in *The Works of Thomas Nashe*, ed. R.B. McKerrow, 5 vols, with corrections and supplementary notes by F.P. Wilson (Oxford: Oxford University Press, 1958), I, 200.

5 *Nashes Lenten Stuffe*, in *Works of Thomas Nashe*, ed. R.B. McKerrow, III, 184–5.

6 [Thomas Dekker], *The Owles Almanacke* (London: 1618), 16.

7 Anthony Munday, *Chrysanleia: The Golden Fishing: or Honour of Fishmongers* (London: 1618).

8 *Owles Almanac*, 24.
9 *Order conceived by the Lordes of her Maiesties Priuie Counsell, and by her Highnesse special direction . . . for the restraint of killing and eating of flesh this next lent* (London: 1598).
10 *A briefe note of the benefits that grow to this Realme, by the observation of Fish daies* (London: 1584).
11 *Muld Sacke, or the Apologie of Hic Mulier* (London: 1620), sig. C.
12 Nashe, *Summers Last Will and Testament*, in *Works of Thomas Nashe*, ed. R.B. McKerrow, III, 285.
13 Nashe, *Summers Last Will*, 287.
14 Nashe, *Summers Last Will*, 286.
15 John Taylor, *The Complaint of Christmas* (London: 1620), 13.
16 Taylor, *Complaint of Christmas*, 15.
17 *A Breefe Discourse, declaring and approuing the necessarie and inviolable maintenance of certain laudable custemes of London* (London: 1584), 3.
18 *A Breefe Discourse*, 5–6.
19 *A Breefe Discourse*, 6–7.

CHAPTER 6   'A COMPLETE EXIT FROM THE PRESENT ORDER OF LIFE'

1 Virgil, *Eclogue* IV, 4–10; Abraham Fraunce, *The Third Part of the Countess of Pembroke's Ivychurch* (London: 1591), sig. C$_3$; H.H. Scullard, *Festivals and Ceremonies of the Roman Republic* (Ithaca: Cornell University Press, 1981), 205–7; see also Robert C. Elliott, 'Saturnalia, Satire, and Utopia', *Yale Review* 55 (1965–6), 521–36; and *The Shape of Utopia: Studies in a Literary Genre* (Chicago: University of Chicago Press, 1970); A.B. Giamatti, *The Earthly Paradise and the Renaissance Epic* (Princeton: Princeton University Press, 1966); Brooks Otis, *Virgil: A Study in Civilized Poetry* (Oxford: Oxford University Press, 1964), 98–144; entry for Saturn in *Larousse Encyclopedia of Mythology* (London: Batchwath Press, 1959), 219.
2 A.L. Morton, *The English Utopia* (London: Lawrence and Wishart, 1952), 11–32; Weimann, *Shakespeare and the Popular Tradition*, 20, et passim.
3 Tillyard, *Shakespeare's History Plays*, 173–88; Weimann, *Shakespeare and the Popular Tradition*, 237–46.
4 Y.S. Brenner, 'The Inflation of Prices in Early Sixteenth Century England', and C.E. Challis, 'The Circulating Medium and the Movement of Prices in Mid-Tudor England', both in Peter H. Ramsey, *The Price Revolution in Sixteenth Century England* (London: Methuen, 1971); R.B. Outhwaite, *Inflation in Tudor and Stuart England* (London: Macmillan, 1969).
5 *Utopia, Yale Edition of the Complete Works of St Thomas More*, IV, 241.
6 J.H. Hexter, Introduction, *Utopia, Yale Edition of the Complete Works of St Thomas More*, IV, xli.
7 J.H. Hexter, Introduction, IV, xliii.

8 Raymond Williams, *The Country and the City* (New York: Oxford University Press, 1973), 44.

9 Frederic Jameson, *The Political Unconscious* (Ithaca: Cornell University Press, 1981), 281–99.

10 Sir Thomas More, *The Apologye of Syr Thomas More*, Knyght, ed. A.I. Taft, EETS (London: Oxford University Press, 1930), 191.

11 *A Breefe Discourse*, 4.

12 *A Breefe Discourse*, 16–17.

13 Nashe, *Lenten Stuffe*, ed. R.B. McKerrow, III, 147. Subsequent references to this work are given in the text.

14 Bakhtin, *Rabelais and His World*, 297 ff.

PART III   THEATER AND THE STRUCTURE OF AUTHORITY

1 Jonas Barish, *The Antitheatrical Prejudice* (Berkeley: University of California Press, 1981); Johannes H. Birringer, 'Marlowe's Violent Stage: "Mirrors" of Honor in *Tamburlaine*', *ELH* 51, (1984), 219–39.

2 John Northbrooke, *A Treatise . . .* , quoted in *Rise of the Common Player*, 69.

3 Harry Levin, 'Dramatic Auspices: The Playwright and his Audience', in *Shakespeare and the Revolution of the Times* (London: Oxford University Press, 1976); Alfred Harbage, *Shakespeare's Audience* (New York: Columbia University Press, 1941), *Shakespeare and the Rival Traditions* (New York: Macmillan, 1952); Andrew Gurr, *The Shakespearean Stage* (Cambridge: Cambridge University Press, 1970); William Hattaway, *Elizabethan Popular Theatre* (London: Routledge & Kegan Paul, 1982).

4 Weimann, *Shakespeare and the Popular Tradition*, 174; Hexter, 'Property, Monopoly, and Shakespeare's *Richard II*', 17.

5 Ann Jennalie Cook, *The Privileged Playgoers of Shakespeare's London, 1576–1642* (Princeton: Princeton University Press, 1981), 272.

CHAPTER 7   AUTHORITY AND THE AUTHOR FUNCTION

1 G.E. Bentley, *The Profession of Dramatist in Shakespeare's Time, 1590–1642* (Princeton: Princeton University Press, 1971), 2–11.

2 Phillip Stubbes, *The Anatomie of Abuses*, 1583 (New York: Johnson Reprint Company, 1972), Sig. Bv.

3 Stubbes, *Anatomie*, Sig. Lv.

4 Stubbes, *Anatomie*, Sig. M.

5 Stubbes, *Anatomie*, Sig. Lv.

6 Henry Chettle, *Kind-Hartes Dreame*, 1592, ed. G.B. Harrison (Edinburgh: Edinburgh University Press, 1966), 39.

7 Chettle, *Kind-Hartes Dreame*, 44.

8 *Bartholomew Faire*, in Ben Jonson, *Works*, ed. C.H. Herford, Percy and Evelyn Simpson (Oxford: Clarendon Press), VI, 14.

9 Jonathan Haynes, 'Festivity and the Dramatic Economy of Jonson's *Bartholomew Faire*', *ELH* (forthcoming).

10 Thomas Hobbes, *Leviathan*, ed. C.B. MacPherson (Harmondsworth: Penguin, 1974), 217.

11 Hobbes, *Leviathan*, 218.

12 Michel Foucault, 'What is an Author?' in *Language, Counter-Memory, Practise*, ed. D.F. Bouchard (Ithaca: Cornell University Press, 1977), 124.

13 Walter Benjamin, 'The Storyteller', in *Illuminations*, 83–111.

14 Bakhtin, *The Dialogic Imagination*, Glossary, 462.

CHAPTER 8   THE DIALECTIC OF LAUGHTER

1 E.R. Curtius, *European Literature and the Latin Middle Ages*, trans. Willard Trask (Princeton: Princeton University Press, 1953); Paul Barolsky, *Infinite Jest: Wit and Humor in Italian Renaissance Art* (London: University of Missouri Press, 1978).

2 V.A. Kolve, *The Play Called Corpus Christi* (London: E. Arnold, 1966), 124–44.

3 Nashe, *Summers Last Will*, 294.

4 Keith Thomas, 'The Place of Laughter in Tudor and Stuart England', *TLS*, 21 January 1977, 76–83.

5 Nashe, *Summers Last Will*, 294.

6 Sir Philip Sidney, *An Apologie for Poetry*, in *Elizabethan Critical Essays*, ed. Gregory Smith, 2 vols (Oxford: Oxford University Press, 1959), I, 201.

7 Sidney, *Apologie*, 301.

8 Sidney, *Apologie*, 199.

9 Hobbes, *Leviathan*, 125.

10 Hobbes, *Leviathan*, 125–6.

11 Erasmus, *The Praise of Folly*, 3. Subsequent references to this work will be given in the text.

12 W. David Kay, 'Erasmus's Learned Joking: The Ironic Use of Classical Learning in the *Praise of Folly*', *Texas Studies in Language and Literature* 19 (1977), 248–9.

13 For a full discussion of this problem see Greenblatt, *Renaissance Self-Fashioning*.

14 Donald G. Watson, 'Erasmus' *Praise of Folly* and the Spirit of Carnival', *Renaissance Quarterly* 32, no. 3 (Autumn, 1979), 333–53.

15 Watson, 'Erasmus and Carnival', 352.

16 Laurent Joubert, *Treatise on Laughter*, trans. Gregory David de Rocher (University of Alabama Press, 1980), 15. Subsequent references to this work are given in the text.

17 Gregory David de Rocher, *Rabelais' Laughters and Joubert's Traité du Ris* (University of Alabama Press, 1979), 31–47.

18 Baldesar Castiglione, *The Book of the Courtier*, trans. George Bull (Harmondsworth: Penguin, 1976), 192.

19 Bakhtin, *Rabelais and His World*, 73.

20 Bakhtin, *Rabelais and His World*, 92.

21 Sigmund Freud, *Wit and Its Relation to the Unconscious*, ed. A.A. Brill (London: Paul, Trench & Trubner, 1922), 110.

CHAPTER 9   CLOWNING AND DEVILMENT

1 Ernst Kantorowicz, *The King's Two Bodies: A Study in Medieval Political Theology* (Princeton: Princeton University Press, 1957), 24–41.

2 Kristeva, *Le Texte du roman*, 162–77.

3 William Kemp, *Kemps nine daies wonder*, ed. G.B. Harrison (Edinburgh: Edinburgh University Press, 1966), 4.

4 *Kemps nine daies wonder*, 9.

5 *Locrine*, I. i. 109–21; in *The Shakespeare Apocrypha*, ed. C. F. Tucker Brooke (Oxford: Oxford University Press, 1903). Subsequent references to this work will be given in the text.

6 Bakhtin, *The Dialogic Imagination*, 35.

7 *Doctor Faustus*, A. 361–73; in *Doctor Faustus: 1604–1616, Parallel Texts*, ed. W.W. Greg (Oxford: Clarendon Press, 1950). Subsequent references to this work will be given in the text.

8 Greenblatt, *Renaissance Self-Fashioning*, 193–222.

9 Judith Weil, *Christopher Marlowe: Merlin's Prophet* (Cambridge: Cambridge University Press, 1977), 68.

PART 4   CARNIVALIZED LITERATURE

1 Robert Bridges, 'The Influence of the Audience on Shakespeare's Drama', in *Collected Essays*, I (London: Oxford University Press, 1927), 29.

2 Foucault, 'What is an Author?', *Archaeology of Knowledge*, trans. A.M. Sheridan Smith (New York: Pantheon Books, 1972), 23–4; Gerald L. Bruns, 'Intention, Authority, and Meaning', *Critical Inquiry* 7 (1980), 297–311.

3 Michael Warren, '*Doctor Faustus*: The Old Man and the Text', *ELR* 11 (1981), 115.

CHAPTER 10   WEDDING FEAST AND CHARIVARI

1 Lawrence Stone, *The Family, Sex, and Marriage in England, 1500–1800* (Harmondsworth: Pelican, 1979), 70 et passim; P. Laslett, et al., *Household and Family in Past Time* (Cambridge: Cambridge University Press, 1972); Jean Louis Flandrin, *Families in Former Times*, trans. Richard Southern (Cambridge: Cambridge University Press, 1979).

2 Natalie Davis, 'Women on Top', in *Society and Culture in Early Modern France* (Stanford: Stanford University Press, 1975); Coppélia Kahn, *Man's Estate: Masculine Identity in Shakespeare* (Berkeley: University of California Press, 1981); Juliet Dusinberre, *Shakespeare and the Nature of Women* (London: Macmillan, 1975); Carolyn Ruth Swift Lenz, Gayle Green, Carol Thomas Neely, eds, *The Woman's Part: Feminist Criticism of Shakespeare* (Urbana: University of Illinois Press, 1980).

3 E.P. Thompson, 'Rough Music: Le Charivari Anglais', *Annales: Economies, Sociétés, Civilizations* 27 (1972); Jean-Claude Margolin, 'Charivari et Marriage Ridicule au Temps de la Renaissance', *Les Fêtes de la Renaissance*, III (Paris: Editions du Centre National de la Recherche Scientifique, 1975), 579–601; Capp, 'English Youth Groups', 127–33; Le Roy Ladurie, *Carnival in Romans*, 211–13.

4 Davis, 'The Reasons of Misrule', 58–73.

5 *The Black Man*, in C.R. Baskerville, *The Elizabethan Jig* (New York: Dover, 1965), 465.

6 *The Black Man*, 466.

7 Le Roy Ladurie, *Carnival in Romans*, 211–13 et passim.

8 *The Merry Devil of Edmonton*, I. i. 71–82; in *The Shakespeare Apocrypha*. Subsequent references to this work will be given in the text.

9 Paul N. Siegel, '*A Midsummer Night's Dream* and the Wedding Guests', *SQ* 4 (1953), 139–44.

10 Orgel, 'Poetics of Spectacle', 367 ff.

11 Bakhtin, *The Dialogic Imagination*, 342 ff.

12 Terence Hawkes, 'Comedy, Orality, and Duplicity: *A Midsummer Night's Dream* and *Twelfth Night*', in *Shakespearean Comedy*, ed. Maurice Charney (New York: New York Literary Forum, 1980), 159.

13 Barber, *Festive Comedy*, 151.

14 J.W. Robinson, 'Palpable Hot Ice: Dramatic Burlesque in *A Midsummer Night's Dream*', *SP* 61 (1966), 192–204; Dieter Mehl, 'Forms and Functions of the Play within a Play', *Renaissance Drama* 7 (1974), 41–62.

CHAPTER 11   TREATING DEATH AS A LAUGHING MATTER

1 Sidney, *Apologie*, 199.

2 Weimann, *Shakespeare and the Popular Tradition*, 237–46.

3 Kantorowicz, *The King's Two Bodies*, 312–31.

4 Kantorowicz, *The King's Two Bodies*, 30.

5 Davis, 'The Reasons of Misrule', 75.

6 Robertson, 'A Medievalist Looks at Hamlet', 317.

7 Weimann, *Shakespeare and the Popular Tradition*, 237–46. See also P.J. Aldus, *Mousetrap: Structure and Meaning in Hamlet* (Toronto: University of Toronto Press, 1977), 151–3; Nigel Alexander, *Poison, Play, and Duel: A Study in Hamlet* (Lincoln: University of Nebraska Press, 1971), 153–73;

Bridget Gellert, 'The Iconography of Melancholy in the Graveyard Scene in Hamlet', *SP* 67 (1972), 34–53; Jacques Lacan, 'Desire and the Interpretation of Desire in Hamlet' *Yale French Studies* 55/56 (1977), 11–52.

8 Thomas Dekker, *The Wonderful Year*, in *Selected Writings*, ed. E.D. Pendry, The Stratford-Upon-Avon-Library (Cambridge, Mass.: Harvard University Press, 1968), 34. Subsequent references to this work will be given in the text.

CHAPTER 12   THE FESTIVE AGON: THE POLITICS OF CARNIVAL

1 Davis, 'The Rites of Violence', 55–65.

2 Girard, *Violence and the Sacred*, 304–5.

3 Lily B. Campbell, *Shakespeare's Histories: Mirrors of Elizabethan Policy* (San Marino: Huntington Library Publications, 1947); David Bevington, *Tudor Drama and Politics* (Cambridge, Mass.: Harvard University Press, 1968).

4 Barber, *Festive Comedy*, 205.

5 Hattaway, *Elizabethan Popular Theatre*, 2.

6 Jan Kott, *Shakespeare Our Contemporary* (New York: Anchor Books, 1966), 3–57.

7 Bakhtin, *The Dialogic Imagination*, 206–8.

8 Claude Gaignebet, 'Le Combat de carnaval et de carême de P. Breughel (1559)', *Annales: Economies, Sociétés, Civilizations* 27 (1972), 313–43; K. Thomas, 'Work and Leisure in Pre-Industrial Society', *Past and Present* 29 (1964), 67–84.

9 Stow, *Survay of London*, 115.

10 Bakhtin, *The Dialogic Imagination*, 171–92; *Rabelais and His World*, 369–437.

11 Thomas Metscher, 'Shakespeare in the Context of Renaissance Europe', *Science and Society* 41 (1977), 17–24; S.H. Steinberg, *The Thirty Years War and the Conflict for European Hegemony: 1600–1660* (London: Edward Arnold, 1966).

12 Turner, 'Variations on a Theme of Liminality', 57.

BIBLIOGRAPHY

PRIMARY MATERIALS

A Breefe Discourse, declaring and approuing the necessarie and inviolable maintenance of certain laudable custemes of London (London: 1584).

A Briefe note of the benefits that grow to this Realme by the observation of Fish-daies (London: 1584).

Castiglione, Baldesar. *The Book of the Courtier*. Trans. George Bull (Harmondsworth: Penguin, 1976).

Chettle, Henrie. *Kind-Hartes Dreame*. Ed. G.B. Harrison (Edinburgh: Edinburgh University Press, 1966).

Dekker, Thomas. *The Dramatic Works of Thomas Dekker*. Ed. Fredson Bowers. 4 vols. (Cambridge: Cambridge University Press, 1953).

   The Owles Almanacke (London: 1618).

   Selected Writings. Ed. E.D. Pendry (Cambridge, Mass.: Harvard University Press, 1968).

Elizabethan Critical Essays. Ed. G. Gregory Smith (Oxford: Oxford University Press, 1959).

Erasmus, Desiderius. *The Praise of Folly*. Trans. John Wilson (Ann Arbor: University of Michigan Press, 1967).

Hic Mulier or the Man-woman (London: 1620).

Hobbes, Thomas. *Leviathan*. Ed. C.B. MacPherson (Harmondsworth: Penguin, 1968).

Joubert, Laurent. *Treatise on Laughter*. Trans. G. D. de Rocher (Montgomery: University of Alabama Press, 1980).

Kemp, William. *Kemps nine daies wonder*. Ed. G.B. Harrison (Edinburgh: Edinburgh University Press, 1966).

Marlowe, Christopher. *Doctor Faustus: 1604–1616. Parallel Texts*. Ed. W.W. Gret (Oxford: Clarendon Press, 1950).

More, Sir Thomas. *The History of King Richard III*. Ed. Richard Sylvester. The Yale Edition of the Works of St Thomas More (New Haven: Yale University Press, 1963).

    Utopia. Ed. Edward Surtz, SJ and J.H. Hexter. The Yale Edition of the Works of St Thomas More (New Haven: Yale University Press, 1965).

The Apologye of Syr Thomas More, Knyght. Ed. A.I. Taft, EETS 180 (Oxford: Oxford University Press, 1930).

Muld Sacke, or the Apologie of Hic Mulier (London: 1620).

Munday, Anthony. *Chrysanleia, The Golden Fishing* (London: 1618).

The Works of Thomas Nashe. Ed. R.B. McKerrow. 5 vols (Oxford: Oxford University Press, 1958).

Order conceived by the Lordes of her Maiesties Privie Counsell . . . for the restraint of killing and eating of flesh this next lent (London: 1598).

The Shakespeare Apocrypha. Ed. C.F. Tucker Brooke (Oxford: Oxford University Press, 1908).

Shakespeare, William. *The Complete Works*. Ed. G.B. Harrison (New York: Harcourt, Brace & World, 1952).

Stow, John. *A Survay of London*. Ed. H. Morley (London: G. Routledge, 1890).

Stubbs, Phillip. *The Anatomie of Abuses*, 1583 (New York: Johnson Reprint Corp., 1972).

Works of John Taylor, the Water Poet. Ed. Charles Hindley (London and Westminster: Reeves & Turner, 1872).

Von Hutten, Ulrich. *Letters of Obscure Men*. Trans. F.G. Stokes (New York: Harper Torchbooks, 1964).

SECONDARY MATERIALS

Aldus, P.J. *Mousetrap: Structure and Meaning in Hamlet* (Toronto: University of Toronto Press, 1977).

Alexander, Nigel. *Poison, Play, and Duel: A Study in Hamlet* (Lincoln: University of Nebraska Press, 1971).

Alford, Violet. *Sword Dance and Drama* (London: Merlin Press, 1962).

Althusser, Louis. *For Marx*. Trans. Ben Brewster (London: Verso, 1977).

Anderson, Perry. *Lineages of the Absolutist State* (London: NLB, 1974).

Anglo, Sydney. *Spectacle, Pageantry, and Early Tudor Policy* (Oxford: Clarendon Press, 1969).

Arden, Heather. *Fools Plays: A Study of Satire in the 'sottie'* (Cambridge: Cambridge University Press, 1980).

Aston, Trevor, ed. *Crisis in Europe, 1560–1660: Essays from 'Past And Present'* (London: Routledge & Kegan Paul, 1965).

Babcock, Barbara, ed. *The Reversible World: Symbolic Inversion in Art and Society* (Ithaca: Cornell University Press, 1978).

Bakhtin, Mikhail. *The Dialogic Imagination*. Trans. Michael Holquist and Caryl Emerson (Austin: University of Texas Press, 1981).

Rabelais and His World. Trans. Hélène Iswolsky (Cambridge, Mass.: MIT Press, 1968).

Barber, C.L. *Shakespeare's Festive Comedies: A Study of Dramatic Form and Its Relation to Social Custom* (New York: Meridian Books, 1963).

Barish, Jonas. *The Antitheatrical Prejudice* (Berkeley: University of California Press, 1981).

Barolsky, Paul. *Infinite Jest: Wit and Humor in Italian Renaissance Art* (London: University of Missouri Press, 1978).

Baskervill, Charles Read. *The Elizabethan Jig and Related Song Drama* (New York: Dover, 1965).

Benjamin, Walter. *Illuminations*. Ed. Hannah Arendt (New York: Schocken Books, 1969).

The Origins of German Tragic Drama. Trans. John Osborne (London: NLB, 1977).

Bentley, G.E. *The Profession of Dramatist in Shakespeare's Time 1590–1642*. (Princeton: Princeton University Press, 1971).

Bercé, Yves-Marie. *Fête et révolte: Des mentalités populaires du XVIe au XVIIIe siècle* (Paris: Hachette, 1976).

Berger, Harry. *The Allegorical Temper* (New Haven: Yale University Press, 1957).

Bergeron, David M. *English Civic Pageantry: 1558–1642* (Columbia: University of South Carolina Press, 1971).

Bethell, S.L. *Shakespeare and the Popular Dramatic Tradition* (London: P.S. King & Staples, 1944).

Bevington, David. *Tudor Drama and Politics* (Cambridge, Mass.: Harvard University Press, 1968).

Birringer, Johannes H. 'Marlowe's Violent Stage: "Mirrors" of Honor in Tamburlaine'. *ELH* 51 (1984), 219–39.

Bradbrook, Muriel. *The Rise of the Common Player* (Cambridge, Mass.: Harvard University Press, 1964).

Brand, John. *Observations on the Popular Antiquities of Great Britain*. 3 vols (London: Henry G. Bohn, 1855).

Braudel, Fernand. *Civilization and Capitalism: 15th–18th Century*. Trans. Siân Reynolds. 3 vols (New York: Harper & Row, 1984).

Brecht, Bertolt. *The Messingkauf Dialogues*. Trans. John Willett (London: Eyre Methuen, 1965).

Bridges, Robert. 'The Influence of the Audience on Shakespeare's Drama'. *Collected Essays* (London: Oxford University Press, 1927).

Bristol, Michael. 'Acting Out Utopia: The Politics of Carnival'. *Performance* 6 (1973), 13–28.

Bruns, Gerald. 'Intention, Authority and Meaning'. *Critical Inquiry* 7 (1980), 291–311.

Burke, Peter, ed. *Economy and Society in Early Modern Europe*. (London: Routledge & Kegan Paul, 1972).
  Popular Culture in Early Modern Europe (New York: New York University Press, 1978).
Caillois, Roger. *Man and the Sacred*. Trans. Meyer Barash (Glencoe, Ill.: Free Press, 1959).
  Man, Play, and Games. Trans. Meyer Barash (New York: Free Press, 1961).
Campbell, Lily B. *Shakespeare's Histories: Mirrors of Elizabethan* Policy (San Marino: Huntington Library Publications, 1947).
Capp, Bernard. 'English Youth Groups and The Pinder of Wakefield'. *Past and Present* 76 (1977), 127–33.
Chambers, E.K. *The English Folk Play* (Oxford: Clarendon Press, 1933).
Clark, P. and P. Slack. *Crisis and Order in English Towns: 1500–1700* (London: Routledge & Kegan Paul, 1972).
Clarkson, L.A. *The Pre-Industrial Economy in England: 1500–1700*. (London: Batsford, 1971).
Colie, Rosalie. *Paradoxica Epidemica: The Renaissance Tradition of Paradox* (Princeton: Princeton University Press, 1966).
  Shakespeare's Living Art (Princeton: Princeton University Press, 1974).
Cook, Ann Jennalie. *The Privileged Playgoers of Shakespeare's London: 1576–1642* (Princeton: Princeton University Press, 1981).
Cox, Harvey. *The Feast of Fools* (Cambridge, Mass.: Harvard University Press, 1969).
Curtius, Ernst. *European Literature and the Latin Middle Ages*. Trans. Willard Trask (Princeton: Princeton University Press, 1953).
Davis, Natalie Zemon. 'The Reasons of Misrule: Youth Groups and Charivaris in Sixteenth Century France'. *Past and Present* 50 (1971), 49–75.
  'The Rites of Violence: Religious Riot in Sixteenth Century France'. *Past and Present* 59 (1973), 51–91.
  Society and Culture in Early Modern France (Stanford: Stanford University Press, 1975).
Dollimore, Jonathan. *Radical Tragedy: Religion, Ideology and Power in the Drama of Shakespeare and his Contemporaries* (Brighton, Sussex: Harvester Press, 1984).
Douglas, Mary. *Implicit Meanings: Essays in Anthropology* (London: Routledge & Kegan Paul, 1975).
Dumouchel, Paul and Jean Pierre Dupuy. *L'Enfer des choses: René Girard et la logique de l'économie* (Paris: Editions du Seuil, 1979).
Dupuy, Jean-Pierre. *Ordres et désordres: Enquête sur un nouveau paradigme* (Paris: Editions du Seuil, 1982).
Durkheim, Emile. *The Elementary Forms of the Religious Life*. Trans. J. Swain (London: George Allen & Unwin, 1915).
Dusinberre, Juliet. *Shakespeare and the Nature of Women* (London: Macmillan, 1975).
Elliott, Robert C. 'Saturnalia, Satire, and Utopia'. *Yale Review* 55 (1965–6), 521–36.

The Shape of Utopia: Studies in a Literary Genre (Chicago: University of Chicago Press, 1970).

Fletcher, Angus. *Allegory: The Theory of a Symbolic Mode* (Ithaca: Cornell University Press, 1964).

Foucault, Michel. *The Archaeology of Knowledge*. Trans. A.M. Sheridan Smith (New York: Pantheon, 1972).

Madness and Civilization: A History of Insanity in the Age of Reason. Trans. Richard Howard (New York: Vintage Books, 1973).

The Order of Things (New York: Vintage Books, 1973).

'What is an Author?'. *Language, Counter-Memory, Practise.* Ed. Donald F. Bouchard (Ithaca: Cornell University Press, 1977).

Freud, Sigmund. *Wit and its Relation to the Unconscious.* Ed. A.A. Brill (London: Paul, Trench & Trubner, 1922).

Gaignebet, Claude. *Le Carnaval: Essais de mythologie populaire* (Paris: Payot, 1974).

'Le cycle annuel des fêtes à Rouen au milieu du XVIe siècle'. *Les Fêtes de la Renaissance*, III (Paris: Editions du Centre National de la Recherche Scientifique, 1975), 569–78.

'Le Combat de Carnaval et de Carême de P. Breughel (1559)'. *Annales: Economies, Sociétés, Civilisations* 27 (1972), 313–43.

Gellert, Bridget. 'The Iconography of Melancholy in the Graveyard Scene in Hamlet'. *SP* 67 (1972).

Giamatti, A. Bartlett. *The Earthly Paradise and the Renaissance Epic* (Princeton: Princeton University Press, 1966).

Ginzburg, Carlo. *The Cheese and the Worms.* Trans. John and Anne Tedeschi (Baltimore: Johns Hopkins University Press, 1980).

Girard, René. *Violence and the Sacred.* Trans. Patrick Gregory. (Baltimore: Johns Hopkins University Press, 1977).

Goldberg, Jonathan. *James I and the Politics of Literature* (Baltimore: Johns Hopkins University Press, 1983).

Gramsci, Antonio. *The Modern Prince and Other Writings* (New York: International Publishers, 1957).

Greenblatt, Stephen. *Renaissance Self-Fashioning: From More to Shakespeare* (Chicago: University of Chicago Press, 1980).

Grinberg, Martine. 'Carnaval et société urbaine à la fin du XVe siècle'. *Les Fêtes de la Renaissance*, III (Paris: Editions du Centre National de la Recherche Scientifique, 1975), 547–53.

Griffin, Alice V. *Pageantry on the Shakespearean Stage* (New Haven: College and University Press, 1951).

Gross, David. 'Culture and Negativity: Notes Toward a Theory of the Carnival'. *TELOS* 36 (1978).

Grossvogel, David I. 'The Depths of Laughter: The Subsoil of a Culture'. *Yale French Studies* 23 (1959), 63–71.

Gurr, Andrew. *The Shakespearean Stage* (Cambridge: Cambridge University Press, 1970).

Gurvitch, Georg. *The Spectrum of Social Time.* Trans. Myrtle Korenbaum. (Dordrecht, Holland: D. Reidel, 1964).

Harbage, Albert. *Shakespeare and the Rival Traditions* (New York: Macmillan, 1952).

Shakespeare's Audience (New York: Columbia University Press, 1941).

Hassel, R.C. *Renaissance Drama and the English Church Year* (Lincoln: University of Nebraska Press, 1979).

Hattaway, William. *Elizabethan Popular Theatre* (London: Routledge & Kegan Paul, 1982).

Hawkes, Terence. 'Comedy, Orality, and Duplicity: *A Midsummer Night's Dream* and *Twelfth Night*'. *Shakespearean Comedy*, ed. Maurice Charney (New York: New York Literary Forum, 1980).

Haynes, Jonathan. 'Festivity and the Dramatic Economy in Jonson's *Bartholomew Faire*'. *ELH* (forthcoming).

Heller, Agnes. *Renaissance Man.* Trans. Richard Allen (New York: Schocken Books, 1981).

Hewitt, Douglas. 'The Very Pompes of the Divell: Popular and Folk Elements in Elizabethan and Jacobean Drama'. *RES* 25 (1949), 10–23.

Hill, Christopher. *Reformation to Industrial Revolution* (London: Weidenfeld & Nicolson, 1967).

The World Turned Upside Down: Radical Ideas during the English Revolution (London: Temple Smith, 1972).

Hilton, Rodney. *The Transition from Feudalism to Capitalism* (London: Verso, 1978).

Holderness, B.A. *Pre-Industrial England: Economy and Society from 1500–1700* (London: J.M. Dent & Sons, 1976).

Holland, Norman. *Laughing: A Psychology of Humor* (Ithaca: Cornell University Press, 1982).

Holquist, Michael. 'Answering as Authoring: Mikhail Bakhtin's Trans-Linguistics'. *Critical Inquiry* 10 (1983), 307–20.

Huizinga, Johan. *Homo Ludens: A Study of the Play Elements in Culture* (New York: Harper & Row, 1970).

James, E.O. *Seasonal Feasts and Festivals* (London: Thames & Hudson, 1961).

Jameson, Frederic. *Marxism and Form* (Princeton: Princeton University Press, 1971).

The Political Unconscious (Ithaca: Cornell University Press, 1981).

Kahn, Coppélia. *Man's Estate:Masculine Identity in Shakespeare* (Berkeley: University of California Press, 1981).

Kantorowicz, Ernst. *The King's Two Bodies: A Study in Medieval Political Theology* (Princeton: Princeton University Press, 1957).

Kay, W. David. 'Erasmus's Learned Joking: The Ironic Use of Classical Learning in *The Praise of Folly*'. *Texas Studies in Language and Literature* 19 (1977).

Kolve, V.A. *The Play Called Corpus Christi* (London: E. Arnold, 1966).

Kott, Jan. *Shakespeare Our Contemporary*. Trans. Boleslaw Taborski (New York: Anchor Books, 1966).

Kristeva, Julia. *Le Texte du roman: approche sémiologique d'une structure discursive et transformationelle* (Paris: Mouton, 1970).

Lacan, Jacques. 'Desire and the Interpretation of Desire in *Hamlet*'. *Yale French Studies* 55/56 (1977), 11–52.

Laslett, P. et al. *Household and Family in Past Time* (Cambridge: Cambridge University Press, 1972).

The World We Have Lost (New York: Scribner, 1965).

Leach, Edmund. *Rethinking Anthropology* (London: Athlone Press, 1961).

Lefebvre, Joël. 'Vie et mort du jeu de Carnival à Nuremberg, Neidhardt et La Violette, de Hans Sachs (1557)'. *Les Fêtes de la Renaissance*, III (Paris: Editions du Centre National de la Recherche Scientifique, 1975), 555–68.

Le Roy Ladurie. *Carnival in Romans*. Trans. Mary Feeney (New York: G. Braziller, 1979).

The Mind and Method of the Historian. Trans. Siân Reynolds (Chicago: University of Chicago Press, 1981).

Levin, Harry. *Shakespeare and the Revolution of the Times* (London: Oxford University Press, 1976).

Manning, Brian. *The English People and the English Revolution* (London: Heinemann, 1976).

Margolin, Jean-Claude. 'Charivari et marriage ridicule au temps de la renaissance'. *Les Fêtes de la Renaissance*, III (Paris: Editions du Centre National de la Recherche Scientifique, 1975), 579–601.

Marx, Karl. *Grundrisse: Foundations of the Critique of Political Economy*. Trans. Martin Nicolaus (New York: Random House, 1973).

McLennan, Gregor. *Marxism and the Methodologies of History* (London: Verso Editions and NLB, 1981).

Medvedev, P.N. and M.M. Bakhtin. *The Formal Method in Literary Scholarship: A Critical Introduction to Sociological Poetics* (Baltimore: Johns Hopkins University Press, 1978).

Mehl, Dieter. 'Forms and Functions of the Play within a Play'. *Renaissance Drama* 7 (1974), 41–62.

Metscher, Thomas. 'Shakespeare in the Context of Renaissance Europe'. *Science and Society* 41 (1977), 17–24.

Montrose, Louis Adrian. 'The Purpose of Playing: Reflections on A Shakespearean Anthropology'. *Helios*, NS 8 (1980), 51–74.

Moore, Barrington. *Social Origins of Dictatorship and Democracy* (Boston: Beacon Press, 1967).

Moore, Sally F. and Barbara G. Myerhoff, eds. *Secular Ritual* (Amsterdam: Van Gorcum, 1977).

Morton, A.L. *The English Utopia* (London: Lawrence & Wishart, 1952).

Neely, Carol Thomas, Gayle Greene and Carolyn Ruth Swift Lenz, eds. *The Woman's Part: Feminist Criticism of Shakespeare* (Urbana: University of Illinois Press, 1980).

Ogilvy, J.D. 'Mimi, Scurrae, Histriones: Entertainers of the Early Middle Ages'. *Speculum* 38 (1963), 603–19.

Orgel, Stephen. *The Illusion of Power: Political Theater in the Renaissance* (Berkeley: University of California Press, 1975).

'The Poetics of Spectacle'. *NLH* 2 (1971), 367–89.

Otis, Brooks. *Virgil: A Study in Civilized Poetry* (Oxford: Oxford University Press, 1964).

Outhwaite, R.B. *Inflation in Tudor and Stuart England* (London: Macmillan, 1969).

Rabkin, Norman. *Shakespeare and the Common Understanding* (New York: Free Press, 1967).

Ramsey, Peter H., ed. *The Price Revolution in Sixteenth Century England* (London: Methuen, 1971).

Righter, Anne. *Shakespeare and the Idea of the Play* (Harmondsworth: Penguin, 1967).

Robertson, D.W. *Essays in Medieval Culture* (Princeton: Princeton University Press, 1980).

Robinson, J.W. 'Palpable Hot Ice: Dramatic Burlesque in *A Midsummer Night's Dream*'. *SP* 61 (1966), 192–204.

de Rocher, Gregory. *Rabelais' Laughers and Joubert's Traité du Ris* (Montgomery: University of Alabama Press, 1980).

Said, Edward W. *Beginnings: Intention and Method* (New York: Basic Books, 1975).

Schechner, Richard. *Essays on Performance Theory: 1970–1976* (New York: Drama Book Specialists, 1977).

Scullard, H.H. *Festivals and Ceremonies of the Roman Republic* (Ithaca: Cornell University Press, 1981).

Siegel, Paul N. '*A Midsummer Night's Dream* and the Wedding Guests'. *SQ* 4 (1953), 139–44.

Stone, Lawrence. *The Causes of the English Revolution: 1529–1642* (New York: Harper & Row, 1972).

The Crisis of the Aristocracy: 1558–1641 (Oxford: Clarendon Press, 1965).

The Family, Sex, and Marriage in England: 1500–1800 (Harmondsworth: Pelican, 1979).

'Social Mobility in England: 1500–1700'. *Past and Present* 33 (1966).

Sweezy, Paul M., ed. *The Transition from Feudalism to Capitalism* (London: NLB, 1976).

Tawney, R.H. *The Agrarian Problem in the Sixteenth Century* (New York: Harper & Row, 1967).

Thomas, Keith. 'The Place of Laughter in Tudor and Stuart England'. *TLS*, 21 January 1977, 76–83.

'Work and Leisure in Pre-Industrial Society'. *Past and Present* 29 (1964).

Thompson, E.P. *The Making of the English Working Class* (Harmondsworth: Penguin, 1968).

'Patrician Society, Plebeian Culture'. *Journal of Social History* 7 (1974), 382–405.

'Rough Music: Le Charivari anglais'. *Annales: Economies, Sociétés, Civilisations* 27 (1972), 285–312.

Tillyard, E.M.W. *The Elizabethan World Picture* (New York: Vintage Books, 1948).

Shakespeare's History Plays (London: Chatto & Windus, 1961).

Turner, Victor. *Dramas, Fields, and Metaphors: Symbolic Action in Human Society* (Ithaca: Cornell University Press, 1974).

From Ritual to Theatre: The Human Seriousness of Play (New York: Performing Arts Journal Publications, 1982).

The Ritual Process: Structure and Anti-Structure (Ithaca: Cornell University Press, 1977).

Tuve, Rosemond. *Allegorical Imagery*. Ed. Thomas P. Roche (Princeton: Princeton University Press, 1966).

Van Gennep, Arnold. *The Rites of Passage*. Trans. Monika Vizedom and Gabrielle Caffee (Chicago: University of Chicago Press, 1960).

Watson, Donald G. 'Erasmus' *Praise of Folly* and the Spirit of Carnival'. *Renaissance Quarterly* 32 (1979), 333–53.

Wallerstein, Immanuel. *The Capitalist World Economy* (Cambridge: Cambridge University Press, 1979).

The Modern World System: Capitalist Agriculture and the Origins of the European World-Economy in the Sixteenth Century (New York: Academic Press, 1974).

Warren, Michael. '*Doctor Faustus*: The Old Man and the Text'. *ELR* 11 (1981), 111–47.

Weil, Judith. *Christopher Marlowe: Merlin's Prophet* (Cambridge: Cambridge University Press, 1977).

Weimann, Robert. *Shakespeare and the Popular Tradition in the Theater*. Ed. Robert Schwartz (Baltimore: Johns Hopkins University Press, 1978).

Welsford, Enid. *The Fool: His Social and Literary History* (New York: Farrar, 1935).

White, Allon. 'Pigs and Pierrots: The Politics of Transgression in Modern Fiction'. *Raritan Review* 2 (1982), 51–71.

Wickham, Glynne. *Early English Stages: 1300–1600*. 3 vols (London: Routledge & Kegan Paul, 1981).

Willeford, William. *The Fool and His Sceptre: A Study in Clowns and Jesters and their Audience* (London: E. Arnold, 1969).

Williams, Raymond. *The Country and the City* (New York: Oxford University Press, 1973).

Problems in Materialism and Culture (London: Verso, 1980).

Zagorin, P., ed. *Culture and Politics from Puritanism to the Enlightment* (Berkeley: University of California Press, 1980).

INDEX